Adventures in Microwave/Convection Cooking

Montgomery Ward

Precautions to Avoid Possible Exposure to Excessive Microwave Energy

(a)   Do not attempt to operate this oven with the door open since open-door operation can result in harmful exposure to microwave energy. It is important not to defeat or tamper with the safety interlocks.

(b)   Do not place any object between the oven front face and the door or allow soil or cleaner residue to accumulate on sealing surfaces.

(c)   Do not operate the oven if it is damaged. It is particularly important that the oven door close properly and there is no damage to the: (1) Door (bent), (2) Hinges and latches (broken or loosened), (3) Door seals and sealing surfaces.

(d)   The oven should not be adjusted or repaired by anyone except properly qualified service personnel.

(e)   Do not operate oven with the Temperature Probe caught between the oven front face and the door.

Some of the recipes contained herein were previously published in Adventures in Microwave Cooking and are reprinted with the permission of Delair Publishing Company, Inc., 420 Lexington Avenue, New York, New York 10170

Adventures in Microwave/Convection Cooking
Marti Murray, Montgomery Ward National Home Economist

Cookbook Development:
Donna Land & Helen Geist, Culinary Arts & Services

Graphic Design/Art Direction:
Marti Walery & Susan Litowitz, ad lib, inc.

Color Photography:
Dick Jones, Dick Jones Studios

Contents

Dear Consumer,

You are holding in your hand the key to successful cooking in your new Montgomery Ward Microwave/Convection Oven. This cookbook contains over 350 recipes from Appetizers to Desserts, all tested in our kitchen. In addition, there are 15 Complete Meals to help you fully use your new oven.

We hope you will find these recipes exciting and that they will entice you to use your microwave/convection oven every day.

Microwave ovens present a new way of cooking for many people. As you adjust to new techniques and timings, you will find that it is really not all that different from conventional cooking. In fact, the biggest difference you will notice is the time you'll save waiting for food to finish cooking. Variable cooking power will give you the flexibility to cook many different types of food with excellent results.

Convection cooking has been used by professional chefs in restaurants for years. As you become familiar with this type of cooking you'll see that it is as easy as cooking in your conventional range.

The truly exciting part of this oven is combination cooking—the speed of microwave cooking plus the browning of convection cooking.

You will notice that the recipes have directions for the type of cooking that gives the best results. Some charts give multiple techniques. This is so you can choose the type of cooking that fits best into your schedule.

Please take the time to read the Operating Manual that came with your Montgomery Ward Microwave/Convection Oven. We suggest keeping this instruction booklet for easy reference. Read the Introduction carefully before starting to cook. If you have any suggestions or ideas that you would like to share with us, please feel free to let us know. If you have a question, please include the model number of your microwave/convection oven when you write.

Marti Murray

Marti Murray
National Home Economist

Address all correspondence to:

Home Economist
Montgomery Ward Plaza
Merchandise Dept. 68, A-4
Chicago, Illinois 60671

Introduction

Cooking Convenience in One Appliance

The Montgomery Ward Microwave/Convection Oven is truly a versatile appliance. This microwave/convection oven lets you cook three ways; microwave, convection, combination. It gives you the speed and convenience to cook foods fast with microwave energy alone. It is also a convection oven! Those foods you like delicately brown and crisp cook with convection heat. Best of all, this oven lets you use microwave and convection heat together—a combination that is truly the best of both!

Microwave Cooking

Cooking with microwaves is fast, convenient and cool. Many foods, particularly vegetables, cook best with microwave cooking techniques. Your microwave oven can be used for more than just the actual primary food preparation. You will discover that using your microwave oven can be a useful part of many recipes. Many of the preparation steps can be accomplished easily and completely in the microwave oven before continuing with either convection or combination cooking.

Convection Cooking

Convection cooking differs from microwave cooking in that heat is used to cook the food. Hot air is circulated through the oven cavity by a high speed fan. This constantly moving air surrounds the food to heat the outer portion quickly, "sealing in" the moisture and juices. This provides the added benefit of elimination of preheating when roasting meats. Baked goods enjoy the benefit of heat for crispy brown foods, especially those baked goods that can not be cooked satisfactorily with microwave cooking alone. And convection, no-turn broiling is sure to be a hit with many cooks. The oven is preheated for fast broiling and less spattering.

Combination Cooking

Combination cooking gives you the best of both types of cooking. It lets you cook with convection heat and microwave energy to cook food fast. This mode automatically alternates between convection and microwave cooking. You will find combination cooking is especially good for foods that cook longer than 30 minutes. The addition of microwave power to convection heat speeds up the cooking process, making the cooking time shorter than for conventional cooking. In addition to faster cooking, you will also notice less drying out of some foods that normally cook a long time.

What Microwaves Are

Microwaves are high frequency electromagnetic waves that are very short; thus the "micro" in the name. They travel invisibly through air just like TV, CB, and radio waves.

The combination of the microwaves' attraction to specific molecules and the high speed at which they vibrate results in the fantastic speed of microwave cooking.

Microwave energy is not absorbed by all materials or substances as it is by food. The metal walls of the microwave oven reflect the microwaves entering from the top, bouncing them all over the oven, and thus enabling them to penetrate the food from all sides. Metal pans, therefore, cannot be used in microwave cooking because the microwaves would bounce off the pans and never reach the food.

Paper, plastic and glass transmit the microwaves. As the microwaves hit any of these substances, they pass through. Consequently, these materials are excellent for microwave cooking utensils.

How Microwaves are Generated

The source of microwave energy in the microwave oven is a magnetron tube. The microwave waves pass from the magnetron tube through a wave guide to the inside of the oven and are distributed by a fanlike stirrer into a pattern inside the microwave oven cavity to cook food evenly. The microwave oven is manufactured to 2450 megahertz (MHZ). That number frequency was assigned by the Federal Communications Commission (FCC) just as they assign the frequencies for radio stations to which you listen. 2450 MHZ means that microwaves vibrate 2450 million times per second.

How Microwaves Cook the Food

The rapid movement of microwaves passing through food causes the molecules in the food to rub against each other. Just as warmth is created when two hands are rubbed together, friction from the vibrating molecules produces heat. It is that heat then that cooks the food. Some molecules heat faster than others. Sugar, fat and salt molecules attract microwaves even more strongly than water molecules. Foods containing them need special attention, such as turning or cooking on lower power settings. The cooking process starts on the surface of the food; only the outer inch or so is actually penetrated by the microwaves. The heat generated at the outer rim of the food moves by conduction toward the center of the food, cooking as it moves.

How Convection Works

Convection heat is forced heated air. A fan circulates the air past the heater to warm it to the set programmed temperature. The hot air is then circulated into the oven cavity by a fan. This system of heating provides very even cooking patterns. The heated air forces away the cold air that normally surrounds the food, thus immediately letting the food get warmer. The total cooking time of some foods, particularly meat and poultry, is faster than with conventional heat. In some cases, this faster cooking lets you eliminate preheating.

How the Combination Settings Work

Combination cooking uses both microwave energy and convection heat. The oven automatically alternates between the two to give you the benefits of both speed and browning.

There are two combination settings on your microwave/convection oven. Combination I (325°F, 10% microwave power) is used primarily for baking and roasting. Combination II (375°F, 30% microwave power) is used for poultry and some additional baking.

Factors That Affect Microwave Cooking

Certain factors affect microwave cooking results. By understanding them, you can make them work for you. These factors affect speed of cooking and how evenly the food cooks.

Amount of Food
Small quantities cook faster than large quantities. One artichoke will take 5 minutes, whereas 4 artichokes will take 12 minutes to cook. The timing must be increased for larger quantities because the microwave energy has more molecules to vibrate to create heat. The amount of power your oven produces is controlled by its wattage, and its cooking power is divided among the items in the oven. One small item will absorb all the energy and cook faster than several small items.

Food Temperature
Warm food cooks more quickly than cold because it has a head start. Refrigerated food takes longer than food at room temperature, and frozen food takes even longer to cook.

Amount of Food

6

Food Shape

Testing for Doneness

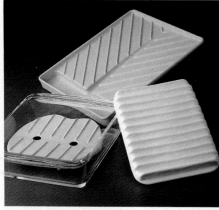

Appropriate Racks

Food Shape

Food with a regular shape cooks more evenly than irregular shapes. Multiple foods can be arranged in a circle to promote even cooking. Irregular shapes can be cooked in the microwave oven but may need shielding with aluminum foil. Simply place strips of aluminum foil where the food is cooking faster than the rest. Round shapes cook more evenly than rectangles; corners may overcook before the center is done. Thin foods cook faster than thick foods. Small pieces of food cook faster than large. Cut up or ground meat, for example, cooks faster than a roast weighing the same amount. That's because there is more surface for the microwave energy to penetrate. Foods that are thicker than two inches rely on heat to be conducted inward from the outside edges. Thick foods need longer standing time after microwave cooking for conduction to complete the cooking process and let the heat equalize throughout.

Testing for Doneness

Porous food cooks faster than more solid food. Cakes, which are airier, for example, cook faster than roasts which are more dense and compact. Test for doneness to be certain that foods are properly cooked. Use a Temperature Probe or a microwave-oven-safe meat thermometer to check roasts. A fork can be used to test doneness in vegetables. For cakes, use a conventional tester, but remember that standing time will help to complete baking.

Appropriate Dishes

Use the dishes recommended in each recipe for the best results. A roast rack, especially designed for microwave use, keeps meat from stewing in its juices and allows air to circulate around heating bread, preventing sogginess. You can improvise a rack by inverting a saucer.

Food Composition

Different types of food cook at different rates of speed. Foods that are sweet and rich tend to cook faster than those that are not. Salt attracts microwaves, so it's a good idea to sprinkle it on food after microwaving.

Power Setting

Most microwave ovens offer a variety of power settings. High settings cook faster than low settings. The lower power levels offer more versatility and control over the speed of cooking.

Oven Wattage

There is some variation among brands in wattage, but most ovens are 600 to 700 watts and will give good results with our recipes. Check the operating instructions. Remember that there can be some variation in electric power delivered depending on time of day. At hours of peak electric usage, power is slightly lower and even our tested recipes may require slightly more time.

Cooking Pattern

Every microwave oven has its own pattern formed by the path the microwaves take. By learning the pattern in your microwave oven, you can promote even cooking. Next time you prepare muffins, notice which ones puff up first. That will tell you where the impact of the microwave energy is the greatest. Because of the random nature of microwave energy, you may need to encourage even cooking. Turning, rearranging and stirring help to equalize the cooking. The center of the oven is usually relatively inactive so when cooking a single item or reheating one cup of coffee, place it slightly to the front off center, or off side.

Timing

Proper cooking time is essential for even cooking, and *standing time* is equally important. Once the microwave oven is off, the microwaves are gone but the heat created by them in the food lingers on. Heat generated at the surface continues to cook food by conduction. Thick and dense foods continue an important part of their cooking during this standing time. A general rule is to allow time equal to one-fourth of the cooking time for standing time.

Utensils

One of the biggest surprises for one accustomed to conventional cooking is learning the variety of containers that can be used for cooking in the microwave oven. Standard metal pots and pans are out, but now "in" are a whole array of materials including glass, paper, many plastics, straw and wood!

Here is a simple test to determine whether a particular dish is microwave-oven-safe or not:
1. Pour one cup of room temperature water into a glass measuring cup.
2. Place it in the microwave oven along with the dish you are testing.
3. Microwave 1 minute at High. If the dish feels warm, it is not microwave-oven-safe, and should not be used in the microwave oven. Be aware, however, that after cooking, even dishes that are microwave safe will warm up from heat conducted by the food. But if the dish has passed the original test, this is no cause for alarm.

Size is an important consideration when choosing a utensil for a microwave recipe; follow the size directions when the recipe gives them. When preparing sauces with fat content such as cream or egg sauces, a container twice the size of the recipe will prevent boiling over.

New shapes, new sizes, and new materials keep cropping up in microwave cookware. They are designed to accommodate the unique features of microwaves. Cake dishes, for example, have higher sides; are ring shaped to provide the ideal shape for microwave cooking, and some are made to be used in both microwave and conventional ovens. Muffin rings are formed in ring shapes for even cooking. Dishes are being designed with handles to make it easy to rotate during cooking, as well as to transfer food in and out of the oven.

Here are some of the materials used in microwave utensils:

Glass, Glass Ceramic and China

Ovenproof glass, sold under such brand names as Pyrex® from Corning and Fire King® from Anchor Hocking, takes naturally to the waves. Utensils made of glass come in designs handsome enough to serve in, and they offer the added bonus of "see through," allowing you to check progress of food as it cooks. Glass measuring cups and glass measuring pitchers make handy cooking utensils as they give a quick check on quantity, and pour easily.

Glass ceramics, such as pyroceram Corning Ware® by Corning, permit cooking, storing and serving, all in the same container. Look for the "Microwave Safe" notation on the label, and make sure that there are no metal parts such as screws on handle, lid or trim.

The browning dish is a special tray made of pyroceram with a tin oxide coating on the bottom. The metal coating attracts microwaves during a preheating period in the oven. It becomes intensely hot so that food placed on it sears and browns by conduction. When returned to the microwave oven, this action continues while the microwaves complete the cooking of the food.

Glass

Pyroceram and Porcelain

Pottery and Stoneware

Shielding

Metal Utensils

Paper

The ceramic, china and earthenware dishes you already have on the shelf can be used in the microwave oven, as long as they have passed the test above. A few kinds of dishes that aren't suitable include:

— Centura® dinnerware by Corning and the closed-handle cup for Corelle® Livingware by Corning (all other Corelle® is acceptable).
— Glass dishes with metal screws, handles or bands.
— Dinnerware with gold or silver trim.
— Lead crystal.

Metal
Metal utensils are unsuitable for microwave and combination cooking because they reflect microwaves away from food. Small amounts of metal, however, can be used to good advantage in special cases.

Small pieces of aluminum foil can be used to shield irregular food shapes (leg and wing tips on poultry) that would otherwise overcook.

One of the conveniences of convection cooking is that the metal baking utensils you now own can all be used. We recommend the use of metal cooking utensils for straight convection cooking. Foods cooked in glass utensils may take longer to cook and have less browning. Metal utensils conduct heat and give the best browning.

The two racks that come with the oven, even though metal, can be used with microwave complete meals, convection and combination cooking. The wire rods have been designed to be just far enough apart so as not to restrict microwaves. The rack placed in the bottom position has many uses; it can be used to cook roasts and broil meats and poultry. It has another function—increased air circulation around the food for convection and combination.

Metal skewers and clamps are safe when the volume of food is considerably greater than the amount of metal. Arrange pieces so that the skewers touch neither the walls of the oven nor each other to prevent *arcing* (sparking). If arcing occurs, stop the oven and rearrange or remove the metal as prolonged arcing can damage the oven.

The foil trays that commercial TV dinners come in, and ready-to-use foil trays less than ¾ inch high can be used in the microwave oven. Since they prevent cooking on the bottom, however, food will cook faster if transferred to a microwave-oven-safe dish, or cooked at the convection setting.

Paper
Paper dishes and napkins are wonderfully convenient microwave ware. Avoid long periods in the oven; they could burn or wax coating melt if left for prolonged cooking. Paper towels and napkins make easy "lids" and help to absorb moisture when heating bread and cakes. Chinese carry-out cartons with metal handles removed are handy for reheating leftovers.

Paper, of course, is not acceptable in convection or combination cooking unless it is one of the new ovenable paperboard containers designed for both convection heat and microwave energy. Using any other paper products could result in a fire, so check carefully.

Not recommended paper products are brown paper bags for corn popping (bags can ignite), towels made from recycled products (may contain metal particles), foil-lined cartons (they shield food from cooking) and newspapers (because some inks absorb microwaves and could ignite).

Plastic Cookware

Plastic Wrap

Plastic

Plastic cookware is so diverse that it is essential to read the label to see just when it can be used for microwave and/or convection heat.

Foam cups and dishes are handy heaters for microwave-only single servings. Plastic stirring spoons can be left in the sauce while cooking, facilitating stirring.

Plastic wrap has proved its value as an instant "lid" in microwave cooking. When covering a dish, however, a small opening is needed for some of the excess steam to escape. Cooking bags and oven film can be used if the foil strip is removed. Plastic bags and pouches should be slit with a knife or punctured before microwave cooking, so steam can escape as it builds up. Since metal twists are taboo, use string or rubber bands.

Combination cooking uses both microwave energy and convection heat. Choose utensils for cooking that can withstand convection heat and also allow for microwave penetration. Thermoset filled polyester utensils (Microware® by Anchor Hocking) and others (for example, Gemstone™ Nordicware by NordicWare®) can be used. These special utensils are very helpful and useful since they come in a variety of sizes and shapes for many of your baking needs.

Plastics to avoid for microwave cooking include melamine dishes, flexible freezer containers such as some Tupperware® and lightweight containers that are not dishwasher safe such as margarine tubs. All plastics that are not high-temperature plastics suitable for conventional cooking should be avoided for combination and convection cooking.

Straw and Wood

Straw and wood items can be used for short microwave heating times, such as for rolls. Wooden spoons can be left in the microwave oven for short times; longer periods are not advised. Don't use wooden cutting boards or baskets with wire in the oven.

How to Choose Utensils

Material	Microwave Cooking Method	Convection Cooking Method	Combination Cooking Method
Glass (oven-proof, heat tempered)	yes	yes	yes
Glass-ceramic (oven-proof, heat tempered)	yes	yes	yes
Metal and foil	no	yes	no
Ovenable paper	yes	yes	yes
Paper (cups, napkins, plates, towels)	yes	no	no
Plastic (conventional oven safe)	yes	yes	yes
Plastic (heat set, dishwasher safe)	yes	no	no
Plastic wrap	yes	no	no
Temperature Probe	yes	yes	yes
Waxed paper	yes	no	no

Techniques

Arrange

Cover

Rearrange

There's nothing complicated about cooking in your new oven. Now that you know the factors that affect its outcome, you can apply the skills you already use in conventional cooking to get the most from your microwave oven. Most of these techniques pertain to microwave cooking. There are a few, however, for convection and combination.

Arrange
For even microwave cooking, place pieces of food in a circular arrangement, leaving the center empty. When cooking several items, such as potatoes, leave at least an inch between them so microwaves can reach them from all sides. Arrange foods with uneven shapes, such as drumsticks, with thicker parts toward the outside. Put food in a dish large enough to permit arranging in a single layer; try not to stack.

Cover
Some foods benefit from the steam cooking that a cover gives. In microwave cooking covers can also reduce spatter and absorb excess moisture. Glass lids, an inverted pie plate or plastic wrap keep in the most heat and steam. When using plastic wrap as a tight-fitting cover, pierce or fold back a vent to let some steam escape. Waxed paper, paper towels or napkins or paper plates can also be used to help absorb moisture. All baked goods reheat nicely, wrapped in paper.

Rearrange
When microwave cooking more than two items, results will be more even if you rearrange them halfway through the cooking period. (See "Arrange" above for repositioning.) If you see that foods aren't cooking evenly, as you rearrange, this is a good time to make adjustments. Rearrange such foods as potatoes, cupcakes in individual baking cups and chicken pieces.

Rotate
This means turning the cooking dish either a quarter- or half-turn. It is the way to reposition food that can't be stirred or rearranged, such as cakes, pies, and some casseroles. Many microwave recipes tell you to rotate. If rotation is needed more than once, do it in even time intervals. It's a good idea to monitor food cooking in the microwave oven, just as you would food on the range top, and rotate as needed.

Adapting Recipes
Conversion of conventional recipes to microwave recipes will become second nature with practice. Here are a few tips:
1. Find a recipe in this book with ingredients similar to the one you want to convert for microwave cooking.
2. Check our recipe to see if the yield is similar to your recipe. If not, multiply or divide to make the two recipes similar in size.
3. Use the cooking method, dish size, cooking time and power level given in our recipe. Start with the shortest cooking time given, and check progress often during cooking. Make notes on your recipe, so next time you prepare the recipe you will be a step ahead.

To adapt your favorite recipes to convection baking, bake at the suggested time and temperature in the charts; preheat the oven if the recipe directs. Foods that cook very quickly (cookies) probably will not cook faster in the convection oven. Large baked items may cook faster. To avoid overcooking, check the foods for doneness as they near the minimum recommended cooking time. Make notes for handy reference next time you prepare the recipe.

To adapt your recipes to combination cooking, find a food similar to your recipe in our recipe sections or charts. Use that information as a guide for time and selection of combination power level. Remember when you are adding microwave power, food will cook faster; Combination I has 10% microwave power and Combination II has 30% microwave power. Combination I will probably be most useful to you when baking delicate foods. Combination II works best with poultry and items that you want to cook fast with deeper browning. Check after half the cooking time has elapsed to prevent overcooking your foods. As a general rule, preheat the oven for baking and broiling but not for roasting.

Standing Time

Standing Time

Standing time is an important part of microwave cooking. Allow from two minutes for smaller foods such as eggs and breads to five minutes for medium quantities of foods such as vegetables and fish. Larger meat roasts and turkeys will need as much as 15 minutes, depending on size, and the internal temperature will rise about 10 to 15 degrees during standing. When cooking by convection heat or combination, the temperature will rise only 5 to 10 degrees. Use the Temperature Probe, to check internal temperature. The heat generated by microwave energy continues to cook by conduction during standing.

Stir

Stir

Liquids and foods in sauces cook along the outside edges first. Stirring is needed to distribute the heat evenly. Move the cooked portion from the outside to the center; move cooler portion out to the edge. When the recipe tells how often to stir; do it at even time intervals. Or if you notice a food bubbling and starting to overcook, stir as needed. Many foods that need constant stirring on the range (candies and sauces, for example) need only occasional stirring in the microwave oven.

Turn

Turn

Dense foods such as meat roasts, chicken and turkey, benefit from being turned over midway during microwave cooking. Smaller foods cook more evenly when turned too. These include hamburgers, steaks and whole vegetables. Often turning, rotating and rearranging are done at the same time.

Rack Position

The rack in the bottom position has many uses. It can be used to cook roasts and broil meats and poultry. It has another function—increased air circulation around the food. Because you cannot use metal baking utensils in combination baking, some foods will brown less on the bottom than when baked in metal pans with convection heat. However, if you place the glass or ceramic utensil on the bottom rack, the air flow around the food and utensil is greatly increased, thereby giving a much browner appearance and more even cooking on the bottom. You will notice that some recipes and foods in the charts call for using the bottom rack. Our testing showed that food cooked for a fairly long time or food that is dense benefited from the additional air circulation.

Convenience Foods

Convenience foods have been commercially processed to go from store to table with the least possible help from the cook. Canned, frozen and shelf-stable prepared packaged foods all belong to the convenience family.

With a microwave oven, these convenience foods become all the more convenient. Many of them come with microwave instructions on the label. Follow the specific instructions, when available. When not provided on the label, use these charts as guidelines. Convenience foods require reheating or rehydrating rather than basic cooking.

Basic microwave methods apply to cooking convenience foods. Cook them in microwave-oven-safe dishes with lids, or cover with waxed paper or plastic wrap to avoid spatters and shorten the cooking time. Be careful to remove covers away from you to prevent steam burns. Check to see if the food is heated to the proper temperature at the minimum time suggested. If not, then add more time. Standing time is an important part of the cooking time. Remember to allow for it before adding extra heating time.

Frozen foods come in a variety of packaging, including paperboard cartons, aluminum foil trays, and plastic pouches. If the container is microwave-oven-safe, the food can be cooked right in the container in the microwave oven. Open the ends of cartons and cut an "X" in pouches before cooking to prevent steam buildup.

Frozen TV dinners and main dishes can be microwave-heated in the foil tray, if it is no higher than ¾ inch, although the food will heat faster if it is transferred to a microwave-oven-safe plate. To heat in the foil tray, remove the foil cover, then cover with waxed paper or return to its original box to keep in the moisture. If bread or dessert is included in the dinner, remove from the tray and heat separately. Heat only one dinner at a time. If the foil tray is higher than ¾ inch, the frozen dinner will not heat properly in the foil tray in the microwave oven. The aluminum would shield too much surface from the microwave action and the sides and bottom would not be heated. Transfer the frozen dinner to a dinner plate that is microwave-oven-safe and the results will be more satisfactory.

Canned foods are the ultimate convenience food; just heat and eat. And the heating is faster than ever in the microwave oven. Merely turn the can contents into a cooking dish, cover with a lid, waxed paper or plastic wrap and set the timer. Or, if your microwave oven has a Temperature Probe, insert it into the center of the canned food in the microwave-oven-safe dish and set it to your preferred temperature, usually 150°F. It is a good idea to stir the food halfway through the cooking to promote even heating and to equalize the heat.

Foods canned in glass jars, such as baked beans, should not be cooked in their original containers. Those glass jars are not designed for cooking. Simply transfer the contents to a microwave-oven-safe dish or casserole and heat in the microwave oven.

Dry mixes are available for everything from scalloped potatoes and macaroni and cheese to gourmet sauces. Heat the water in a glass measuring pitcher in the microwave oven, add the dry mix and complete the dish. Follow the package suggestions as guidelines for stirring and for cooking. These foods requiring rehydration will need almost as much time in the microwave oven as they do when prepared conventionally.

Many foods now list microwave directions right on the packages, or the companies will supply directions on request. New products are being developed especially for the microwave oven, so keep a watchful eye in your supermarket for the newest in convenience foods.

How to Cook Convenience Foods

Food	Amount	Cook at High	Cooking Directions
Frozen Foods			
Beef stew	10-ounce pouch	7 to 8 minutes	Cut an "X" in the pouch and place pouch "X" side down in a glass casserole. Cook 5 minutes. Remove pouch, cover and continue cooking. Stir once.
Breakfast in aluminum tray	4½ ounces	2 to 3 minutes	Remove aluminum foil top and cover with waxed paper or plastic wrap.
Cabbage rolls (stuffed)	14 ounces	8 to 10 minutes	Place cabbage rolls in a 1½-quart glass casserole and cover. Turn cabbage rolls over once during the cooking period.
Chicken à la king	5 ounces	3 to 4 minutes	Cut an "X" in the pouch and place pouch "X" side down in a glass casserole.
batter fried	16 ounces	6 to 9 minutes	Place chicken in a glass baking dish with thin portion of chicken pieces toward the center. Do *not* pile chicken.
creamed	6½ ounces	3 to 4 minutes	Place pouch on microwave-oven-safe plate. Pierce 3 to 4 times.
Kiev	6 ounces	2 to 3 minutes	Defrost first 2 to 3 minutes at Medium-Low. Remove from bag. Place in microwave-oven-safe dish.

Food	Amount	Cook at High	Cooking Directions
Fish sticks (breaded)	4 fish sticks	1½ to 2½ minutes	Arrange fish sticks in a circle on a paper plate. Cook uncovered until fish flakes easily.
French toast	9 ounces	1 to 1½ minutes	Place 2 slices on a plate.
Fruit pie	one	8 to 10 minutes	Preheat conventional oven to 450°F. Remove frozen pie from the aluminum pie plate and place in a 7½-inch glass pie plate. Cook uncovered in microwave oven; rotate pie plate halfway through cooking period. Quickly transfer pie to preheated conventional oven and bake until golden brown (about 10 minutes).
Lasagna	21 ounces	13 to 15 minutes	Place lasagna in a glass baking dish. Cover with plastic wrap and heat for 7 minutes. Rotate the dish one-half turn. Continue to heat 6 to 8 minutes, or until heated through.
Macaroni and cheese	12 ounces	8 to 9 minutes	Place macaroni and cheese in a 1½-quart glass casserole. Cover. Stir once.
and beef and tomatoes	11½ ounces	7 to 8 minutes	Place macaroni casserole in a 1½-quart glass casserole. Cover. Stir once.
Pancakes	10½ ounces	1¼ to 1½ minutes	Place 2 pancakes on a glass plate.
		2½ to 2¾ minutes	Place 4 pancakes on a glass plate.
		3½ to 4 minutes	Place 8 pancakes in a circle on a glass plate.
Peppers (stuffed)	2 servings	8 to 10 minutes	Place peppers in a glass casserole and cover. Stir sauce once.
Pie shell	12 ounces	4 to 5 minutes	Remove from foil pan and place in a glass pie plate. Cook 1 minute. Pierce with a fork and flute edge. Cook 3 to 4 minutes, or until done; turn once.
Pot pie	8 ounces	8 to 10 minutes	Remove pot pie from aluminum foil container and place in a glass casserole. If additional browning is desired, place in conventional oven at 425°F for an additional 15 minutes.
Potatoes (baked, stuffed)	2	7 to 8 minutes	Place potatoes in a glass baking dish and cover with waxed paper. Turn once.
Rice (frozen cooked)	10-ounce pouch	5 to 6 minutes	Cut an "X" in the pouch and place pouch "X" side down in a glass casserole.
Salisbury steak with gravy	14 ounces	8 to 9 minutes	Place steaks in a glass baking dish and cover with plastic wrap. After 5 minutes separate steaks and turn over.
Scallops or shrimp (breaded)	8 ounces	1 to 2 minutes	Arrange fish in a circle on a paper plate and cook uncovered.
Waffles	12 ounces	30 to 50 seconds	Place one or two waffles on microwave-oven-safe dinner plate.

Food	Amount	Cook at High	Cooking Directions
TV Dinners			
Burritos	12 ounces	3 to 4 minutes	Wrap each in plastic wrap leaving ends open. Rotate once.
Complete dinner: meat, vegetable and dessert	15 ounces	7 to 8 minutes	Place food in a nonmetal cooking utensil or plate. Cover with waxed paper.
Meat and potato entrée	8 to 8¾ ounces	6 to 7 minutes	Remove aluminum foil cover and cover with waxed paper or plastic wrap. Or, food can be transferred to a nonmetal cooking utensil or plate; reduce cooking time 1 minute.
and two vegetables	12 ounces	7 to 8 minutes	Same as above.
Tuna-noodle casserole	11½ ounces	8 to 9 minutes	Transfer contents of package to a 1½-quart glass casserole. Cover. Stir once.
Canned Foods			
Baked beans	21 ounces	5 to 7 minutes	Empty beans into a 1½-quart glass casserole; cover. Stir once.
Beef gravy	10½ ounces	3 to 4 minutes	Empty gravy into a 2-cup glass measuring cup. Stir once.
stew	24 ounces	7 to 9 minutes	Empty stew into a 2-quart glass casserole; cover. Stir twice.
Potato salad (German style)	15 ounces	5 to 6 minutes	Empty potato salad into a 1½-quart glass casserole; cover. Stir once.
Sauce	8 ounces	1½ to 2 minutes	Empty sauce into a 2-cup glass measuring cup. Stir once.
Soup	10¾ ounces	3 to 4 minutes	Add milk or water to soup in a 2-quart glass casserole; cover. Stir once or twice.
Spaghetti with meat balls	15 ounces	5 to 6 minutes	Empty spaghetti into a 1½-quart glass casserole; cover. Stir once.
Vegetables	8 ounces	1½ to 2 minutes	Empty vegetables into a 1-quart glass casserole; cover. Stir once during cooking period and before serving.
	12 ounces	2 to 2½ minutes	Same as above.
	16 ounces	2½ to 3½ minutes	Empty vegetables into a 1½-quart glass casserole; cover. Stir once during cooking period and before serving.

How to Cook Pizza

Type	Method	Preheat and Oven Temperatures	Rack Position	Time
Pizza frozen, packaged	Convection	Follow package directions	Bottom	Follow package directions

Food	Amount	Cook at High	Cooking Directions
Dry Mixes			
Dehydrated soup mix	2½-ounce packages with 4 cups water	6 to 8 minutes to heat water; 4 to 5 minutes to heat soup	Pour water into a 2-quart glass casserole and heat to boiling. Add soup mix. Stir once.
Gravy mix	1½ ounces	3 to 4 minutes	Pour water into a 2-cup glass measuring cup. Stir in gravy mix. Stir once during cooking.
Hamburger Helper	1 package	5 minutes to cook meat; 18 to 22 minutes	Cook meat first in a 3-quart glass casserole. Add mix and water according to package directions. Cover and cook. Stir occasionally.
Hash brown potatoes	6 ounces	12 minutes	Follow instructions for rehydrating. Stir once.
Instant mashed potatoes	3 to 4 servings	2 to 3 minutes	Heat water, butter and salt in microwave oven.
Noodles Romanoff mix	6¼ ounces	10 minutes	Add 1½ cups water and ½ cup milk to mix in a 2-quart glass casserole. Cover and cook. Stir occasionally.
Scalloped potatoes mix	5⅛ ounces	15 to 18 minutes	Follow package instructions and place all ingredients in a 3-quart glass casserole. Cover and cook until potatoes are tender. Stir occasionally.
Skillet casserole mixes	12 to 18 ounces	5 minutes to cook meat; 7 minutes to cook casserole	Cook meat first in a 2-quart glass casserole. Add remaining ingredients, reducing liquid by ¼ cup. Cover and cook. Stir occasionally.
Tuna Helper	1 package	18 to 22 minutes	Place tuna in a 3-quart glass casserole. Add mix and water according to package directions. Cover and cook. Stir occasionally.

Defrosting and Reheating

The microwave oven and freezer go together today just as horse and carriage did in yesteryear. With a freezer, you can cook meals with old-fashioned appeal to enjoy later. The microwave oven lets you put them on the table in record time.

Become familiar with these defrosting charts so that next time you need to defrost in a hurry, you'll be ready. Defrosting is usually done in several intervals, with time out for *turning* food and *standing time* after defrosting.

Most foods can be defrosted right in the freezer wrap, except for aluminum foil. Metal on packages, such as twist ties, should be removed. Plastic pouches can be used in the microwave, with an ''X'' cut in the side to let steam escape.

Some foods, such as hot dogs and other meat in casings, have their own natural envelope that needs to be pierced, also to let steam escape.

Meat roasts take longer than smaller cuts to defrost. If the meat is irregularly shaped, the thin portions may start to cook before the rest is defrosted. Frozen turkeys present a similar problem. *Shield* protruding parts with pieces of foil to prevent this. Unwrapped meat should be covered with waxed paper.

Ground meat defrosts first on the surface. Remove defrosted parts to prevent cooking. Similarly, fish that is frozen in blocks should be tested during defrosting to see if the block can be pulled apart and some pieces removed. When just a few ice crystals remain in the center portions, defrosting can be finished by holding the fish pieces under cold running water.

Defrost turkey in its original plastic wrapper (with holes pierced to let steam escape) in a large dish. As it defrosts, pour off the liquid that accumulates.

Fruit needn't be defrosted completely; flex the package when partially defrosted to equalize the temperature.

Bread and cake defrost quickly; take care not to overdo them.

Reheating leftovers is a joy with a microwave oven, because ''leftover taste'' is avoided. Cleanup is a breeze. Follow the charts carefully so you won't cook food more, but simply heat it.

How to Defrost Foods

The Medium-Low control automatically cycles the microwave energy on and off for defrosting. Some foods will require additional attention during the defrost cycle to prevent cooking on the outside. Refer to the chart for direction.

Set oven control **at Medium-Low** for all foods in this chart, unless otherwise designated. At the end of the defrost cycle, some ice crystals should remain in the center of the food. The food will finish defrosting during the standing time. If corners begin to cook, protect those areas with small pieces of foil.

Most foods can be defrosted in their original package, as long as there is no metal. *Be sure to remove metal twist ties from any paper or plastic wrappers. Food in metal containers more than ¾ inch high should be transferred to a glass container for defrosting.*

Food	Amount	Power Setting	Defrosting Time and Directions
Meat			
Bacon	1 pound	Medium-Low	Defrost 3 minutes. Turn package over. Defrost 2 minutes, or until bacon slices can be separated.
Chops	1 pound	Medium-Low	Defrost 4 minutes. Separate and turn meat over. Defrost 2 minutes. Let stand 5 minutes.
	2 pounds	Medium-Low	Defrost 6 minutes. Separate and turn meat over. Defrost 4 minutes. Let stand 5 minutes. Defrost 2 minutes. Let stand 5 minutes.
Ground meat, beef or pork	1 pound	Medium-Low	Defrost 3 minutes. Remove defrosted portion. Defrost 2 minutes. Remove defrosted portion. Defrost 1 minute. Let stand 5 minutes.
	2 pounds	Medium-Low	Defrost 5 minutes. Remove defrosted portion. Defrost 3 minutes. Remove defrosted portion. Defrost 2 minutes. Remove defrosted portion. Defrost 1 minute. Let stand 5 minutes.
	4 patties	Medium-Low	Defrost 3 minutes. Let stand 5 minutes.
Hot dogs	1 pound	Medium-Low	Defrost 4 minutes. Let stand 3 minutes, or until hot dogs can be separated.
Roast	2 pounds	Medium-Low	Defrost 8 minutes. Turn meat over. Let stand 10 minutes. Shield warm areas with foil. Defrost 4 minutes. Let stand 10 minutes.
	3 pounds	Medium-Low	Defrost 10 minutes. Turn meat over. Let stand 10 minutes. Shield warm areas with foil. Defrost 6 minutes. Let stand 10 minutes.
Sausage, pork, bulk	1 pound	Medium-Low	Defrost 4 minutes. Separate sausage. Defrost 2 minutes. Let stand 3 minutes.
Spareribs, pork	3 pounds	Medium-Low	Defrost 6 minutes. Separate and turn meat over. Defrost 4 minutes. Let stand 10 minutes.

Food	Amount	Power Setting	Defrosting Time and Directions
Steak (sirloin or round)	1 to 1½ pounds	Medium-Low	Defrost 5 minutes. Turn meat over. Defrost 2 minutes. Let stand 10 minutes.
Stew meat	1½ pounds	Medium-Low	Defrost 5 minutes. Separate meat. Defrost 3 minutes. Let stand 5 minutes.
Poultry			
Chicken pieces	2½ to 3¼ pounds	Medium-Low	Defrost 8 minutes. Separate chicken pieces. Defrost 3 minutes. Remove wings. Defrost 2 minutes. Let stand 10 minutes.
whole	2 pounds	Medium-Low	Defrost 6 minutes. Turn chicken over. Shield warm areas with foil. Defrost 4 minutes. Let stand 10 minutes.
	3 pounds	Medium-Low	Defrost 8 minutes. Turn chicken over. Shield warm areas with foil. Defrost 4 minutes. Let stand 10 minutes. Defrost 4 minutes. Let stand 10 minutes.
			Note: If chicken is not thawed enough to remove giblets, run under cold water.
Cornish hen	1-pound hen	Medium-Low	Defrost 5 minutes. Turn hen over. Defrost 3 minutes. Let stand 5 to 10 minutes.
	2 1-pound hens	Medium-Low	Defrost 8 minutes. Turn hens over. Defrost 6 minutes. Let stand 10 minutes.
Duckling	4 to 5 pounds	Medium-Low	Defrost 10 minutes. Let stand 10 minutes; shield warm areas with foil. Defrost 8 minutes. Let stand in cold water 30 minutes.
Turkey leg	2 (10 ounces each)	Medium-Low	Defrost 5 minutes. Let stand 5 minutes.
roast	2½ to 3 pounds	Medium-Low	Defrost 8 minutes. Let stand 10 minutes. Defrost 6 minutes. Let stand 10 minutes.
whole	12 pounds	Medium-Low	Defrost 20 minutes. Turn turkey over. Let stand 10 minutes; shield warm areas with foil. Defrost 15 minutes. Let stand in cold water 1 hour, or until defrosted; remove giblets.
Seafood			
Crab (pouch)	6 ounces	Medium-Low	Defrost 2 minutes. Separate pieces.
Fish fillets	1 pound	Medium-Low	Defrost 2 minutes. Turn fish over. Defrost 2 minutes. Let stand 5 minutes.
whole	12 ounces	Medium-Low	Defrost 4 minutes. Turn fish over. Defrost 4 minutes. Rinse cavity in cold water until defrosted.
Lobster tail	8 ounces	Medium-Low	Defrost 3 minutes. Let stand 5 minutes.
Shrimp	1 pound	Medium-Low	Defrost 1 minute. Separate shrimp. Defrost 1 minute. Let stand 5 minutes.

Food	Amount	Power Setting	Defrosting Time and Directions
Bread			
Dinner rolls	12	High	Remove any metal twist ties. Defrost 1 to 2 minutes. Let stand 5 minutes.
Frozen Bread Dough	12 ounces	Medium-Low	See recipe on page 47.
Loaf, small	1 pound	High	Remove any metal twist ties. Defrost 1½ to 2 minutes. Let stand 5 minutes.
Desserts			
Brownies	12¼ ounces	High	Remove from foil pan. Defrost 1 to 1½ minutes. Let stand 10 minutes.
Cake	17 to 20 ounces	High	Remove from foil pan. Defrost 1 to 2 minutes. Let stand 10 minutes.
Cheese cake	23 ounces	Medium-Low	Remove from foil pan. Defrost 3 to 4 minutes. Cut into pieces and let stand 15 minutes.
Fruit	16 ounces	High	Defrost 1 to 2 minutes. Let stand 5 minutes.
Non-dairy whipped topping	4 ounces	High	Defrost 30 to 45 seconds. Stir well.
	9 ounces	High	Defrost 45 to 60 seconds. Stir well.
Miscellaneous			
Egg substitute	8½ ounces	Medium-Low	Open carton. Defrost 2½ to 3½ minutes. Shake well and let stand 10 minutes.
Frozen orange juice	6 ounces	High	Remove metal lid from one end. Defrost 1½ to 2½ minutes. Let stand 3 minutes.
	12 ounces	High	Remove metal lid from one end. Defrost 1½ to 2½ minutes. Let stand 3 minutes.
Hash brown potatoes	12 ounces	Medium-Low	Defrost 5 minutes. Stir halfway through and let stand 5 minutes.
Pancake batter	7 ounces	Medium-Low	Open carton. Defrost 2 to 3 minutes. Shake well and let stand 10 minutes.

How to Reheat Foods

The following is a basic chart for foods frequently reheated in the microwave oven. The times are based on 1 serving. For each additional serving, increase the time by ⅔ of the original time. For example, if one serving takes 45 seconds to reheat, 2 servings will take 1 minute 15 seconds and 3 servings will take 1 minute 45 seconds.

A rule of thumb for reheating foods that are not on the chart is 1½ minutes per cup measure or 1½ minutes per 8 ounces of weight.

To keep the food from drying out, cover with an all-glass lid, plastic wrap or waxed paper, unless otherwise indicated.

The times in this chart are a guide and may vary depending on amount and temperature of food to be reheated. Check after minimum time has elapsed to avoid overheating.

Food	Amount	Reheat at High	Reheating Directions
Meat and Eggs			
Bacon	3 slices	20 to 30 seconds	Place bacon on a paper plate or paper towel. Cover with a paper towel.
Casserole	1 serving	45 seconds to 1½ minutes	Cover and stir once during the heating period. Additional servings may require additional stirring.
Chicken	6 to 8 ounces	45 seconds to 1¼ minutes	Place chicken on a plate or in a glass utensil and cover with waxed paper.
Fish	3 to 4 ounces	30 to 45 seconds	Place fish on a plate or in a glass utensil and cover with waxed paper.
Hamburger	4 ounces	45 seconds to 1½ minutes	Place hamburger on a plate or in a glass utensil and cover.
Omelet	1 serving	45 to 60 seconds	Heat covered on a microwave-oven-safe serving plate.
Roast beef	1 slice	30 to 45 seconds	Place beef on a plate or in a glass utensil and cover with plastic wrap.
Steaks and chops	1	45 seconds to 1½ minutes	Place meat on a plate or in a glass utensil and cover.
Scrambled eggs	1 serving	20 to 30 seconds	Cover and stir once during the heating period.
Vegetables			
Vegetables	4 ounces	30 to 45 seconds	Cover and stir once during the heating period. Additional servings may require additional stirring.
Mashed potatoes	1 serving	45 seconds to 1 minute	Cover and stir once during the heating period. Additional servings may require additional stirring.
Breads			
Bread slice	1	10 to 15 seconds	Place bread on a paper towel.
Pastries includes pie and cake	1 serving	15 to 30 seconds	Place pastries on a paper towel.
Roll	1	5 to 10 seconds	Place roll on a paper towel.
Sandwich	1	20 to 30 seconds	Wrap sandwich in waxed paper or a paper napkin.
Sweet roll	1	5 to 10 seconds	Place roll on a paper towel.

Spiced
Toasty Nuts

Mini-Pizzas

Nachos

Appetizers

Ever notice how new microwave cooks seem to have stars in their eyes? It's not unusual to find one as happy as a child with a new bike. Showing off their new microwave oven makes party cooking fun to do.

Use it to make appetizers and you can share your excitement with your guests. You can count on a double bonus if you do. It will literally melt the ice and when guests get involved in the preparation, it will save you work.

Do Ahead
The more appetizer preparation steps you can get out of the way before guests arrive, the better. That's true of all party food but especially so of appetizers. When the door bell is ringing and guests are arriving you want to be available, not fussing with food.

Appetizer ingredients need attention; cutting, measuring and stirring takes time, with or without a microwave oven. But with the work done before the party and ingredients lined up in the refrigerator, it's a breeze to do last minute touches after guests arrive.

Best Microwave Choices
Some of the easiest appetizers work best in the microwave oven. Small slices of cheese on crackers, for example, are simple to assemble and serve. Let guests watch as the appetizers heat and bubble, and your microwave oven becomes a star attraction.

The cheeses that are best suited to microwave heating are the ones that melt easily such as Swiss, Monterey Jack, and process cheese spreads. Harder cheeses, such as aged Cheddar, work better in the microwave oven when shredded and added to sauces.

The best crackers for microwave use are the crisp ones, such as shredded wheat crackers, Melba toast, and crisp rye crackers. They will stay crisper if you wait to add spreads until party time. A paper towel placed under the crackers while microwaving helps absorb extra moisture. If the serving tray is microwave-oven-safe you can heat cheese-crackers right on it. Arranging them in a circle on the plate will encourage even cooking.

A number of snack foods benefit from a quick microwave heating, even some you might not normally think of heating. A bowl of salted nuts, for example, takes on newly-roasted freshness with a little microwave heating. Many dips are more interesting hot than cold. You can overcook with microwaves, just as you can with other cooking methods. Set the timer for your appetizers for the shortest time given in the recipe. The oven turns itself off when it reaches the end of the cooking time. Add more time if needed after checking. This feature is especially helpful when you're giving a party and have other things on your mind.

Best Convection Choices
Some appetizers benefit from convection cooking. Those with a pastry crust are better baked in the convection oven for the dry heat they need for crispness. The circulating heated air enables two layers of appetizers to bake evenly at the same time so you can make larger quantities to feed your hungry guests.

Choose the method of preparation to best fit each recipe. For quick appetizers use microwave cooking. Crispy appetizers are cooked best with convection heat.

Cheese Crisps

¼ cup sliced green onion
1½ cups (6 ounces) shredded Cheddar cheese
½ teaspoon paprika
¼ teaspoon salt
¾ cup mayonnaise
1 loaf thin-sliced party rye bread (about 48 slices)

1. Preheat convection oven to 450°F.

2. Combine green onion, cheese, paprika, salt and mayonnaise. Spread one heaping teaspoon mixture on each slice of bread. Place 12 on each of two ungreased round metal trays.

3. Place one tray on each metal rack. Cook in convection oven **4 to 5 minutes at 450°F**. Repeat with remaining cheese mixture and bread slices.

About 4 dozen

Cheese Straws

1 cup plus 2 tablespoons all-purpose flour
1 tablespoon paprika
½ teaspoon salt
½ cup (2 ounces) shredded sharp Cheddar cheese
1 package (3 ounces) cream cheese
⅓ cup vegetable shortening
2 tablespoons water

1. Preheat convection oven to 425°F.

2. Combine flour, paprika, salt and Cheddar cheese in a bowl. Cut in cream cheese and shortening with a pastry blender or two knives until mixture is crumbly. Stir in water until well mixed.

3. Turn dough onto a lightly floured surface. Roll dough to ¼-inch thickness and a 12x10-inch rectangle. Cut into narrow strips (about 4x½ inch).

4. Place straws on two ungreased round metal trays.

5. Place one tray on each metal rack. Cook in convection oven **10 minutes at 425°F**, or until flaky.

About 60 straws

Shrimp Roll-Ups

2 packages (8 ounces each) refrigerated crescent roll dough
6 tablespoons butter or margarine, softened
1 cup coarsely chopped cooked shrimp
3 tablespoons thinly sliced green onion
1 teaspoon dill weed
1 small clove garlic, minced
½ teaspoon Worcestershire sauce

1. Preheat convection oven to 375°F.

2. Separate crescent dough into 8 rectangles; pinch seams to seal. Set aside.

3. Combine remaining ingredients. Spread 2 tablespoons mixture to edge of each rectangle.

4. Roll each filled rectangle of dough tightly; start from long side. Pinch to seal seams.

5. Slice each roll into 6 pieces. Place 24 seam-side-down on each of two ungreased round metal trays.

6. Place one tray on each metal rack. Cook in convection oven **13 to 14 minutes at 375°F**, or until golden brown.

4 dozen

Salami Biscuits

1 package (7½ ounces) flaky
refrigerated biscuits (10)
5 slices salami, quartered
5 slices pasteurized process
American cheese, quartered
1 tablespoon butter or
margarine, melted
Poppy seed or sesame seed

1. Preheat convection oven to 400°F.

2. Cut biscuits into quarters and flatten each piece of dough. Top half of dough pieces with a piece of salami and a piece of cheese. Top with remaining dough pieces. Seal edges.

3. Put onto two ungreased round metal trays. Brush tops with melted butter. Sprinkle with poppy seed or sesame seed.

4. Place one tray on each metal rack. Cook in convection oven **10 to 15 minutes at 400°F**, or until biscuits are golden brown.

20 biscuits

Mini-Pizzas

4 English muffins
1 can (8 ounces) tomato sauce
½ teaspoon oregano leaves
Dash garlic powder
1 cup (4 ounces) shredded
mozzarella cheese

Optional ingredients:
Green pepper strips
Pepperoni
Italian sausage, cooked
Pimiento-stuffed green
olives, sliced
Sliced small mushrooms
Grated Parmesan cheese
Chopped onion

1. Split English muffins in half and toast in toaster.

2. Mix tomato sauce, oregano and garlic powder. Spread on toasted muffin halves. Sprinkle with shredded cheese.

3. Top with desired optional ingredients.

4. Cut each muffin half into 4 pieces. Place 8 pieces in a circle on 2 individual paper plates. For each plate, cook uncovered in microwave oven **1 minute at High**, or until cheese is melted.

32 appetizers

Hint: For convection oven cooking, preheat oven to 400°F. Arrange appetizers on ungreased round metal trays. Place one tray on each metal rack. Cook in convection oven **about 4 minutes at 400°F**, or until cheese is melted.

Meatballs and Sweet-Sour Sauce

1 pound ground beef
1 tablespoon finely chopped onion
1 tablespoon finely chopped parsley
½ cup soft bread crumbs
1 egg, slightly beaten
2 tablespoons milk
1 teaspoon salt
¼ teaspoon garlic salt
⅛ teaspoon ground allspice
⅛ teaspoon ground cloves
1 cup unsweetened pineapple juice
2 tablespoons brown sugar
1 tablespoon cornstarch
1 tablespoon lemon juice

1. Combine ground beef, onion, parsley, bread crumbs, egg, milk, salt, garlic salt, allspice and cloves.

2. Form into 40 balls (about 1 inch in diameter). Place 8 balls in a circle on 5 individual paper plates lined with a double thickness of paper towels; cover with waxed paper. For each plate, cook in microwave oven **1½ minutes at High**.

3. Combine pineapple juice, brown sugar and cornstarch in a 2-cup glass measuring cup. Cook uncovered in microwave oven **2 minutes at High**, or until thickened; stir once. Stir in lemon juice. Serve with meatballs.

About 40 meatballs

Hint: Meatballs can be prepared ahead, frozen or refrigerated and cooked at serving time. If frozen, cooking time will be **2½ to 3 minutes at High**; if refrigerated, **2 to 2½ minutes at High**.

Stuffed Mushrooms

32 fresh medium mushrooms
1 package (10 ounces) frozen chopped broccoli
½ cup fine soft bread crumbs
2 tablespoons chili sauce
2 tablespoons lemon juice
1 teaspoon salt
⅛ teaspoon pepper
1 tablespoon chopped parsley
2 tablespoons butter or margarine
⅓ cup minced onion
Grated Parmesan or Romano cheese

1. Clean mushrooms; remove and chop stems.

2. Pierce broccoli package with fork and place on a paper towel in microwave oven. Cook **5 minutes at High**. Drain.

3. Combine drained broccoli, chopped mushroom stems, bread crumbs, chili sauce, lemon juice, salt, pepper and parsley in a bowl.

4. Put butter and onion into a 2-cup glass measuring cup. Cook uncovered in microwave oven **3 minutes at High**.

5. Add butter and onion to ingredients in bowl; mix.

6. Stuff the mushroom caps generously.

7. Put 8 mushrooms in a circle on 4 individual paper plates lined with a double thickness of paper towels. Sprinkle with Parmesan cheese. Cover with waxed paper. For each plate, cook in microwave oven **2 minutes at High**, or until hot; rotate plate one-half turn after 1 minute.

32 stuffed mushrooms

Rumaki

½ pound chicken livers
2 tablespoons vegetable oil
1½ tablespoons honey
1 tablespoon soy sauce
½ clove garlic, crushed in a garlic press
9 slices bacon, cut in halves
1 can (6 ounces) whole water chestnuts, drained

1. Rinse chicken livers under running cold water and drain on paper towels; cut livers in half and put into a bowl.

2. Pour a mixture of oil, honey, soy sauce and garlic over the liver pieces; cover. Let stand about 1 hour, turning pieces occasionally. Remove from marinade and set on paper towels.

3. Place bacon slices on a microwave-oven-safe roast rack set in a glass baking dish. Cover with paper towels. Cook in microwave oven **2½ to 3 minutes at High**, or until partially cooked. Pat bacon with paper towels.

4. Hold liver and water chestnut together, wrap a piece of bacon around both and secure with a wooden pick.

5. Place 6 appetizers in a circle on individual paper plates lined with a triple thickness of paper towels. For each plate, cover with a double thickness of paper towels and cook in microwave oven **3 minutes at High**, or until bacon is done; rotate plate one-half turn after 1½ minutes.

About 18 appetizers

Beef Teriyaki Kabobs

¼ cup bottled Italian salad dressing
½ cup soy sauce
¼ cup white wine
2 tablespoons honey
½ teaspoon ground ginger
2 pounds boneless beef loin sirloin steak, cut ¾ inch thick
1 can (20 ounces) unsweetened pineapple chunks, drained; reserve juice
1 package (6 ounces) dried apricots
24 fresh mushrooms, halved
1 can (8 ounces) whole water chestnuts, drained and halved

1. Combine Italian dressing, soy sauce, wine, honey and ginger in a 1-quart glass casserole. Stir marinade.

2. Cut steak into ¾-inch cubes and put into marinade in casserole; stir. Cover and marinate in refrigerator at least 1 hour.

3. Put apricots and reserved pineapple juice into a 1-quart glass casserole. Cook in microwave oven **3 minutes at High**. Let cool in liquid.

4. Remove beef cubes from marinade and thread on bamboo skewers, alternating each cube with a piece of pineapple, apricot, mushroom or water chestnut.

5. Place kabobs in a large baking dish. Cover with waxed paper. Cook in microwave oven **2½ minutes at High**. Turn each kabob over and rearrange; continue cooking **2½ minutes at High**, or until done as desired. Serve hot.

About 24 kabobs

Hint: Kabobs can be done in 3 batches. For each batch cook **1½ minutes at High**. Turn kabobs over and continue cooking **1 to 1½ minutes at High**, or until done.

Fruit-Shrimp Kabobs

1 can (8 ounces) unsweetened pineapple chunks
1 firm ripe small cantaloupe
1 medium green pepper, cored and cut in 32 pieces
32 cooked medium shrimp
¼ cup firmly packed brown sugar
2 tablespoons cider vinegar

1. Drain pineapple; reserve pineapple juice. Cut cantaloupe into quarters lengthwise. Using a melon baller, cut 32 melon balls.

2. Place green pepper in a 1-quart glass casserole. Cook in microwave oven **1 to 2 minutes at High**, or until tender. Cool.

3. Alternate cantaloupe, green pepper, pineapple and shrimp on bamboo skewers. Put 4 kabobs into a 1½-quart glass baking dish.

4. Mix reserved pineapple juice, brown sugar and vinegar; pour one-fourth of liquid over kabobs. Heat uncovered in microwave oven **3 to 4 minutes at Medium-High**; turn and rearrange kabobs after 1½ minutes.

5. Repeat procedure for remaining kabobs.

16 kabobs

**Spiced Nuts
and Raisins**

Spiced Toasty Nuts

**Mexicali
Chicken Drumettes**

Nachos

Spiced Nuts and Raisins

2 tablespoons butter or margarine
2 tablespoons confectioners' sugar
½ teaspoon onion or garlic powder
½ teaspoon ground red pepper
½ teaspoon ground ginger
4 cups (1 pound) mixed nuts
1 cup raisins

1. Melt butter in a 1-cup glass measuring cup in microwave oven (**about 30 seconds at High**). Add sugar, onion powder, red pepper and ginger; stir well.

2. Put nuts into a 1-quart glass casserole. Pour butter mixture over nuts and mix well. Cook uncovered in microwave oven **6 to 7 minutes at High,** or until hot; stir once. Cool, stirring frequently. Stir in raisins until well mixed.

5 cups

Spiced Toasty Nuts

2 tablespoons butter or margarine
1 tablespoon sugar
1 teaspoon garlic salt
½ teaspoon curry powder
½ teaspoon ground cinnamon
4 cups (1 pound) mixed nuts

1. Melt butter in a 1-cup glass measuring cup in microwave oven (**about 30 seconds at High**). Add sugar, garlic salt, curry powder and cinnamon; stir well.

2. Put nuts into a 1-quart glass casserole. Pour butter mixture over nuts and mix well. Cook uncovered in microwave oven **6 to 7 minutes at High,** or until hot; stir once. Cool, stirring frequently.

4 cups nuts

Mexicali Chicken Drumettes

2½ to 3 pounds chicken drumettes
1 package (1¼ to 1½ ounces) taco seasoning mix
1 can (8 ounces) tomato sauce
2 tablespoons chopped onion
1 tablespoon chopped green chilies

1. Place chicken drumettes in a plastic bag. Add taco seasoning mix and shake to coat well.

2. Arrange half of chicken drumettes on a microwave-oven-safe platter in spoke fashion with meaty portion to outside of platter. Cook uncovered in microwave oven **9 minutes at High;** turn over once. Repeat with remaining drumettes.

3. Combine tomato sauce, onion and green chilies. Serve with drumettes.

About 20 drumettes

Nachos

1 package (8 ounces) round tortilla chips
¼ cup finely chopped onion
1 can (4 ounces) chopped green chilies, drained
1 can (3¼ ounces) pitted medium ripe olives, drained and sliced
1 jar (2 ounces) pimiento-stuffed green olives, drained and sliced
2 cups (8 ounces) shredded Cheddar cheese

1. Arrange about one-third of tortilla chips on a microwave-oven-safe glass platter. Sprinkle with about one-third of chopped onion, one-third of chopped green chilies, one-third of ripe and green olives and about one-third of cheese.

2. Cook uncovered in microwave oven **1½ minutes at High,** or until cheese is melted. Repeat with remaining chips, onion, chilies, olives and cheese.

About 12 servings

Toasty Squash Seeds

1 cup squash or pumpkin seeds
2 tablespoons butter or margarine
½ teaspoon salt

1. Rinse seeds, removing fibers.

2. Melt butter in a 1-quart glass casserole in microwave oven (**about 30 seconds at High**). Stir in seeds and salt. Cook uncovered **6 to 7 minutes at High**, or until seeds are crisp to the bite; stir 3 times. Cool, stirring occasionally.

About 1 cup seeds

Crispy Nibblers

1½ cups stick pretzels
1 cup ready-to-eat corn cereal squares
1 cup ready-to-eat rice cereal squares
1 cup dry-roasted peanuts
¼ cup (½ stick) butter or margarine
1 tablespoon Worcestershire sauce
½ teaspoon celery salt
½ teaspoon onion salt
½ teaspoon garlic salt

1. Combine pretzels, cereal and peanuts in a large glass microwave-oven-safe bowl.

2. Melt butter in a 2-cup glass measuring cup in microwave oven (**about 1 minute at High**). Add seasonings; stir and pour over cereal mixture while tossing. Heat uncovered **3 to 4 minutes at High**; stir well after 2 minutes.

About 4 cups

Bacon-Wrapped Oysters

12 oysters in shells
Freshly ground pepper
12 slices bacon
1 lemon, thinly sliced

1. To open oysters, place 6 oysters in an 8-inch round glass cake dish. Heat uncovered in microwave oven **45 seconds to 1 minute at High** (time depends on size of the oysters), or until shells open slightly; do not cook oysters.

2. Remove oysters from shells; discard shells. Season oysters with pepper.

3. Arrange 6 slices bacon on a microwave-oven-safe roast rack set in a glass baking dish. Cover with a paper towel. Partially cook bacon in microwave oven **3½ minutes at High**; rearrange bacon as necessary. Repeat with remaining bacon. Pat bacon with paper towels.

4. Wrap a slice of bacon around each oyster; secure with a wooden pick. Arrange on the roast rack. Cover with a paper towel.

5. Cook in microwave oven **3½ to 4½ minutes at High** (time depends on size of oysters), or until oysters are cooked; rotate dish one-half turn halfway through cooking period.

6. Serve with lemon slices.

12 appetizers

Barbecued Hot Dogs

½ cup ketchup
¼ cup chili sauce
¼ cup water
1 tablespoon Worcestershire sauce
1 teaspoon prepared mustard
Several drops liquid pepper sauce
8 hot dogs, quartered, or 32 cocktail hot dogs

1. Combine all ingredients except hot dogs in an 8-inch round glass cake dish.

2. Add hot dogs to sauce in dish and stir to coat with sauce. Cover with waxed paper. Heat in microwave oven **4 to 5 minutes at High**; stir once.

32 appetizer hot dogs

Chicken Liver Pâté

½ cup (1 stick) butter or margarine
¼ cup chopped onion
1 clove garlic, minced
½ teaspoon salt
⅛ teaspoon pepper
¼ cup brandy
1 pound chicken livers
Crackers

1. Combine butter, onion and garlic in a 1½-quart glass casserole. Cover with an all-glass lid or plastic wrap. Cook in microwave oven **2 minutes at High**.

2. Stir in salt, pepper and brandy.

3. Trim and cut away membrane from livers. Cut livers in half. Pierce livers with fork. Stir into brandy mixture. Cover and cook in microwave oven **12 to 14 minutes at Medium**, or until livers are cooked; stir twice.

4. Cool chicken livers 20 minutes. Purée in a blender or food processor. Refrigerate overnight and serve with crackers.

About 2½ cups

Creamy Corn Fondue

2 tablespoons butter or margarine
2 tablespoons finely chopped green pepper
¼ cup all-purpose flour
¼ teaspoon salt
⅛ teaspoon ground red pepper
1½ cups chicken broth (homemade, canned or from bouillon cubes)
1 cup (4 ounces) shredded Swiss cheese
1 cup (8-ounce can) cream-style corn
4 drops liquid pepper sauce
Fresh vegetable pieces for dipping

1. Put butter and green pepper into a 2-quart glass measuring pitcher. Cook uncovered in microwave oven **1 minute at High**.

2. Add flour, salt and red pepper to mixture in pitcher; stir. Blend chicken broth into flour mixture. Cook uncovered in microwave oven **5½ to 6½ minutes at High**, or until thickened; stir once.

3. Add cheese to sauce and stir until melted. Stir in corn and liquid pepper sauce. Heat uncovered in microwave oven to serving temperature (**1½ to 2 minutes at High**). Serve with fresh vegetables.

About 3 cups

Hint: Fondue can be prepared ahead and refrigerated. At serving time, reheat in microwave oven.

Hot Clam and Cheese Spread

¼ cup (½ stick) butter or margarine
1 small onion, finely chopped
½ small red or green pepper, finely chopped
1 can (8½ ounces) minced clams, drained
1 pound pasteurized process American cheese, diced
½ cup ketchup
1 teaspoon lemon juice
1 tablespoon dry sherry
¼ teaspoon ground red pepper
Crackers or Melba toast rounds

1. Put butter, onion and pepper into a 1½-quart glass casserole. Cook uncovered in microwave oven **3 to 4 minutes at High**.

2. Add drained minced clams and remaining ingredients except crackers; mix well. Cook uncovered in microwave oven **4 to 5 minutes at High**, or until cheese melts; stir twice.

3. Serve on crackers or Melba toast rounds.

About 3 cups

French
Onion Soup

Spiced Citrus
Tea Mix

Beverages and Soups

"We'll take a cup o' kindness yet . . . for auld lang syne?"

The universal symbol of friendliness is the offer of a beverage. In the mind's eye, a curl of steam drifts just above the cup, because that brew has to be as warm as its message.

Entertaining the kaffee klatsch? You can serve each guest according to special order. In three minutes or less, you can bring a cup of water to boiling. Drop in a tea bag, or a teaspoon of instant coffee or cocoa, and it's ready to serve. Since you can make each beverage right in its own microwave-oven-safe cup, clean-up is a snap.

For fancier parties, you can prepare a hot punch such as spiced cider or wassail, right in a microwave-oven-safe punch bowl. Or ladle into cups and reheat as needed.

Heating Beverages

Using the microwave oven for heating beverages makes everyday living easy too. Now you can brew a whole pot of coffee without worrying about leftovers or stale coffee. Simply turn off the pot and reheat individual cups as needed. There is no leftover taste.

Microwave cooks tell us that one of their favorite uses for the microwave oven is keeping their coffee or tea at just the right temperature; no need now to tolerate a lukewarm cup! With the Temperature Probe, it's extra simple. Just set the temperature for 150°F (or the degree of your choice) and let the microwave oven do the rest.

A milk-based beverage is easy to prepare in the microwave oven too, but it is an exception to the "Fix it in the serving cup" rule. Milk tends to boil over in the microwave oven, so it's a good idea to heat it in a container about twice the size of the milk mixture.

An exception to the exception: If you merely want to take the chill from an ice-cold glass of milk, set it (glass and all) into the microwave oven for a few seconds of heating, and stir before serving.

Stirring, by the way, is advisable for all heated beverages, as it helps to distribute the heat evenly.

Soups

Many folks would like to say "Make mine soup" when warm beverages are offered. That kind of wish fulfillment is what the microwave oven does best. Just add an instant soup mix or a bouillon cube to a cup of microwave-heated water, and you're in business.

The Temperature Probe can be used to good advantage in soup making. The microwave oven stops when the probe measures precisely the right temperature. Lacking a probe, a microwave thermometer will give an instant reading.

Soups can also be made from scratch in the microwave oven. Vegetable soups are especially successful, as microwave-cooked vegetables retain their bright color. Soups require little attention other than occasional stirring to promote even cooking.

When making soup in the summertime, the microwave oven is definitely the way to go, for the kitchen and the cook will stay cool.

Spiced Citrus Tea Mix

1 cup orange-flavored breakfast drink mix
1 package (about 3 ounces) sugar-sweetened lemonade mix
¼ cup instant tea
¼ teaspoon ground cinnamon
¼ teaspoon ground cloves
Cinnamon stick

1. Combine all ingredients except cinnamon stick, mixing thoroughly.

2. To serve, pour water (see chart on page 38) into a microwave-oven-safe serving cup. Add 1½ teaspoons mix or more to taste; stir. Heat uncovered in microwave oven to serving temperature (**1½ to 2 minutes at High**).

3. Stir well before serving. Serve with cinnamon stick.

About 1½ cups mix

Hot Chocolate

2 ounces (2 squares) unsweetened chocolate
1 cup water
3 to 4 tablespoons sugar
Dash salt
3 cups milk
Marshmallows

1. Put chocolate and water into a 2-quart glass measuring pitcher. Heat uncovered in microwave oven until chocolate melts (**4 to 5 minutes at High**); stir once.

2. Stir chocolate mixture; add sugar and salt. Stir in milk gradually. Heat uncovered in microwave oven to boiling (**6 to 8 minutes at High**); stir once.

3. Beat hot chocolate with rotary beater. Pour over marshmallows in mugs.

About 1 quart

Hot Chocolate Mocha Drink

2 ounces (2 squares) unsweetened chocolate
1 cup water
¼ cup sugar
2 teaspoons instant coffee
½ teaspoon ground cinnamon
Dash salt
3 cups milk

1. Put chocolate and water into a 2-quart glass measuring pitcher. Heat uncovered in microwave oven until chocolate melts (**4 to 5 minutes at High**); stir once.

2. Stir chocolate mixture; add sugar, instant coffee, cinnamon and salt. Stir in milk gradually. Heat uncovered in microwave oven to boiling (**7 to 9 minutes at High**); stir once.

3. Beat hot chocolate with rotary beater before serving.

About 1 quart

Hot Butterscotch Milk

1 **quart milk**
½ **cup butterscotch-flavored pieces**
  Miniature marshmallows

1. Combine milk and butterscotch pieces in a 2-quart glass measuring pitcher. Heat uncovered in microwave oven until butterscotch pieces are melted (**about 8 minutes at High**); stir once.

2. Stir beverage. Pour into glasses or mugs and top with marshmallows.

About 4½ cups

Hot Pink Drink

½ **cup water**
¼ **cup red cinnamon candies**
2 **tablespoons sugar**
2 **tablespoons whole cloves**
⅛ **teaspoon salt**
1 **quart milk**
  Cinnamon sticks

1. Combine water, candies, sugar, cloves and salt in a 2-quart glass measuring pitcher. Heat uncovered in microwave oven to simmering (**about 5 minutes at High**); stir once.

2. Strain mixture and return liquid to pitcher. Stir in milk. Heat uncovered in microwave oven to serving temperature (**6 to 8 minutes at High**, or if using Temperature Probe, set at **160°F and at High**).

3. Stir beverage and pour into glasses or mugs. Serve with cinnamon sticks.

About 4½ cups

Double Orange Delight

1 **quart milk**
1 **package (4-serving-size) vanilla instant pudding and pie filling mix**
6 **tablespoons defrosted orange juice concentrate**
1 **tablespoon honey**
  Orange slices

1. Combine all ingredients except orange slices in a 2-quart glass measuring pitcher. Heat uncovered in microwave oven to serving temperature (**about 10 minutes at High**, or if using Temperature Probe, set at **160°F and at High**); stir once.

2. Stir beverage and pour into glasses or mugs. Garnish with orange slices.

About 1 quart

Cranberry-Orange Punch

1 quart cranberry juice cocktail
1 can (12 ounces) frozen orange
  juice concentrate, defrosted
2 cups water
½ teaspoon ground allspice
¼ teaspoon salt
  Cinnamon sticks

1. Combine all ingredients except cinnamon sticks in a 3-quart glass microwave-oven-safe bowl. Heat uncovered in microwave oven to serving temperature (**7 to 10 minutes at High**, or if using Temperature Probe, set at **160°F and at High**).

2. Serve hot with cinnamon sticks as stirrers.

About 2 quarts

Buttered Rum Toddy

1 cup rum
2 tablespoons butter
1 cup water
  Grated nutmeg

1. Divide rum and butter in 4 mugs or old-fashioned glasses.

2. Measure water in a glass measuring cup. Heat in microwave oven to boiling (**about 2½ minutes at High**). Pour ¼ cup boiling water into each mug; stir well. Sprinkle with nutmeg.

About 2 cups

Hot Spiced Apple Cider

2 quarts sweet apple cider
1 teaspoon whole allspice
1 teaspoon whole cloves
2 cinnamon sticks
¼ cup packed light brown sugar
  Dash salt
  Red apple slices

1. Combine apple cider, allspice, cloves, cinnamon sticks, brown sugar and salt in a heat-resistant glass punch bowl. Heat uncovered in microwave oven to serving temperature (**about 15 minutes at High**, or if using Temperature Probe, set at **160°F and at High**).

2. Stir cider. Remove spices. Serve hot, garnished with apple slices.

About 2 quarts

How to Heat Beverages

1. Fill microwave-oven-safe cup or cups each with one cup of beverage.

2. Heat in microwave oven as directed below.

Amount of Cups	Cook at High
1	1½ to 2 minutes
2	2½ to 3 minutes
3	4 to 4½ minutes
4	5 to 5½ minutes

Old English Wassail

3 cans (12 ounces each) ale
¾ to 1 cup sugar
10 thin strips lemon peel
3 whole cloves
3 whole allspice
1 small cinnamon stick
1 small whole nutmeg, cracked (optional)
1½ cups dry sherry
Small baked apples or lemon slices (optional)

1. Pour 1 can of ale into a heat-resistant glass punch bowl. Stir in sugar, lemon peel and spices. Heat uncovered in microwave oven to simmering (3 to 4 minutes at High).

2. Stir in sherry and remaining ale. Heat uncovered in microwave oven to serving temperature (about 10 minutes at High, or if using Temperature Probe, set at 160°F and at High).

3. Stir wassail. Remove spices and peel. If desired, float small baked apples or lemon slices in wassail. Serve in heat-resistant punch cups.

About 1½ quarts

Fresh Vegetable Soup

Beef Broth:
1½ pounds beef shank cross cuts, trimmed of excess fat
1 tablespoon butter or margarine
1 onion, peeled and cut in quarters
1 small clove garlic, peeled
1 small bay leaf
¾ teaspoon thyme leaves
1 sprig parsley
3 beef bouillon cubes
3 peppercorns
1 teaspoon salt
2 quarts water
Vegetables for soup:
1½ cups chopped cabbage
1 cup fresh green beans, cut in 1-inch pieces
¾ cup sliced celery
¾ cup sliced pared carrot
2 large potatoes, pared and cut in ½-inch cubes
1 teaspoon salt
2 tomatoes, peeled and chopped

1. For broth, put meat and butter into a 4-quart microwave-oven-safe casserole. Cover with microwave-oven-safe lid. Cook in microwave oven 6 minutes at High, or until meat starts to brown; turn meat over once.

2. Add remaining ingredients for broth. Cook covered 15 minutes at High, or until mixture boils.

3. Stir broth. Cook covered in microwave oven 45 minutes at High, or until meat is fork-tender; stir twice. Remove from oven.

4. Combine cabbage, green beans, celery, carrot and potato in a 2-quart glass casserole. Add 1 cup broth. Cover with an all-glass lid or plastic wrap. Cook in microwave oven 12 minutes at High, or until tender; stir once.

5. Remove meat from broth and cut meat into pieces. Add to broth along with cooked vegetables, salt and tomatoes; stir. Heat covered in microwave oven to serving temperature (about 6 minutes at High, or if using Temperature Probe, set at 160°F and at High); stir once.

About 3 quarts

Clam Chowder

1¾ cups milk
1 cup half-and-half
2 tablespoons butter or margarine
½ cup diced celery
¼ cup minced onion
¼ cup minced green pepper
3 tablespoons all-purpose flour
½ cup diced potato
2 cans (6½ ounces each) minced clams, drained; reserve liquid
½ teaspoon salt
⅛ teaspoon thyme leaves
½ teaspoon Worcestershire sauce
3 drops liquid pepper sauce

1. Combine milk and half-and-half in a 1-quart glass measuring cup. Heat uncovered in microwave oven until very hot (about 3 minutes at High). Set aside.

2. Put butter, celery, onion and green pepper into a 3-quart glass casserole. Cook uncovered in microwave oven 3 minutes at High, or until vegetables are tender; stir once.

3. Blend flour into the vegetable-butter mixture. Add the hot milk and half-and-half gradually, stirring constantly. Cook uncovered in microwave oven 4½ minutes at High, or until boiling; stir once.

4. Stir potato, reserved clam liquid, salt and thyme into sauce. Cook uncovered in microwave oven 3 minutes at High, or until boiling. Stir. Cook uncovered 10 minutes at Medium; stir once.

5. Add clams, Worcestershire sauce and pepper sauce to mixture in casserole; stir. Heat uncovered in microwave oven to serving temperature (about 1½ minutes at High, or if using Temperature Probe, set at 160°F and at High).

About 5 cups

Shrimp Gumbo

Vegetable-Oyster Soup

Cheddar Cheese Soup

Shrimp Gumbo

¼ cup (½ stick) butter or margarine
1 onion, peeled and chopped
½ stalk celery, thinly sliced
2 tablespoons all-purpose flour
2 cups chicken broth (homemade, canned or from bouillon cubes)
1 can (16 ounces) tomatoes (undrained), coarsely chopped
1 can (14 ounces) sliced okra (undrained)
¼ teaspoon thyme leaves
1 small bay leaf
¼ teaspoon salt
Dash ground red pepper
12 medium peeled and deveined shrimp
1 cup cooked rice (see page 59)

1. Put butter, onion and celery into a 3-quart microwave-oven-safe casserole. Cook uncovered in microwave oven **3 to 4 minutes at High,** or until tender; stir once.

2. Mix flour into onion mixture. Add chicken broth gradually, stirring constantly. Cook uncovered in microwave oven **5 to 6 minutes at High,** or until slightly thickened; stir once.

3. Add undrained tomatoes, undrained okra, seasonings and shrimp to sauce; stir. Cook uncovered in microwave oven **12 minutes at High,** or until shrimp are tender and gumbo is hot.

4. Put ¼ cup cooked rice into each large soup bowl; ladle hot gumbo into bowls.

About 1½ quarts

Vegetable-Oyster Soup

4 cups chopped head lettuce
2 cups chopped spinach
1 cup chopped carrot
½ cup chopped onion
1½ cups chicken broth (homemade, canned or from bouillon cubes)
10 ounces fresh oysters in their own liquid
2 tablespoons butter or margarine
2 tablespoons all-purpose flour
1 teaspoon salt
2 cups milk
1 teaspoon grated lemon peel
1 tablespoon lemon juice
Freshly ground pepper
Lemon slices
Parsley

1. Put lettuce, spinach, carrot, onion and ½ cup chicken broth into a 4-quart microwave-oven-safe casserole or soup tureen. Cover with waxed paper. Cook in microwave oven **12 to 14 minutes at High,** or until carrots are crisp-tender; stir once.

2. Turn half of mixture into blender or food processor container and blend a few seconds. Return to casserole. Set aside.

3. Melt butter in a 1-quart glass measuring pitcher in microwave oven (**about 30 seconds at High**). Stir in flour and salt. Add milk and remaining 1 cup chicken broth gradually, stirring constantly. Cook uncovered **about 10 minutes at High,** or until thickened; stir once.

4. Add milk mixture to vegetable mixture. Stir in oysters in liquid, lemon peel, lemon juice and pepper. Heat uncovered in microwave oven to serving temperature (**3 to 4 minutes at High,** or if using Temperature Probe, set at **160°F and at High**).

5. Garnish with lemon slices and parsley.

About 1½ quarts

Cheddar Cheese Soup

6 cups milk
2 tablespoons butter or margarine
1½ cups thinly sliced celery
2 tablespoons chopped onion
⅓ cup all-purpose flour
3 tablespoons chicken seasoned stock base
1¼ teaspoons dry mustard
¼ teaspoon garlic powder
¼ teaspoon paprika
2 teaspoons Worcestershire sauce
2 cups (8 ounces) shredded Cheddar cheese
Chopped red and green pepper or cooked crumbled bacon for garnish

1. Pour milk into a 2-quart glass measuring pitcher. Heat uncovered in microwave oven until hot (**about 3 minutes at High**). Set aside.

2. Put butter, celery and onion into a 4-quart microwave-oven-safe casserole. Cook uncovered in microwave oven **4 minutes at High,** or until tender; stir once.

3. Stir flour, chicken stock base, mustard, garlic powder and paprika into onion butter. Add 3 cups heated milk gradually, stirring constantly until well mixed. Stir in Worcestershire sauce. Cook uncovered in microwave oven **10 minutes at High,** or until slightly thickened; stir 3 times.

4. Stir cheese and remaining milk into sauce. Heat uncovered in microwave oven to serving temperature (**about 8 minutes at High,** or if using Temperature Probe, set at **160°F and at High**); stir twice.

5. Serve soup topped with desired garnish.

About 7 cups

French Onion Soup

2 tablespoons butter or margarine
3 medium onions, peeled and sliced
⅓ cup sliced celery
4 cups beef broth (homemade, canned or from bouillon cubes)
4 to 6 French bread slices, toasted
Grated Parmesan or Romano cheese

1. Put butter, onion and celery into a 3-quart glass casserole. Cover with an all-glass lid or plastic wrap. Cook in microwave oven **7 to 8 minutes at High**, or until vegetables are tender; stir once.

2. Add broth to onion mixture. Heat covered in microwave oven to serving temperature (**6 to 8 minutes at High**, or if using Temperature Probe, set at **160°F and at High**).

3. Ladle soup into bowls and add toasted bread slices. Sprinkle with cheese.

About 1½ quarts

Easy Vegetable Soup

1 package (10 ounces) frozen chopped broccoli
1 can (8½ ounces) cut green beans (undrained)
2 cups thinly sliced cabbage
1 cup chopped celery
1 tablespoon instant minced onion
2 cups beef broth (homemade, canned or from bouillon cubes)
1 cup tomato juice

1. Heat frozen broccoli uncovered in a 3-quart glass casserole in microwave oven just until defrosted (**3 to 4 minutes at High**); stir once to separate.

2. Add green beans with liquid, cabbage, celery, onion and broth. Cover with an all-glass lid or plastic wrap. Cook in microwave oven **16 to 18 minutes at High**, or until vegetables are tender.

3. Stir in tomato juice. Season soup to taste.

About 1½ quarts

Corn Chowder

3 cups milk
3 tablespoons butter or margarine
½ cup thinly sliced onion
¼ cup all-purpose flour
1 teaspoon salt
⅛ teaspoon white pepper
1 can (16 ounces) whole kernel golden corn (undrained)
1 tablespoon chopped chives

1. Pour milk into a 1-quart glass measuring cup. Heat uncovered in microwave oven until very hot (**about 3 minutes at High**).

2. Put butter and onion slices, separated in rings, into a 2-quart glass casserole. Cook uncovered in microwave oven **3½ to 4 minutes at High**, or until onion is soft; stir once.

3. Blend flour, salt and pepper into butter-onion mixture. Add the hot milk gradually, stirring constantly. Stir in undrained corn. Cook uncovered in microwave oven **about 14 minutes at High**, or until boiling and slightly thickened; stir 3 times. Serve garnished with chives.

About 5 cups

Split Pea Soup

1 pound (2 cups) dried green split peas
1 quart water
⅔ cup chopped onion
¼ cup sliced carrot
3 sprigs parsley
1 teaspoon salt
⅛ teaspoon pepper
⅛ teaspoon ground thyme
1 can (13¾ ounces) chicken broth (about 1½ cups)
2 cups water
1 medium smoked ham hock
Croutons (see page 47)

1. Put split peas into a large bowl, add water to cover peas and cover bowl tightly; let soak overnight.

2. Drain peas and put into a 3-quart glass casserole and pour 1 quart water over peas. Cook uncovered in microwave oven **40 minutes at High**.

3. Add remaining ingredients except croutons to casserole. Cover with plastic wrap. Cook in microwave oven **20 minutes at Medium**. Remove ham hock; cut off and reserve meat. Purée soup in blender or food processor.

4. Return soup to casserole and add reserved meat. Heat uncovered in microwave oven to serving temperature (**about 10 minutes at High**, or if using Temperature Probe, set at **160°F and at High**). Serve garnished with croutons.

About 2 quarts

Egg Drop Soup

6 cups chicken broth
(homemade, canned or from
bouillon cubes)
1 slice ginger root
(1x¾x¼ inch)
1 tablespoon dry sherry
1 tablespoon soy sauce
3 tablespoons cold water
1 tablespoon cornstarch
2 eggs
2 teaspoons water
Chopped parsley

1. Pour broth into a 3-quart glass casserole. Add ginger root slice. Cover with plastic wrap. Cook in microwave oven **12 to 14 minutes at High**, or until boiling.

2. Remove ginger root from broth. Stir in sherry and soy sauce. Blend 3 tablespoons water with the cornstarch until smooth; stir into broth. Cook uncovered in microwave oven **3 minutes at High**; stir once.

3. Beat eggs and 2 teaspoons water and pour into broth slowly, stirring constantly to form shreds. Garnish with parsley.

About 1½ quarts

Chicken-Asparagus Soup

¼ cup chopped onion
2 tablespoons butter or
margarine
2 tablespoons all-purpose flour
1½ cups chicken broth
(homemade, canned or from
bouillon cubes)
2 cups coarsely chopped
cooked chicken
(see page 133)
2 tablespoons chopped parsley
1 tablespoon lemon juice
2 tablespoons butter or
margarine
2 tablespoons all-purpose flour
1 cup milk
1 package (10 ounces) frozen
asparagus spears, cooked
(see page 148) and cut in
chunks
⅛ teaspoon salt
Dash white pepper

1. Put onion and 2 tablespoons butter into a 3-quart glass casserole. Cook uncovered in microwave oven **3 minutes at High**, or until onion is tender; stir once.

2. Stir flour into onion-butter mixture. Cook uncovered in microwave oven **1 minute at High**.

3. Add broth gradually, stirring constantly. Stir in chicken, parsley and lemon juice. Set aside.

4. Melt 2 tablespoons butter in a 1-quart glass measuring pitcher in microwave oven (**about 30 seconds at High**). Stir in flour. Cook uncovered **30 seconds at High**.

5. Add milk gradually to butter-flour mixture, stirring constantly. Cook uncovered in microwave oven **3 minutes at High**, or until slightly thickened; stir twice.

6. Reserve asparagus tips for garnish. Stir remaining asparagus, salt and pepper into sauce. Add to chicken mixture and mix well. Heat uncovered in microwave oven to serving temperature (**about 8 minutes at High**, or if using Temperature Probe, set at **160°F and at High**); stir twice. Garnish with reserved asparagus tips.

About 1 quart

Apple-Raisin Muffins

Basic Yeast Bread

Date-Nut Bread

Canadian Mushroom Sandwich

Breads and Sandwiches

Microwave cooking has given new meaning to the term "quick bread." In the past, the "quick" referred to the method when some leavening agent other than yeast was used and no rising time was needed. Now, thanks to the microwave oven, "quick" applies to cooking time too. A loaf of cornbread, for example, made in the conventional oven, takes about a half hour to bake. Our Cornbread Ring (page 48) takes just 5 minutes!

Quick Breads

The coffee cake and muffin recipes that follow are quick breads. The coffee cakes take less than 10 minutes in the microwave oven and muffins even less, so they do live up to their name.

Why do coffee cakes take longer to cook than muffins? Smaller shapes cook more quickly than larger shapes. That's true of pieces of meat and vegetables, just as it is of batter amounts. Even when the same amount of batter is used, it will bake faster in muffin cups than in loaves, rectangular or large circular shapes. Microwaves start the cooking at the outer edges of food, and several muffins have more exposed surfaces than one large cake. Also, a cake will need more standing time for the heat generated at the outside to cook the center by conduction.

Quick breads rise to greater heights when cooked in the microwave oven. For that reason, baking dishes and muffin cups should be filled only halfway, or they will spill over the sides when baking. The *test for doneness* is the same as for conventional quick breads. Insert a wooden pick into the center of the cake, and if it comes out clean, the cake is done.

Some of the recipes that follow will give you microwave directions for speedy, cool cooking and also convection directions for a more traditional browned quick bread. Decide on the best method as to just how "quick" you need them.

Yeast Breads

Yeast bread dough needs the hot dry air from the convection oven to produce a loaf with golden brown crustiness. Follow your conventional recipe for baking temperatures and times to try in the convection oven. The microwave oven can save preparation time by speeding up the proofing of the dough.

You can also capitalize on microwave speed when using frozen bread dough. The method on page 47 shortens the otherwise all-day process of thawing and baking to about an hour and a half from start to finish.

Freeze and Reheat

Bread you've baked and frozen, as well as frozen bakery goods, can be defrosted quickly by using the microwave oven too. Remove any foil wrap and metal twist ties. Plastic wraps should have air vents so steam can escape as frozen breads become warm.

You can heat rolls and freshen day-old bread by placing them on paper towels to absorb moisture. Easy does it on the time, as they take only seconds to freshen. Heat only until they feel warm to the touch. Whoops—they went just a little too long? All is not lost. Use dried bread for croutons on soup or salad.

Sandwiches

Sandwiches become sensational with a little microwave heating. Gone are the days of the cold sandwich! The same precautions for heating bread apply to sandwiches. Place them on a paper towel so they don't become soggy underneath. Overcooking will make them tough, dry and unappealing.

As for the novice in any new endeavor, once you've learned the timing, you can feel confident of success. Until it becomes second nature, it will help to follow the charts on pages 46 and 51 for heating breads and sandwiches.

Crescent Dinner Rolls

Basic Yeast Bread (see page 47)

1. Prepare Basic Yeast Bread dough and knead; let rise (in a bowl) as in step 5. Punch dough down and divide in half. Roll one-half of dough on floured surface into a 10x8-inch rectangle..Cut into 4 smaller rectangles (5x4 inches each). Cut each smaller rectangle diagonally to form 2 triangles. Roll up each triangle, beginning at wide edge; curve to form crescent. Repeat with remaining dough.

2. Arrange 8, points down, on each of two ungreased round metal trays. Cover with a towel and let rise in warm place about 20 minutes.

3. Preheat convection oven to 375°F.

4. Place one tray on each metal rack. Cook in convection oven **15 minutes at 375°F**, or until golden brown.

16 rolls

How to Bake Yeast Breads and Rolls

1. Follow conventional recipe or package directions for baking temperature.

2. Preheat convection oven to temperature.

3. Use bottom metal rack for best results for loaves and coffee cakes. Use both metal racks for dinner or breakfast rolls.

4. Follow recipe or package directions for baking time.

How to Heat Rolls and Muffins

1. Place rolls or muffins on a paper towel on microwave oven tray.

2. Heat as directed below.

Amount	Cook at High
1	5 to 10 seconds
6	30 seconds
12	45 to 60 seconds

Herb Bread

1 loaf French or Vienna bread
½ cup (1 stick) butter or margarine, softened
2 teaspoons chopped parsley
½ teaspoon salt
½ teaspoon basil leaves
½ teaspoon paprika

1. Cut bread diagonally, almost through to bottom crust, in 12 equal slices.

2. Cream butter with parsley, salt, basil and paprika. Spread herb butter on each slice of bread and over top of loaf. Place on a paper towel and heat in microwave oven **1 minute at Medium-High**.

1 loaf

Onion Bread: Follow recipe for Herb Bread; omit herbs and paprika and add 3 tablespoons minced onion to butter.

Basic Yeast Bread

1 **package active dry yeast**
½ **cup warm water (110°F)**
½ **cup milk**
1 **tablespoon butter or margarine**
1 **tablespoon sugar**
1 **teaspoon salt**
2½ **to 3 cups all-purpose flour**

1. Dissolve yeast in warm water; set aside.

2. Measure milk in a 1-cup glass measuring cup. Heat uncovered in microwave oven until hot (**about 45 seconds at High**). Add butter, sugar and salt. Cool to room temperature.

3. Combine 1½ cups flour, dissolved yeast and milk mixture in a mixer bowl. Beat with mixer until well blended (about 1½ minutes). Stir in enough remaining flour to make a soft dough.

4. Turn dough onto a floured surface. Knead 4 to 5 minutes, or until smooth and elastic. Shape into a loaf and place in a greased 1½-quart glass loaf dish.

5. Measure 1½ cups water in a 2-cup glass measuring cup. Heat uncovered in microwave oven to boiling (**3½ to 4 minutes at High**). Place bread dough in microwave oven next to water. Cook uncovered in microwave oven **5 minutes at Low**. Leave in microwave oven until doubled in bulk (about 30 minutes).

6. Remove water from microwave oven; set bread aside away from drafts.

7. Preheat convection oven to 375°F.

8. Place bread dough on bottom metal rack. Cook in convection oven **30 to 40 minutes at 375°F**, or until top of bread sounds hollow when tapped. Loosen edges with spatula and remove bread to cooling rack for 30 minutes.

1 loaf

Baked Bread (Frozen Dough)

1 **loaf frozen bread dough**

1. Put greased bread dough into a well-greased 1½-quart glass loaf dish. Heat in microwave oven **4 to 5 minutes at Medium-Low**, or Until defrosted at edges; turn loaf over each minute. Dough will still be frozen in center. Remove from microwave oven and allow to stand covered with plastic wrap.

2. Measure 1½ cups water in a 2-cup glass measuring cup. Heat uncovered in microwave oven **4 minutes at High**.

3. Place bread dough in loaf dish in microwave oven in front of water. Heat uncovered **5 minutes at Low**. Let stand in microwave oven until doubled in bulk (1½ to 2 hours). Remove bread dough from microwave oven.

4. Preheat convection oven to 375°F.

5. Place loaf dish on bottom metal rack.

6. Bake bread in convection oven **30 to 40 minutes at 375°F**. Remove from dish to rack and cool before slicing.

1 loaf

Croutons and Dry Bread Crumbs

2 **slices bread**

1. Cut bread into cubes. Place in a single layer on paper towels on the microwave oven tray.

2. Heat uncovered in microwave oven **1 to 2 minutes at High**; rearrange once. Let stand 5 minutes. During standing time, bread will completely dry.

3. For croutons, combine dry bread cubes with desired seasoning and melted butter, if desired.

4. For bread crumbs, place dry cubes in blender or food processor with steel blade to crumb.

About 1½ cups croutons or ½ cup dry bread crumbs

Cornbread Ring

2 tablespoons fine corn flake crumbs
1 cup all-purpose flour
1 cup yellow cornmeal
1 tablespoon baking powder
1 tablespoon sugar
1 teaspoon salt
2 eggs
⅔ cup milk
½ cup vegetable oil

1. Sprinkle corn flake crumbs in an oiled 5½- to 6-cup microwave-oven-safe ring mold.

2. Combine flour, cornmeal, baking powder, sugar and salt. Add eggs, milk and oil; mix well. Pour into ring mold.

3. Cook uncovered in microwave oven **5 minutes at High**, or until a cake tester comes out clean; rotate one-half turn once. Immediately invert on serving platter.

1 cornbread ring

Raisin-Bran Muffins

2½ cups all-purpose flour
1½ cups sugar
1 teaspoon ground cinnamon
2½ teaspoons baking soda
1 teaspoon salt
2 eggs
2 cups buttermilk
½ cup vegetable oil
3½ cups bran cereal flakes with raisins

1. Combine flour, sugar, cinnamon, baking soda and salt in a bowl.

2. Combine eggs, buttermilk and oil, mixing well. Add to dry ingredients and mix just until dry ingredients are moistened. Stir in bran flakes. Cover bowl and set in refrigerator for 24 hours.

3. Fill 6 paper-lined microwave-oven-safe muffin-ring cups half full with batter.

4. Cook uncovered in microwave oven **5½ to 6 minutes at Medium-High**, or until a cake tester comes out clean and tops of muffins appear slightly moist, but not wet.

5. Repeat steps 3 and 4 using remaining batter.

2 dozen

Hint: For convection oven cooking, preheat oven to 375°F. Spoon batter into 24 paper baking cups set in two metal muffin pans. Place one pan on each metal rack. Cook in convection oven **20 to 25 minutes at 375°F**, or until a cake tester comes out clean.

Apple-Raisin Muffins

¼ cup vegetable shortening
1½ cups all-purpose flour
⅓ cup sugar
2 teaspoons baking powder
½ teaspoon salt
½ teaspoon ground cinnamon
1 cup finely chopped apple (cored but not pared)
½ cup raisins
¾ cup milk
1 egg, beaten

1. Preheat convection oven to 375°F.

2. Melt shortening in a 2-cup glass measuring cup in microwave oven (**1 minute and 30 seconds at High**). Set aside.

3. Combine flour, sugar, baking powder, salt, cinnamon, apple and raisins in a bowl.

4. Combine milk and egg. Add to melted shortening. Stir egg mixture into dry ingredients just until moistened.

5. Spoon into 12 paper baking cups set in a metal muffin pan.

6. Place muffin pan on bottom metal rack. Cook in convection oven **25 to 30 minutes at 375°F**, or until a wooden pick inserted in center comes out clean.

12 muffins

Old-Fashioned Popovers

2 tablespoons butter or
  margarine
2 eggs
1 cup milk
½ teaspoon salt
1 cup all-purpose flour

1. Preheat convection oven to 400°F. Put ½ teaspoon butter in each of 12 metal muffin pan cups. Place muffin pan in convection oven during preheat time to melt butter.

2. Beat eggs in a bowl with milk and salt. Add flour and beat just until mixture is smooth.

3. Spoon batter evenly into the 12 buttered muffin cups.

4. Place muffin pan on bottom metal rack. Cook in convection oven **30 to 35 minutes at 400°F**, or until deep golden brown and set.

12 popovers

Almond-Apricot Coffee Cake

2 cups all-purpose flour
¼ cup sugar
1 tablespoon baking powder
½ teaspoon salt
¼ cup (½ stick) butter or
  margarine
1 egg, beaten
¾ cup milk
¼ teaspoon almond extract
1 cup apricot preserves
½ cup sliced almonds

1. Preheat convection oven to 350°F.

2. Combine flour, sugar, baking powder and salt in a bowl. Cut in butter with a pastry blender or two knives until mixture resembles coarse crumbs.

3. Combine egg, milk and almond extract. Stir into dry mixture just until moistened. Spread half of batter in a greased 10¾x7x1½-inch metal baking pan. Spread preserves over batter in pan. Drop remaining batter by spoonfuls onto filling; spread carefully. Sprinkle with almonds.

4. Place on bottom metal rack. Cook in convection oven **30 to 35 minutes at 350°F**, or until a wooden pick inserted near center comes out clean.

8 servings

Sour Cream Coffee Cake

1 cup all-purpose flour
1 teaspoon baking powder
½ teaspoon baking soda
¼ teaspoon salt
¼ cup (½ stick) butter or margarine
1 teaspoon vanilla extract
½ cup sugar
1 egg
½ cup dairy sour cream
½ cup finely chopped walnuts
1½ teaspoons sugar
1 teaspoon ground cinnamon

1. Combine flour, baking powder, baking soda and salt.

2. Cream butter, vanilla extract and ½ cup sugar thoroughly in a bowl. Add egg and beat well. Alternately add dry ingredients and sour cream to creamed mixture, beating until blended after each addition.

3. Spoon half of batter into a greased 8-inch round glass cake dish.

4. Mix walnuts, 1½ teaspoons sugar and cinnamon. Spoon half of nut mixture over batter in dish. Spoon remaining batter into dish and top evenly with remaining nut mixture.

5. Cook uncovered in microwave oven **7 to 8 minutes at Medium-High**; rotate dish one-half turn after 4 minutes.

6. Cover with plastic wrap and let stand 10 minutes in dish. Serve warm.

One 8-inch coffee cake

Hint: For convection oven cooking, preheat oven to 375°F. Use a greased 8-inch round metal cake pan. Place pan on bottom metal rack. Cook in convection oven **20 to 25 minutes at 375°F**, or until done.

How to Bake Quick Breads

Type	Method	Preheat and Oven Temperatures	Rack Position	Time
Biscuits				
recipe	Convection	Follow recipe directions	Both	Follow recipe
packaged	Convection	Follow package directions	Both	Follow package
Muffins				
recipe	Convection	Follow recipe directions	Bottom	Follow recipe
packaged	Convection	Follow package directions	Bottom	Follow package
Nut bread				
recipe	Convection	Follow recipe directions	Bottom	Follow recipe
	Combination	325°F—Combination I	Bottom	24 to 35 minutes
packaged	Convection	Follow package directions	Bottom	Follow package
	Combination	325°F—Combination I	Bottom	35 minutes
Coffee cake				
recipe	Convection	Follow recipe directions	Both	Follow recipe
packaged	Convection	Follow package directions	Bottom	Follow package

Date-Nut Bread

1 package (8 ounces) pitted dates, chopped
¾ cup water
¾ cup sugar
3 tablespoons butter or margarine
2 eggs, beaten
1½ cups all-purpose flour
1 teaspoon baking soda
½ teaspoon salt
½ cup finely chopped walnuts
1 teaspoon vanilla extract

1. Combine dates, water, sugar and butter in a 2-quart glass measuring pitcher. Cook uncovered in microwave oven **8 minutes at High**. Cool to lukewarm.

2. Preheat convection oven to 325°F.

3. Stir eggs into date mixture. Combine flour, baking soda and salt; add to date mixture and stir to blend well. Stir in walnuts and vanilla extract.

4. Spread mixture evenly in a greased 2-quart glass loaf dish.

5. Place loaf dish on bottom metal rack. Cook in microwave/convection oven **30 to 35 minutes at Combination I**, or until a wooden pick inserted near center comes out clean. Let stand 5 minutes. Remove from dish to cooling rack.

1 loaf

How to Heat Sandwiches

1. Make sandwiches with favorite filling.

2. Wrap each one in a paper towel. If heating more than one sandwich, arrange in a circle in microwave oven.

3. Let sandwiches stand about 30 seconds before serving.

Amount of Sandwiches	Cook at High
1	30 seconds
4	1½ to 2 minutes
6	2½ to 3 minutes
8	3 to 3½ minutes

Canadian Mushroom Sandwiches

6 kaiser rolls
Butter or margarine, softened
1 tablespoon chopped uncooked bacon
2 tablespoons chopped onion
1 jar (2½ ounces) sliced mushrooms, drained
1 teaspoon snipped parsley
18 slices (about 16 ounces) Canadian-style bacon, cut ⅛ inch thick
6 slices (1 ounce each) Swiss cheese
6 thin green pepper rings
Paprika

1. Split rolls; if desired, reserve tops to accompany open-face sandwiches. Spread roll bottoms with butter.

2. Combine bacon, onion, mushrooms and parsley in a 2-cup glass measuring cup. Cook uncovered in microwave oven **about 2 minutes at High**, or until onion is tender; stir once.

3. Arrange 3 slices Canadian bacon on each buttered roll and top with mushroom mixture and 1 slice cheese. Place 1 green pepper ring on each cheese slice; sprinkle with paprika.

4. Place sandwiches on paper towels on microwave-oven-safe roast rack set in a glass baking dish. Heat uncovered in microwave oven **2½ to 3½ minutes at High**, or until cheese melts and meat is hot.

5. If using roll tops, heat uncovered in microwave oven **15 seconds at High**.

6 sandwiches

Hot Dogs

4 hot dogs (franks)
4 hot dog buns
Prepared mustard, ketchup
  or chili sauce

1. Place each hot dog in a bun, spread as desired and wrap in a paper towel.

2. Heat in microwave oven **at High** as follows: 1 sandwich **30 seconds**, 2 sandwiches **1 minute**, 3 sandwiches **1½ minutes** and 4 sandwiches **2 minutes**.

4 sandwiches

Ham 'n' Swiss Cheese Sandwiches

¼ cup (½ stick) butter or
  margarine, softened
2 tablespoons grated onion
2 tablespoons prepared
  mustard
6 large buns
6 slices cooked ham
6 slices Swiss cheese

1. Cream butter with onion and mustard.

2. Spread butter mixture on cut sides of buns. Put ham on bottom halves of buns, cover with cheese and top with bun halves.

3. Wrap each sandwich in a paper towel. Heat 3 sandwiches at a time in microwave oven **1 minute at Medium-High**, or until cheese is melted.

6 sandwiches

Cheese 'n' Tuna Salad Sandwiches

1 cup diced or shredded
  Cheddar cheese
3 eggs, hard cooked
  (see page 68) and chopped
1 can (6½ or 7 ounces) tuna,
  drained and flaked
1 teaspoon lemon juice
2 tablespoons chopped green
  pepper
2 tablespoons chopped onion
2 tablespoons chopped
  pimiento-stuffed green olives
2 tablespoons chopped sweet
  pickle
½ cup mayonnaise
8 buns, split and lightly
  toasted

1. Combine all ingredients for filling and mix lightly.

2. Fill buns. Wrap each sandwich in a paper towel. Heat 4 sandwiches at a time in microwave oven **3 to 3½ minutes at Medium-High**.

8 sandwiches

Bacon Cheese-Melt Sandwiches

6 slices bacon, halved
4 slices bread, toasted and lightly buttered
4 large tomato slices
4 pasteurized process American cheese slices
Sweet pickle slices

1. Arrange bacon on a microwave-oven-safe roast rack set in a glass baking dish. Cover with paper towels. Cook in microwave oven **5 minutes at High**. Remove bacon and place on paper towels to drain.

2. Put toast on clean roast rack and top with bacon pieces. Put a tomato slice on each toast slice and then a slice of cheese. Heat uncovered in microwave oven **1 minute at High**, or until cheese melts. Garnish with sweet pickle slices. Serve immediately.

4 sandwiches

Corned Beef and Slaw on Rye

3½ cups shredded cabbage
½ cup white vinegar
1 teaspoon caraway seed
⅓ cup chopped onion
¼ teaspoon salt
Dash pepper
12 to 16 thin slices cooked corned beef (about 8 ounces)
4 slices dark rye bread

Horseradish Sauce:
1 cup dairy sour cream
1 tablespoon prepared horseradish
Dash Worcestershire sauce
Dash salt

1. Put cabbage, vinegar, caraway, onion, salt and pepper into a 1½-quart glass casserole. Cover with an all-glass lid or plastic wrap. Cook in microwave oven **9 minutes at High**; stir once.

2. Put corned beef slices into a 1½-quart glass baking dish. Cover dish with waxed paper. Heat in microwave oven **1 to 1½ minutes at High**, or until warm.

3. Combine ingredients for sauce.

4. Put 3 or 4 slices corned beef on each rye bread slice. Top each with hot slaw. Serve with sauce.

4 sandwiches

Sloppy Joes

1 tablespoon butter or margarine
¾ cup chopped celery
½ cup chopped onion
1 pound ground beef
½ teaspoon salt
¼ teaspoon pepper
¾ cup chopped green pepper
1 cup chili sauce
1 cup ketchup
6 buttered toasted hamburger buns

1. Put butter, celery and onion into a 2-quart glass casserole. Cook uncovered in microwave oven **4 minutes at High**, or until onion is soft; stir after 1 minute.

2. Add meat and cook uncovered in microwave oven **5 minutes at High**, or until meat is no longer pink; stir twice and separate meat into small pieces. Drain off fat.

3. Blend in remaining ingredients except buns. Cover with waxed paper. Cook in microwave oven **8 to 10 minutes at High**; stir once.

4. Serve on buns.

4 cups

**Hot Hero
Sandwich**

**Vegetable-Cheese
Pita Sandwich**

**Open-Face Crab
Meat Sandwich**

Hot Hero Sandwiches

2 mini loaves French bread
(½ pound each)
Butter or margarine
2 cups (8 ounces) shredded
Cheddar cheese
1 cup chopped salami
½ cup mayonnaise
¼ cup chopped onion
¼ cup sliced ripe olives
2 tablespoons prepared
mustard

1. Slice each French loaf horizontally in half, then crosswise in thirds. Butter slices of bread.

2. Combine remaining ingredients for filling. Spread filling on bread and wrap each sandwich in a paper towel. Heat 3 sandwiches at a time in microwave oven until hot (**2½ to 3 minutes at High**).

6 sandwiches

Vegetable-Cheese Pita Sandwiches

1 tablespoon butter or
margarine
1 cup sliced cauliflower
1 cup sliced broccoli
1 cup sliced carrots
½ cup sliced green onions
1 cup chopped tomatoes
¼ teaspoon oregano leaves
¼ teaspoon basil leaves
1 cup (4 ounces) shredded
Cheddar cheese
4 pita bread loaves

1. Put butter, cauliflower, broccoli and carrots into a 2-quart glass casserole. Cover with an all-glass lid or plastic wrap. Cook in microwave oven **3 to 4 minutes at High**, or until tender.

2. Toss sautéed vegetables with green onions, tomatoes, oregano, basil and cheese.

3. Cut pita bread loaves in half. Divide vegetable mixture evenly in all pita bread halves.

4. Wrap each sandwich in a paper towel and place cut-side-up in a glass baking dish. Heat sandwiches in microwave oven to serving temperature (**about 3½ minutes at High**).

8 sandwiches

Open-Face Crab Meat Sandwiches

1 can (6 ounces) crab meat,
drained and flaked
2 tablespoons chopped green
onion
2 tablespoons mayonnaise
1 tablespoon lemon juice
¼ teaspoon salt
Dash pepper
4 slices bread, toasted and
lightly buttered
4 large tomato slices
4 Swiss cheese slices

1. Combine crab meat, green onion, mayonnaise, lemon juice, salt and pepper.

2. Put toast on a microwave-oven-safe roast rack set in a glass baking dish. Put a tomato slice on each toast slice. Top with crab meat salad and a cheese slice. Heat uncovered in microwave oven **1 to 1½ minutes at High**, or until cheese melts. Serve immediately.

4 sandwiches

Hot Tuna Open-Face Sandwiches

2 tablespoons butter or
margarine
6 slices bread, toasted
1 can (6½ ounces)
water-packed tuna, drained
½ cup chopped celery
2 tablespoons chopped
pimiento
2 tablespoons chopped onion
½ teaspoon salt
2 tablespoons chopped parsley
¼ cup mayonnaise

1. Melt butter in a small glass dish in microwave oven (**about 30 seconds at High**). Brush melted butter on toast.

2. Combine remaining ingredients in a 1-quart glass casserole. Cover with waxed paper.

3. Heat in microwave oven to serving temperature (**about 2 minutes at High**); stir once.

4. Spread on toast slices and serve at once.

6 sandwiches

Ravioli with
Ricotta Filling

Confetti
Rice Ring

Honey Granola

Cereal, Rice and Pasta

Does the confusion level shift into high gear during your breakfast hour? If so, a microwave oven can turn that level down a few notches.

It has already worked wonders in households in which everyone wants a different hot cereal. In the past, accommodating them meant using every pan in the house. With a microwave oven, you can make the quantity to suit individual appetites, right in the serving dish. There are no pans to wash, and there are no leftovers. Who wants leftover oatmeal?

Cooking Cereal

See our chart for amounts and times, and start sending everyone off with the breakfast of his or her choice. Precautions to take: Make the cereal in a bowl of generous size (twice the size of the recipe if milk is used) because cereals tend to bubble over in the microwave oven. Allow for the *standing time* shown in the chart; cooking is completed as the cereal stands before serving.

The time savings are not as dramatic when cooking rice and pasta in the microwave oven as for many other food categories. In fact, when cooking large quantities, there may not be any time saved at all. There are other considerations, however, that do make microwave cooking advantageous. Being aware of them will help you to consider the options.

Rice

Rice has a more distinct shape and texture when cooked in the microwave oven. When cooked by any method, rice expands so it's necessary to use a bowl at least twice the size of the amount that goes into the oven. A teaspoon of butter added to the cooking water prevents clumping of rice grains. Best of all, the timer automatically turns the microwave oven off. No more scorched pans to clean!

Cooked rice is better reheated in the microwave oven than by conventional cooking. No additional water needs to be added when reheating—just cover, and the moisture in the rice will create enough steam to warm without drying out. Stirring once during reheating will promote an even temperature.

Many recipes that use cooked rice as an ingredient, such as Confetti Rice Ring, can be completed in a fraction of the time conventional cooking takes to complete.

Whether cooking rice from scratch or reheating, allow *standing time.* This is needed to complete cooking and to spread the heat evenly throughout the rice.

Perfect Pasta

Pasta is unlike rice in one respect; it does not need a standing time. When it is cooked to your taste, it is ready to drain and serve.

Pasta and rice are alike, however, in that cooking with water rehydrates and makes them tender. When deciding whether to cook by microwave or conventional means, the decision will ultimately hinge on personal preference.

If you prefer, use your range-top for cooking rice or pasta while you prepare a sauce in the microwave. See our chapter on Sauces (page 187) for some inspiration.

How to Cook Cereal

1. Measure liquid and salt in a microwave-oven-safe serving dish (for one serving) or a 2-quart glass casserole (for four servings).

2. Heat liquid to boiling uncovered (**about 2 minutes** for one serving; **about 8 to 10 minutes** for four servings).

3. Add cereal to boiling liquid; stir. Cook uncovered (**about 30 seconds** for one serving; **about 1 to 2 minutes** for four servings); stir once during cooking.

4. Let stand covered about 3 to 5 minutes before serving.

Type of Cereal	Serving Amount	Cereal Amount	Liquid Amount	Salt
Cream of Wheat quick-cooking	1 serving	2½ tablespoons	¾ cup water or milk	⅛ teaspoon
	4 servings	½ cup	2½ cups water or 3 cups milk	1 teaspoon
Quick-Cooking Grits white hominy grits	1 serving	3 tablespoons	⅔ cup hot tap water	⅛ teaspoon
	4 servings	1 cup	1 quart hot tap water	1 teaspoon
Quick-Cooking Oatmeal	1 serving	¼ cup	⅔ cup hot tap water	⅛ teaspoon
	4 to 6 servings	1½ cups	3 cups hot tap water	¾ teaspoon
Cornmeal	4 servings	1 cup	3 cups cold water	1 teaspoon

Combine all ingredients in a 1½-quart glass casserole. Cover with an all-glass lid or plastic wrap. Cook in microwave oven **9 minutes at High**; stir after 5 minutes. Let stand covered 5 minutes before serving.

Honey Granola

2 cups uncooked old-fashioned oats
¾ cup wheat germ
½ cup chopped almonds or filberts
¼ cup sesame seed
¼ cup vegetable oil
⅓ cup honey
Raisins or snipped dried apricots (optional)

1. Combine oats, wheat germ, nuts and sesame seed in a 2-quart glass casserole. Pour oil and honey over mixture; stir to coat. Heat uncovered in microwave oven **5 minutes at High**; stir twice.

2. Turn mixture into a storage container; cool, stirring occasionally. Store covered.

3. If desired, serve granola topped with raisins or snipped dried apricots.

About 4 cups

How to Cook Rice

1. Combine water, 1 teaspoon salt and 1 teaspoon butter or margarine in a 2-quart glass casserole. Cover with an all-glass lid or plastic wrap. Heat in microwave oven to boiling (**about 4 to 5 minutes at High**).

2. Add rice to boiling water; stir.

3. Cook as directed below.

4. Let stand covered 5 to 10 minutes before serving.

About 4 servings

Type of Rice	Liquid Amount	Rice Amount	Cooking Directions
Brown Rice	3 cups hot tap water	1 cup	Cover and cook **about 45 minutes at Medium**, or until water is absorbed.
Long Grain Rice	2 cups hot tap water	1 cup	Cover and cook **15 minutes at Medium**.
Quick-Cooking Rice	1½ cups hot tap water	1½ cups	Let stand.
Wild Rice	2½ cups hot tap water	1 cup	Cover and cook **about 40 minutes at Medium**, or until rice is fluffy and water is absorbed.

Confetti Rice Ring

4½ cups cooked rice
¼ cup (½ stick) butter or margarine
¾ cup snipped parsley
1 jar (2 ounces) chopped pimiento, drained

1. Prepare rice. While hot, stir in butter, parsley and pimiento.

2. Pack rice mixture into a buttered 5½- to 6-cup microwave-oven-safe ring mold. Cover with plastic wrap. Heat thoroughly in microwave oven (**5 to 6 minutes at Medium-High**).

3. Remove from oven and remove plastic wrap; let stand 3 minutes. Unmold on a warm serving plate. Fill ring as desired.

8 servings

Oriental Brown Rice

3 cups hot tap water
1 teaspoon salt
1 cup uncooked brown rice
1 package (6 ounces) frozen pea pods
1 package (10 ounces) frozen Chinese vegetables
1 tablespoon soy sauce
¼ teaspoon ground ginger

1. Combine water and salt in a 2-quart glass casserole. Cover with an all-glass lid or plastic wrap. Heat in microwave oven to boiling (**about 8 minutes at High**).

2. Add rice to boiling water; stir. Cover and cook in microwave oven **about 45 minutes at Medium**, or until water is absorbed.

3. Remove from oven and let stand covered 10 minutes.

4. Meanwhile, put pea pods and Chinese vegetables into a 2-quart glass casserole. Heat uncovered in microwave oven **5 minutes at High**; stir once.

5. Add vegetables, soy sauce and ginger to rice; stir. Heat uncovered in microwave oven **2 minutes at High**. Stir.

4 servings

Spanish Rice

2 cups cooked rice
4 slices bacon
2 tablespoons bacon drippings, butter or margarine
½ cup chopped onion
½ cup chopped green pepper
1 can (16 ounces) tomatoes (undrained)
½ teaspoon salt
¼ teaspoon pepper
¼ teaspoon chili powder
1 drop liquid pepper sauce

1. Prepare rice and set aside.

2. Arrange bacon on a microwave-oven-safe roast rack set in a glass baking dish. Cover with a paper towel. Cook in microwave oven **4 minutes at High,** or until done. Crumble bacon and set aside.

3. Combine bacon drippings, onion and green pepper in a 2-quart glass casserole. Cook uncovered in microwave oven **4 minutes at High;** stir once.

4. Chop tomatoes. Add chopped tomatoes, tomato liquid, seasonings and cooked rice to casserole; stir. Cover and heat in microwave oven to serving temperature (**5 to 6 minutes at High**).

5. Sprinkle bacon over top.

6 servings

Rice Pilaf

1½ cups uncooked long grain white rice
⅓ cup finely chopped onion
¼ cup (½ stick) butter or margarine
½ teaspoon salt
3 cups chicken broth (homemade, canned or from bouillon cubes)
1 cup golden raisins
½ cup coarsely chopped pecans
1 teaspoon butter or margarine

1. Put rice, onion and ¼ cup butter into a 2-quart glass casserole. Cook uncovered in microwave oven **5 minutes at High,** or until rice is lightly browned; stir once.

2. Add salt, broth and raisins to rice mixture; stir. Cover with an all-glass lid or plastic wrap. Cook in microwave oven **10 to 12 minutes at Medium,** or until rice is tender and liquid is absorbed. Remove from oven.

3. Put pecans and 1 teaspoon butter into a 1-cup glass measuring cup. Cook uncovered in microwave oven **2 to 3 minutes at High;** stir twice. Sprinkle pecans over rice.

6 to 8 servings

Green Rice Casserole

2 cups cooked rice
1 package (10 ounces) frozen chopped broccoli, cooked (see chart on page 148)
½ cup chopped onion
1 tablespoon butter or margarine
1 can (10¾ ounces) condensed cream of mushroom soup
1 cup (4 ounces) shredded pasteurized process American cheese

1. Prepare rice and broccoli; set aside.

2. Put onion and butter into a 1½-quart glass casserole. Cook uncovered in microwave oven **4 minutes at High;** stir once.

3. Add cooked rice, cooked broccoli and soup to onion-butter mixture; mix well. Sprinkle cheese over the top. Cover with an all-glass lid or plastic wrap. Cook in microwave oven **10 minutes at High;** rotate casserole one-quarter turn halfway through cooking period.

6 servings

How to Cook Pasta

1 **quart hot tap water**
1 **teaspoon salt**
8 **ounces manicotti shells or
lasagna noodles, spaghetti,
macaroni or noodles**

1. Combine water and salt in a microwave-oven-safe utensil. For manicotti shells or lasagna noodles, use a 2-quart glass baking dish; for spaghetti, use a 2-quart glass measuring pitcher; for macaroni or noodles, use a 3-quart glass casserole. Cover with an all-glass lid or plastic wrap. Heat in microwave oven to boiling (**8 to 10 minutes at High**).

2. Add pasta. For spaghetti, macaroni or noodles, stir through water. Cover and cook in microwave oven **6 to 10 minutes at Medium**, or until tender. For manicotti shells or lasagna noodles, rearrange noodles once halfway through cooking. Drain.

About 4 servings

Lasagna noodles

Macaroni

Spaghetti

Homemade Pasta

2 **cups all-purpose flour**
⅛ **teaspoon salt**
3 **eggs**
2 **tablespoons water**
1 **teaspoon olive oil**
2 **tablespoons all-purpose flour**
1 **quart hot tap water**
1 **teaspoon salt**

1. Combine 2 cups flour and ⅛ teaspoon salt in a bowl. Make a well in center of flour. Beat eggs with water and oil, pour into well and mix until blended.

2. Knead dough on a lightly floured surface, working in 2 tablespoons flour, until dough is smooth. Divide dough in 4 equal pieces. Flour each piece to prevent sticking, then wrap each in plastic wrap.

3. Roll one piece of dough at a time on a floured surface into a very thin rectangle (about 14x12 inches). Cut into ¼-inch-wide noodles.

4. Arrange half the noodles in a single layer on paper towels on the microwave oven tray. Cover with paper towels. Cook in microwave oven **2 minutes at Medium-Low**. Turn noodles over, cover and cook **2 minutes at Medium**. Remove from oven; let cool 5 minutes. Repeat with remaining noodles.

5. Combine 1 quart water and 1 teaspoon salt in a 3-quart glass casserole. Cover with an all-glass lid or plastic wrap. Heat in microwave oven to boiling (**about 9 minutes at High**). Add half of noodles and stir through water. Cover and cook in microwave oven **3 to 4 minutes at Medium**, or until noodles are tender; stir once.

6. Remove noodles with tongs to a colander to drain.

7. Add remaining noodles to hot water in casserole, cover and cook **3 to 4 minutes at Medium**, or until tender. Drain and rinse with warm water.

5 cups cooked noodles

Hint: For food processor pasta dough, put steel blade in place in container. Put all ingredients for dough into container. Process until a ball of dough forms. Continue processing 15 to 20 seconds.

Hint: If using electric pasta machine, it may be necessary to increase flour to 2½ cups.

Vermicelli with Vegetables

1 quart hot tap water
1 teaspoon salt
8 ounces vermicelli (thin spaghetti)
1 cup fresh broccoli flowerets
1 cup fresh cauliflower flowerets
4 ounces fresh mushrooms, cleaned and sliced lengthwise
1 small zucchini, sliced
¾ cup cooked ham strips
½ cup whipping cream
3 tablespoons butter or margarine
1 teaspoon chopped chives
¼ teaspoon dried basil leaves
⅛ teaspoon pepper
Dash ground nutmeg
¼ cup grated Parmesan or Romano cheese

1. Combine water and salt in a 2-quart glass measuring pitcher. Cover with plastic wrap. Heat in microwave oven to boiling (**about 9 minutes at High**).

2. Add vermicelli to boiling water; stir. Cook covered in microwave oven **6 minutes at High**.

3. Remove from oven and let stand covered 5 minutes; drain.

4. Meanwhile, put vegetables into a 2-quart glass measuring pitcher. Cover with plastic wrap. Cook in microwave oven **6 minutes at High**; stir once.

5. Add ham to cooked vegetables; stir. Let stand covered while preparing sauce.

6. Combine cream, butter, chives, basil, pepper and nutmeg in a 1-quart glass measuring cup. Cook uncovered **3 minutes at High**; stir once.

7. Add vegetables and ham to drained vermicelli. Add sauce and cheese; toss until coated.

6 servings

Linguine with White Clam Sauce

¼ cup olive oil
1 clove garlic, thinly sliced
1 tablespoon chopped parsley
½ teaspoon salt
¼ teaspoon oregano leaves
¼ teaspoon pepper
1 can (10 ounces) baby clams (undrained)
8 ounces linguine, cooked (see page 61)

1. Put olive oil and garlic into a 1-quart glass measuring pitcher. Cook uncovered in microwave oven **3 minutes at High**, or until garlic is lightly browned.

2. Add parsley, salt, oregano, pepper and clams with liquid to garlic and oil; stir. Heat in microwave oven to serving temperature (**2 to 3 minutes at High**). Serve on cooked linguine.

4 servings

Lasagna

1½ teaspoons olive oil
½ pound ground beef
½ cup grated Parmesan or Romano cheese
1 egg, slightly beaten
2 cups ricotta cheese
2 teaspoons dried parsley flakes
1 jar (32 ounces) spaghetti sauce (about 3½ cups)
6 uncooked lasagna noodles
1½ cups (6 ounces) shredded mozzarella cheese
2 tablespoons shredded or grated Parmesan or Romano cheese

1. Put olive oil and ground beef into a 9-inch glass pie plate. Cover with waxed paper. Cook in microwave oven **2 minutes at High**, or until meat is no longer pink; stir and break meat apart with a wooden spoon once. Drain off fat from meat. Set aside.

2. Combine ½ cup Parmesan cheese, the egg, ricotta cheese and parsley flakes.

3. Pour 1 cup spaghetti sauce over bottom of a 1½-quart glass baking dish. Put one-third of uncooked lasagna noodles (break to fit dish if necessary) in a layer on sauce. Layer with half each of mozzarella cheese, cooked beef and cheese mixture. Repeat layers. Put remaining noodles over cheese mixture. Spread remaining sauce on top. Cover with waxed paper. Cook in microwave oven **15 minutes at High**; rotate dish one-quarter turn. Cook covered **20 minutes at Medium**, or until noodles are done.

4. Remove dish from oven; cover with aluminum foil and let stand 20 minutes. Before serving, sprinkle remaining Parmesan cheese over top.

6 servings

Fettuccine

8 ounces fine egg noodles,
  cooked (see page 61)
3 tablespoons butter or
  margarine
¼ cup grated Parmesan or
  Romano cheese

1. Prepare noodles and return drained noodles to the casserole.

2. Add butter and cheese and toss lightly until butter is melted. Serve hot.

About 4 servings

Meat-Stuffed Manicotti

6 manicotti shells, cooked
  (see page 61)
1 cup Thin White Sauce
  (see page 188)
2 tablespoons olive oil
8 ounces fresh spinach leaves,
  washed, dried and finely
  chopped
2 tablespoons chopped onion
½ teaspoon salt
¼ teaspoon oregano leaves
½ pound ground beef
2 tablespoons fine dry bread
  crumbs
1 egg, slightly beaten
2 tablespoons tomato paste

1. Prepare manicotti and white sauce. Set aside and keep hot.

2. Combine olive oil, chopped spinach, onion, salt, oregano and ground beef in a 2-quart glass casserole. Cover with waxed paper. Cook in microwave oven **3 minutes at High**, or until meat is no longer pink; stir once.

3. Remove from oven; set aside to cool slightly. Add bread crumbs, egg and tomato paste; mix well. Stuff manicotti with mixture and put side-by-side in a 1½-quart glass baking dish.

4. Pour white sauce over stuffed manicotti. Cover with waxed paper. Cook in microwave oven **3 minutes at High**, or until thoroughly heated.

6 stuffed manicotti

Ravioli with Ricotta Filling

1 **pound ricotta cheese**
1 **tablespoon chopped parsley**
¼ **teaspoon thyme leaves**
⅛ **teaspoon oregano leaves**
  Homemade Pasta
  (see page 61)
1 **quart hot tap water**
1 **teaspoon salt**

1. For filling, combine ricotta cheese, parsley, thyme and oregano in a bowl, mixing thoroughly; set aside.

2. Follow steps 1 and 2 in recipe for Homemade Pasta. Roll one piece of dough at a time on a floured surface into a very thin rectangle, 15 inches long. Cut dough lengthwise with knife or pastry cutter into 5-inch-wide pieces. Place 1 tablespoon filling ½ inch from narrow end in center of strip. Continue along the strip, placing 1 tablespoon filling 1 inch apart 6 more times. Fold strip in half lengthwise covering the mounds of filling. Press gently between mounds to form rectangles about 2½x2 inches. Cut apart with knife or pastry cutter and press the edges of rectangles with tines of fork to seal. Place ravioli on lightly floured towel; cover loosely with second towel. Repeat with remaining dough.

3. Combine water and salt in a 3-quart glass casserole. Cover with an all-glass lid or plastic wrap. Heat in microwave oven to boiling (**about 9 minutes at High**).

4. Add 7 ravioli to boiling water; stir through water. Cover and cook in microwave oven **5 to 6 minutes at High**, or until tender. Remove with slotted spoon. Add 7 more ravioli to same water and continue to cook **5 to 6 minutes**. Repeat with remaining ravioli, cooking 7 ravioli at a time.

28 ravioli

How to Make Ravioli

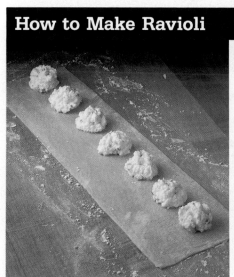

1. Place 1 tablespoon filling ½ inch from narrow end in center of strip.

2. Fold strip in half lengthwise covering the mounds of filling. Press gently between mounds to form rectangles.

3. Cut apart with knife or pastry cutter and press with tines of fork to seal.

Macaroni and Cheese

3 **cups cooked elbow macaroni**
  (see page 61)
3 **tablespoons butter or**
  margarine
3 **tablespoons all-purpose flour**
½ **teaspoon salt**
  Dash pepper
2 **cups milk**
2 **cups (8 ounces) shredded**
  sharp Cheddar cheese

1. Prepare macaroni and set aside.

2. Melt butter in a 2-quart glass casserole in microwave oven (**about 1 minute at High**). Add flour, salt and pepper; mix well. Add milk gradually, stirring constantly. Cook uncovered **6 minutes at High**; stir every 2 minutes.

3. Add cheese to sauce; stir. Cook uncovered in microwave oven **1 minute at High**.

4. Add cooked macaroni to cheese sauce; mix. Cook uncovered in microwave oven **8 minutes at Medium-High**; stir halfway through cooking period.

6 servings

Crustless
Quiche Lorraine

Eggs and Cheese

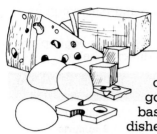

Quiche, soufflé, fondue, omelets—a whole array of gourmet show stoppers are basically egg and cheese dishes. Even if you've never prepared them before, you'll be proud of the results, using the recipes in this chapter. Eggs and cheese are both sensitive to high temperatures, so these recipes have been developed with that in mind.

Proper Settings For Eggs And Cheese

Both eggs and cheese contain fat which has a special attraction for microwave energy. And both contain protein, which can get rubbery when overcooked.

Avoid that disappointment by learning the proper power setting on your oven. Medium-High, Medium or Medium-Low, will work well for most egg and cheese dishes. One exception to the "reduced power" rule is scrambled eggs. They can be microwave-cooked on full power because they can be stirred, equalizing the heat.

Cook Briefly

Set the timer for the shortest time given in the recipe; then check. That's a good habit to form right from the start with all microwave recipes, but especially important when working with these delicate ingredients. You can always cook longer, but you can't "undo" overcooking.

Standing time is an important part of cooking time. The heat inside will continue to cook the food as it stands on the counter so let it rest after that minimum cooking time. If it still looks undercooked, put it back for a short bit of additional cooking.

Eggs

The possibilities for sensational egg dishes from the microwave oven are so varied that it is worthwhile learning the techniques that insure success.

It helps to understand that the composition of yolk and white is different. The fat content in the yolk has a strong attraction for microwaves, so it cooks before the whites. When making poached, soft or hard cooked eggs (never in the shell, but cracked open and placed in a microwave-oven-safe dish) pierce the membrane of the yolk gently to let steam escape.

Any egg recipe, such as scrambled eggs and omelets, in which the yolk and whites are stirred together, cook very well in the microwave oven. Since most breakfast egg dishes can be cooked in individual dishes to suit special requests, it's easy to cater to personal preferences.

Cheese

Some cheeses cook better than others in the microwave oven. Process cheese (soft cheeses not labeled "aged", available under various brand names) melt easily and are less likely to become stringy than aged natural cheeses, such as Cheddar and Edam.

Natural cheeses can be used in other recipes, so don't rule them out altogether. When natural cheese is shredded, for example, it melts easily if stirred into a hot sauce. Or sprinkle it over a casserole that has just come piping hot from the microwave oven, and it will melt while the casserole completes cooking during standing time. Once the cheese is sprinkled on, cover the hot dish with a glass lid or plastic wrap to hold in steam and hasten the melting.

Cheese slices work best when layered between other ingredients before heating. Place between the slices of bread for a melted cheese sandwich. In the time the cheese melts, the bread is heated just right.

With a package of cheese and a carton of eggs, you can turn out some of the best eating this side of haute cuisine restaurants, right in your own kitchen. And with a microwave oven, the job is quicker than you might think.

Soft-Cooked and Hard-Cooked Eggs

1. Break each egg into a 6-ounce glass custard cup and pierce egg yolk. Cover with plastic wrap.

2. Arrange custard cups in microwave oven. For one or two eggs, place off-center; for 4 eggs arrange in a circle. Cook as directed below.

Type of Egg	Amount	Cook at Medium	Standing Time
Soft	1 egg	40 to 45 seconds	3 minutes
	2 eggs	45 to 60 seconds	3 minutes
	4 eggs*	2½ to 2¾ minutes	3 minutes
Hard	1 egg	55 to 60 seconds	3 minutes
	2 eggs	60 to 75 seconds	3 minutes
	4 eggs*	3 to 3¼ minutes	3 minutes

*Rearrange 4 eggs once during cooking period.

Pierce egg yolk.

Cover with plastic wrap.

Soft-cooked egg

Hard-cooked egg

Poached Eggs

2 cups hot tap water (or enough to cover eggs)
4 eggs

1. Put water into a deep 1½-quart glass casserole. Cover with an all-glass lid or plastic wrap. Heat in microwave oven to boiling (**4 to 5 minutes at High**).

2. Break eggs, one at a time, into a saucer or small dish. Slip each egg carefully into hot water. Cover and cook in microwave oven **1½ to 2 minutes at Medium**, or until whites are almost set.

3. Remove from oven and let stand covered a few minutes before serving.

4 servings

Eggs Florentine

1 **package (10 ounces) frozen chopped spinach**
1 **tablespoon butter or margarine**
½ **cup chopped onion**
4 **ounces fresh mushrooms, cleaned and sliced lengthwise**
½ **teaspoon salt**
⅛ **teaspoon pepper**
2 **teaspoons butter or margarine**
4 **eggs**
2 **slices (1 ounce each) Swiss cheese, cut in 4 strips**
Salt and pepper (optional)

1. Pierce frozen spinach package with a fork. Set on a paper towel in microwave oven and heat **3 minutes at High**, or until defrosted.

2. Remove from oven; drain spinach and set aside.

3. Put 1 tablespoon butter, onion and mushrooms into a 1½-quart glass casserole. Cook uncovered in microwave oven **3 to 3½ minutes at High**, or until onion and mushrooms are soft; stir once.

4. Add drained spinach, ½ teaspoon salt and ⅛ teaspoon pepper to casserole; mix well. Divide mixture equally in four 10-ounce glass dishes. Make a depression in each. Set aside.

5. Butter bottoms of four 6-ounce glass custard cups. Slip an egg into each cup and pierce egg yolk. Cover with plastic wrap. Cook in microwave oven **6 to 7 minutes at Medium-Low**, or until almost set; rotate and rearrange custard cups after 2 minutes and after 4 minutes.

6. Remove eggs from oven and set aside.

7. Heat the 4 dishes with spinach mixture uncovered in microwave oven **2 minutes at High**, or until spinach is hot. Slip an egg into each depression. Crisscross 2 strips of cheese on each egg. Heat uncovered **1 to 1½ minutes at High**, or until cheese begins to melt.

8. Sprinkle salt and pepper over eggs, if desired.

4 servings

Denver Omelet

2 tablespoons butter or
margarine
3 tablespoons chopped green
pepper
3 tablespoons chopped green
onion
4 eggs
⅛ teaspoon salt
⅛ teaspoon pepper
3 tablespoons chopped
pimiento
½ cup finely diced cooked ham

1. Put butter, green pepper and green onion into a 9-inch glass pie plate. Cook uncovered in microwave oven **3 minutes at High**, or until green pepper is soft; stir after 1 minute.

2. Beat eggs slightly in a bowl and mix in salt, pepper, pimiento and ham. Pour into pie plate with vegetables; mix well. Cover with plastic wrap. Cook in microwave oven **4 to 5 minutes at Medium-High**, or until almost set. As edges of omelet begin to thicken, draw cooked portions toward the center with a spoon or fork to let uncooked mixture flow to bottom; tilt pie plate as necessary, but do not stir.

3. Remove from oven and fold omelet in half. Let stand covered a few minutes before serving.

2 servings

Citrus Omelet

4 eggs
2 tablespoons half-and-half
2 tablespoons orange juice
1 tablespoon sugar
1 tablespoon butter or
margarine
¼ cup orange marmalade

1. Beat eggs, half-and-half, orange juice and sugar together in a bowl.

2. Melt butter in a 9-inch glass pie plate (**about 30 seconds at High**). Add egg mixture. Cover with plastic wrap. Cook in microwave oven **4 to 5 minutes at Medium-High**, or until almost set. Draw cooked portions to center with spoon or fork to let uncooked mixture flow to bottom; tilt pie plate as necessary, but do not stir.

3. Remove from oven and let stand 1 minute. Loosen edges with rubber spatula. Spread orange marmalade in middle of omelet. Fold omelet in thirds to enclose filling.

2 servings

Crustless Quiche Lorraine

8 slices bacon, cooked
(see page 113)
1 cup (4 ounces) shredded
Swiss cheese
3 green onions, thinly sliced
4 eggs
1 cup half-and-half
½ teaspoon salt
⅛ teaspoon pepper
⅛ teaspoon ground nutmeg

1. Prepare bacon; crumble 2 slices bacon and reserve for garnish. Crumble remaining 6 slices bacon and sprinkle over bottom of 9-inch glass quiche dish. Sprinkle cheese and sliced green onion over bacon.

2. Mix eggs, half-and-half, salt, pepper and nutmeg. Pour over ingredients in quiche dish. Cover with plastic wrap. Cook in microwave oven **7 to 8 minutes at Medium-High**, or until center is almost set; rotate dish one-quarter turn once.

3. Remove from oven; let stand covered on a flat surface 5 minutes before cutting into wedges. Garnish with reserved crumbled bacon.

6 servings

Hint: For microwave/convection oven cooking, preheat convection oven to 325°F. Place filled quiche dish on bottom metal rack. Cook in microwave/convection oven **25 to 30 minutes at Combination I**, or until center is set. Let stand 5 minutes.

Ham and Cheddar Quiche

1 cup chopped cooked ham
1 cup (4 ounces) shredded
Cheddar cheese
1 baked pastry shell in 9-inch
glass pie plate
4 eggs, beaten
1 cup undiluted evaporated
milk
¼ teaspoon salt
⅛ teaspoon pepper
2 teaspoons spicy prepared
mustard

1. Preheat convection oven to 325°F.

2. Sprinkle ham and cheese over baked pastry shell.

3. Combine remaining ingredients in a 1-quart glass measuring pitcher. Pour over cheese.

4. Place pie plate on bottom metal rack. Cook in microwave/convection oven **25 to 30 minutes at Combination I**, or until center is set. Let stand 5 minutes.

6 servings

Broccoli-Mushroom Quiche

1 package (10 ounces) frozen
chopped broccoli
8 ounces fresh mushrooms
¼ cup chopped onion
2 tablespoons butter or
margarine
2 tablespoons all-purpose flour
1 cup (4 ounces) shredded
Swiss cheese
1 baked pastry shell in 9-inch
glass pie plate
3 eggs, beaten
⅔ cup half-and-half
1 teaspoon salt
½ teaspoon dry mustard
⅛ teaspoon pepper

1. Pierce package of broccoli with a fork. Cook in microwave oven **5 minutes at High**; drain. Set aside.

2. Clean mushrooms and slice lengthwise. Put mushrooms, onion and butter into a 2-quart glass measuring pitcher. Cook uncovered in microwave oven **3 minutes at High**. Remove from oven; stir in flour. Add broccoli and cheese; stir well.

3. Preheat convection oven to 325°F.

4. Spread broccoli mixture in baked pastry shell.

5. Combine remaining ingredients and pour over broccoli mixture.

6. Place pie plate on bottom metal rack. Cook in microwave/convection oven **30 to 35 minutes at Combination I**, or until center is set. Let stand 5 minutes.

6 servings

Country-Style Eggs

4 slices bacon
2 tablespoons butter or margarine
6 ounces frozen hash brown potatoes
¼ cup chopped onion
¼ cup chopped green pepper
6 eggs
¼ cup milk
½ teaspoon salt
Dash pepper
1 cup (4 ounces) shredded mild Cheddar cheese

1. Arrange bacon on a microwave-oven-safe roast rack set in a glass baking dish. Cover with a paper towel. Cook in microwave oven **4 minutes at High**, or until done. Crumble bacon and set aside.

2. Put butter, potatoes, onion and green pepper into an 8-inch round glass cake dish. Cook uncovered in microwave oven **6 minutes at High**, or until vegetables are tender; stir once.

3. Mix eggs, milk, salt and pepper. Flatten potato mixture and pour egg mixture over top. Cover with plastic wrap. Cook in microwave oven **6 to 7 minutes at Medium-High**, or until egg mixture is almost set; stir once.

4. Sprinkle bacon and cheese over egg mixture. Heat uncovered in microwave oven **1 minute at Medium-High**, or until cheese just starts to melt.

5. Remove from oven and let stand 5 minutes. Cut into wedges to serve.

4 to 6 servings

Eggs 'n' Mushrooms in Cheese Sauce

1 cup sliced fresh mushrooms
1 tablespoon butter or margarine
1 small can (⅔ cup) evaporated milk
2 cups (8 ounces) shredded pasteurized process American cheese
4 eggs, hard cooked (see page 68) and cut in pieces
Bread slices, toasted

1. Put mushrooms and butter into a 1-quart glass measuring pitcher. Cook uncovered in microwave oven **2 minutes at High**; stir once.

2. Pour evaporated milk into a 1½-quart glass casserole. Heat in microwave oven **1½ minutes at High**. Add cheese, egg pieces and cooked mushrooms; stir. Heat uncovered to serving temperature (**about 4 minutes at Medium-High**); stir every 2 minutes. Serve on toast.

4 to 6 servings

Creamed Eggs

6 eggs, hard cooked
(see page 68)
2 cups Medium White Sauce
(see page 188)
Salt and pepper (optional)
Bread slices, toasted

1. Prepare eggs and sauce.

2. Dice hard-cooked eggs into ½-inch pieces. Put egg pieces into white sauce in measuring pitcher and add seasoning, if desired; mix well. Cover with plastic wrap. Heat in microwave oven to serving temperature (**2½ to 3 minutes at Medium-High**). Serve on toast.

6 servings

Scrambled Eggs

4 eggs
¼ cup milk or cream
1 tablespoon butter or
margarine

1. Beat eggs; mix in milk.

2. Melt butter in a 1-quart glass casserole in microwave oven (**about 30 seconds at High**). Pour egg mixture into dish. Cook uncovered **3 minutes at High**, or until almost set; stir after 2 minutes.

3. Remove from oven; stir and let stand covered a few minutes before serving. Season to taste.

2 servings

Zesty Scrambled Eggs

4 eggs
¼ teaspoon salt
Dash pepper
¼ teaspoon Worcestershire
sauce
⅓ cup chopped peeled tomato
¼ cup finely shredded Cheddar
cheese
1½ tablespoons butter or
margarine

1. Put all ingredients except butter into a bowl and beat with a fork until blended.

2. Melt butter in a 1-quart glass casserole in microwave oven (**about 30 seconds at High**). Pour egg mixture into casserole. Cook uncovered **3 to 4 minutes at High**, or until almost set; stir twice during cooking period.

3. Remove from oven; stir and let stand covered a few minutes before serving.

2 servings

Bacon and Cream Cheese Eggs

4 slices bacon
¼ cup milk or cream
2 ounces cream cheese
3 tablespoons butter or
margarine
4 eggs
¼ teaspoon salt
⅛ teaspoon pepper

1. Arrange bacon on a microwave-oven-safe roast rack set in a glass baking dish. Cover with a paper towel. Cook in microwave oven **4 minutes at High**, or until done. Crumble bacon and set aside.

2. Put milk, cream cheese and butter into a 1-quart glass casserole. Heat uncovered in microwave oven **30 seconds at High**, or until cream cheese is softened; stir to blend.

3. Beat eggs, salt and pepper until blended. Add egg mixture and bacon to cheese mixture; stir. Cook uncovered in microwave oven **3 minutes at High**, or until eggs are almost set; stir after 2 minutes.

4. Remove from oven; stir and let stand covered a few minutes before serving.

2 servings

Brunch Eggs

4 tablespoons shredded
  Cheddar cheese
4 eggs
⅛ teaspoon salt
4 slices cooked bacon,
  crumbled

1. Preheat convection oven to 325°F.

2. Divide cheese evenly among 4 glass custard cups.

3. Separate eggs; reserve yolks individually. Beat egg whites with salt until stiff, not dry, peaks form. Fold in bacon. Divide evenly in custard cups. Make an indentation in egg whites; drop one yolk in each one.

4. Place cups on bottom metal rack. Cook in microwave/convection oven **9 to 10 minutes at Combination I**, or until whites are set and very lightly brown.

4 servings

Corned Beef Hash and Eggs

1 can (15½ ounces) corned
  beef hash
½ teaspoon Worcestershire
  sauce
4 eggs
  Salt and pepper
  Chopped parsley

1. Combine corned beef hash and Worcestershire sauce. Divide the mixture evenly in four 10-ounce glass casseroles. Make a well with back of spoon in each portion of hash. Break eggs, one at a time, and slip into wells. Sprinkle eggs with salt and pepper. Pierce egg yolks. Cover with all-glass lids or plastic wrap.

2. Cook in microwave oven **8 to 9 minutes at Medium**, or until eggs are almost set; rearrange and rotate casseroles one-quarter turn twice.

3. Remove from oven and let stand covered about 1 minute before serving. Sprinkle with parsley.

4 servings

Eggs Benedict

4 (¼-inch) slices
   Canadian-style bacon
4 Poached Eggs (see page 68)
   Hollandaise Sauce
   (see page 191)
2 English muffins, split and
   toasted

1. Put Canadian bacon slices into a 9-inch glass pie plate. Cover with waxed paper. Heat in microwave oven **about 2 minutes at High**. Set aside.

2. Prepare Poached Eggs and Hollandaise Sauce.

3. Put warm toasted muffin halves on individual plates; top with Canadian bacon slices, poached eggs and sauce. Serve immediately.

4 servings

Bologna-Egg Cups

4 slices bologna
4 eggs

1. Fit bologna into four 6-ounce glass custard cups. Slip an egg into each lined cup and pierce egg yolk. Cover with plastic wrap.

2. Cook in microwave oven **3½ to 4½ minutes on Medium**; rearrange the cups once. Season to taste.

4 servings

Crab Soufflé

6 tablespoons butter or
   margarine
6 tablespoons all-purpose flour
1 teaspoon paprika
¼ teaspoon salt
1½ cups milk
2 tablespoons sherry
1 cup (4 ounces) shredded
   Muenster cheese
1 can (6 ounces) crab meat,
   drained
6 eggs, separated

1. Melt butter in a 1-quart glass measuring pitcher in microwave oven (**about 1 minute at High**).

2. Stir in flour, paprika and salt; mix well. Add milk gradually, stirring until smooth. Cook uncovered in microwave oven **3 to 3½ minutes at High**, or until thickened; stir twice. Add sherry and cheese; stir until cheese is partially melted.

3. Preheat convection oven to 300°F.

4. Stir crab meat into cheese sauce. Beat egg yolks in a bowl until lemon colored. Slowly add cheese sauce, stirring constantly.

5. Beat egg whites until stiff, not dry, peaks form. Stir about one-third of beaten egg whites into egg yolk mixture. Gently spread egg yolk mixture on remaining egg whites; fold in gently just until blended. Turn mixture into an ungreased 2-quart soufflé dish. Insert tip of knife into mixture about 1 inch from outside edge and circle the mixture.

6. Place dish on bottom metal rack. Cook in convection oven **70 to 75 minutes at 300°F**, or until set (metal knife inserted near center comes out clean).

8 servings

Cheese Souffle

Cheese Rarebit

Swiss Cheese Fondue

Cheese Soufflé

¼ cup all-purpose flour
½ teaspoon dry mustard
¾ teaspoon salt
⅛ teaspoon paprika
¼ teaspoon liquid pepper sauce
1 can (13 fluid ounces) evaporated milk
2 cups (8 ounces) shredded sharp Cheddar cheese
6 eggs, separated
1 teaspoon cream of tartar

1. Mix flour, dry mustard, salt and paprika in a 1-quart glass measuring pitcher. Add pepper sauce and then evaporated milk gradually, stirring until smooth. Cook uncovered in microwave oven **3 minutes at High**, or until sauce thickens; stir after 2 minutes, then every 30 seconds.

2. Add cheese to sauce and stir until melted. Set aside.

3. Beat egg whites and cream of tartar in a large bowl until stiff, not dry, peaks form.

4. Beat egg yolks in a medium bowl until thick and lemon colored. Add cheese sauce gradually to egg yolks until thoroughly blended. Fold sauce carefully into beaten egg whites. Turn mixture into an ungreased 2-quart glass soufflé dish.

5. Cook uncovered in microwave oven **15 minutes at Medium**, or until set at edges; rotate dish one-quarter turn twice. Cook uncovered **10 to 15 minutes at Medium-Low**, or until top is no longer moist; rotate dish one-quarter turn every 5 minutes.

6 to 8 servings

Cheese Rarebit

1½ teaspoons butter or margarine
2 cups (8 ounces) shredded sharp Cheddar cheese or pasteurized process American cheese
¼ teaspoon Worcestershire sauce
¼ teaspoon dry mustard
   Dash ground red pepper
⅓ cup milk
   Bread slices, toasted

1. Melt butter in a 1-quart glass casserole in microwave oven (**about 15 seconds at High**). Add cheese and heat uncovered **1 minute at High**, or until cheese begins to melt; stir once.

2. Add Worcestershire sauce, dry mustard and red pepper to cheese. Add milk gradually, stirring constantly. Heat uncovered in microwave oven to serving temperature (**2 to 3 minutes at Medium-High**); stir every 30 seconds. Serve immediately on hot toast.

4 to 6 servings

Swiss Cheese Fondue

4 cups (16 ounces) shredded Swiss cheese
¼ cup all-purpose flour
¼ teaspoon salt
¼ teaspoon ground nutmeg
⅛ teaspoon pepper
1 clove garlic, cut in half
1½ cups dry white wine
   French bread cubes for dipping

1. Combine cheese, flour, salt, nutmeg and pepper. Set aside.

2. Rub cut sides of garlic over inside of a 2-quart glass casserole. Pour in wine. Heat in microwave oven until very hot (**3 to 4 minutes at Medium-High**). Add the cheese mixture; stir well.

3. Cook uncovered in microwave oven **5 to 7 minutes at Medium-High**, or until bubbly.

4. Stir fondue until smooth. Keep warm in a fondue pot. Serve with bread cubes.

About 6 servings

Shrimp in Patty Shells

Halibut Steaks Poached in Wine

Deviled Crab

Fish and Shellfish

Learning to use your microwave oven pays off most handsomely in fish cookery. Cooked in the microwave oven fish has the qualities fish lovers cherish most; true flavor, mild taste and delicate tenderness.

Fish cookery puts into practice all of the microwave techniques. Start cautiously, undercooking at first, and adding more time in short intervals, until the fish is cooked just right.

Before you put fish into the microwave oven, consider *arrangement.* If you are cooking several small fish or steaks cut from a large fish, arrange them in a circular pattern in the cooking dish with thick parts turned outward and thinner parts inward. Leave spaces between and don't stack, so that all surfaces will be exposed to the microwave energy.

Poached or Baked Fish

Covering the fish before cooking is important, and the type of cover will determine whether the fish will be poached or baked. For poached fish, cover the utensil with a lid or plastic wrap, vented so that some steam can escape. With this covering, the fish will cook both by microwave energy and trapped steam; ideal for producing tender poached fish. For baked fish, just place waxed paper over the fish in the dish. The waxed paper will prevent spattering, and will help to distribute the heat evenly.

Cooking time: For either baked or poached fish, timing is the key to success. Set the timer for the minimum time given in the recipe, or if using the Temperature Probe (a good method with large whole fish) set the probe for the recommended temperature.

Fish benefits from one or more rotations of the dish during cooking. The larger the quantity, of course, the longer the cooking time and the more turns that will be needed for evenness. *Rearrange* and *turn over* whole fish during cooking time.

When the minimum cooking time or temperature is reached, make the first *doneness test.* Is the flesh of the fish beginning to turn from transparent to opaque? *Standing time* will help to complete the cooking process, so unless the fish appears very underdone, let it stand on the counter a minute or so and check the appearance again. Still underdone? Put it back in the microwave oven for brief, additional cooking.

Doneness test: When the fish acquires a milky-white look, give it another test by inserting a fork in the thickest part. If the fish meat breaks apart or "flakes" easily, it's ready to serve.

Fish unadorned is ideal for the dieter. For everyone else, fish rates highest served with accompaniments as simple as lemon butter or as imaginative as the sauces in Chapter 11.

Shellfish

Shellfish can also be successfully cooked in the microwave oven. Since the shells are invisible to microwave energy, they can be used as cooking utensils. No need to cook shellfish in large quantities of water; they steam right in their shell in the microwave oven. Oysters can be heated in the microwave oven just until the shells open; then served with sauce or on the half shell.

Doneness test: For the shellfish the flesh will be opaque. The shells of shrimp, crab and lobster will also turn red.

Cooking Frozen Fish? Defrost it completely before cooking. Defrost it partially in the microwave oven. Defrosting can be completed under running cold water.

Crispy Fish Fillets Italiano

1 package (16 ounces) frozen
  fillet of sole, defrosted
1 egg, beaten
2 tablespoons water
½ cup dry bread crumbs
¼ cup grated Parmesan cheese
2 teaspoons chopped parsley
½ teaspoon oregano leaves
½ teaspoon basil leaves
½ teaspoon marjoram leaves
½ teaspoon paprika
¼ teaspoon garlic salt

1. Preheat convection oven to 325°F.

2. Separate fillets; cut into serving pieces. Combine egg and water in a shallow bowl. Combine remaining ingredients in another shallow bowl. Dip fish pieces first in egg mixture, then in crumb mixture; turn to coat evenly.

3. Arrange fish on a roast rack suitable for microwave and convection heat; set in a 2-quart glass baking dish.

4. Place dish on bottom metal rack. Cook in microwave/convection oven **12 to 15 minutes at Combination I**, or until fish flakes easily when tested with a fork.

4 servings

Hint: To defrost fish, follow directions in Defrosting Chart (see page 21).

Salmon Croquettes

1 can (15½ ounces) salmon
¼ cup milk
1 egg, beaten
1¼ cups coarse unsalted cracker
  crumbs
1 tablespoon lemon juice
1 tablespoon finely chopped
  onion
1 teaspoon dried parsley flakes
¼ teaspoon salt
⅛ teaspoon pepper

1. Preheat convection oven to 400°F.

2. Drain salmon; reserve liquid in a 1-cup measuring cup; add water, if necessary, to measure ½ cup liquid. Discard skin and bones, if desired. Flake salmon and combine with salmon liquid and remaining ingredients. Shape into eight balls and arrange on ungreased round metal tray.

3. Place tray on bottom metal rack. Cook in convection oven **20 to 25 minutes at 400°F**, or until firm.

8 croquettes

Hint: If desired, serve with Cucumber Sauce (see page 83).

Stuffed Whole Fish

1 dressed whitefish or other
  whole fish (1 pound)
¼ cup (½ stick) butter or
  margarine
1 teaspoon salt
2 tablespoons grated onion
2 cups seasoned croutons

1. Wash fish and pat dry.

2. Melt butter in a 2-cup glass measuring cup in microwave oven **(about 1 minute at High)**.

3. Brush inside of fish with 1 tablespoon melted butter and sprinkle with salt.

4. Combine 2 tablespoons melted butter and onion in a 1-quart glass casserole. Cook uncovered in microwave oven **2 minutes at High**.

5. Add croutons to onion and butter and stir. Fill cavity of fish with stuffing. Lace cavity closed using wooden picks and string.

6. Brush fish with remaining melted butter. Shield head and tail with pieces of aluminum foil.

7. Put fish on a microwave-oven-safe platter. Cover with plastic wrap. Cook in microwave oven **7 to 9 minutes at Medium-High**, or until fish flakes easily when tested with a fork; turn fish over and rotate dish one-half turn once. Or if using Temperature Probe, insert just above the gill into the meatiest area parallel to backbone (be sure it does not touch foil around head). Cover with plastic wrap. Cook in microwave oven set at **140°F and at Medium-High**.

About 2 servings

Hint: Any whole fish suitable for baking can be cooked following these directions. Stuffing may be omitted. Allow approximately 7 to 9 minutes per pound of fish when cooking at Medium-High in microwave oven. For convection oven cooking, preheat oven to 375°F. Put butter-brushed fish on an ovenproof platter and place on bottom metal rack. Cook in convection oven **about 20 minutes at 375°F**, or until fish tests done.

Buttered Fish Fillets

2 tablespoons butter or
  margarine
1¼ pounds whitefish fillets
  Salt and pepper
  Paprika

1. Melt butter in a 1-cup glass measuring cup in microwave oven (**about 30 seconds at High**).

2. Arrange fish in an 8-inch square or a 2-quart glass baking dish, brush with melted butter and sprinkle with salt, pepper and paprika. Cover with waxed paper. Cook in microwave oven **3 to 4 minutes at High**, or until fish flakes easily when tested with a fork.

4 or 5 servings

Hint: Other fish fillets such as halibut, haddock and flounder can be cooked using these directions.

Sunshine Fish Fillets

1½ **pounds red snapper or other fish fillets**
2 **tablespoons butter or margarine**
2 **teaspoons grated orange peel**
3 **tablespoons orange juice**
½ **teaspoon salt**
  Dash pepper
  Dash freshly ground nutmeg

1. Arrange fish fillets in a 1½-quart glass baking dish.

2. Melt butter in a small glass bowl in microwave oven (**about 30 seconds at High**). Add remaining ingredients, mix well and spoon over fish. Cover with waxed paper.

3. Cook in microwave oven **6½ to 7½ minutes at High**, or until fish flakes easily when tested with a fork; rearrange fillets halfway through cooking period.

About 6 servings

Red Snapper Veracruz Style

2 **tablespoons olive oil**
1 **cup chopped onion**
1 **clove garlic, minced**
1 **can (16 ounces) tomatoes, drained and coarsely chopped**
1 **teaspoon salt**
¼ **teaspoon pepper**
1½ **pounds red snapper fillets**
¼ **cup sliced pimiento-stuffed green olives**

1. Combine oil, onion and garlic in a 1-quart glass measuring pitcher. Cover with plastic wrap. Cook in microwave oven **2 minutes at High**; stir after 1 minute.

2. Add tomatoes, salt and pepper to mixture in pitcher; stir. Cook covered in microwave oven **3 minutes at High**.

3. Arrange red snapper fillets skin-side-down in an 8-inch square or a 2-quart glass baking dish with thicker portions to the outside. Pour sauce over fish. Sprinkle with olives. Cover with plastic wrap.

4. Cook in microwave oven **8 to 9 minutes at High**, or until fish flakes easily when tested with a fork; rotate dish one-half turn once.

5. Remove from oven and let stand covered 4 minutes.

About 6 servings

Halibut Steaks Poached in Wine

4 halibut steaks (about
  2 pounds), fresh or
  frozen
¾ cup dry white wine
¼ cup water
2 tablespoons olive oil
2 teaspoons lemon juice
1 clove garlic, minced
¼ teaspoon dry mustard
¼ teaspoon marjoram
½ teaspoon salt
⅛ teaspoon pepper

1. If fish is frozen, defrost in microwave oven following directions in Defrosting Chart on page 21.

2. Arrange halibut steaks in an 8-inch square or a 2-quart glass baking dish.

3. Combine white wine, water, olive oil, lemon juice, garlic, dry mustard, marjoram, salt and pepper in a 2-cup glass measuring cup. Drizzle over halibut. Cover with waxed paper.

4. Cook in microwave oven **6 to 8 minutes at High**, or until fish flakes easily when tested with a fork.

4 servings

Salmon Steaks 'n' Cucumber Sauce

1 cup dairy sour cream
1 cup chopped pared cucumber
1 tablespoon sugar
2 tablespoons prepared
  horseradish
1 tablespoon vinegar
  Salt to taste
  Dash ground red pepper
4 salmon steaks (about
  2 pounds)

1. For sauce, combine all ingredients except salmon in a bowl; cover and chill.

2. Arrange salmon steaks, alternating thick and thin ends, in a 1½-quart glass baking dish. Cover with waxed paper.

3. Cook in microwave oven **4 minutes at High**. Turn salmon steaks over and rearrange. Continue cooking covered **3 to 4 minutes at High**, or until fish flakes easily when tested with a fork.

4. Remove from oven; let stand covered 2 minutes. Serve with cucumber sauce.

4 to 6 servings

Perch with Parsley and Dill

¼ cup finely snipped parsley
1¼ pounds perch fillets
½ teaspoon salt
⅛ teaspoon pepper
2 tablespoons snipped parsley
1 teaspoon dill seed

1. Sprinkle ¼ cup parsley over bottom of a buttered 1½-quart glass baking dish. Arrange fish in dish and season with salt and pepper. Top fish with 2 tablespoons parsley and the dill seed. Cover with waxed paper.

2. Cook in microwave oven **6 minutes at High**, or until fish flakes easily when tested with a fork.

4 servings

Salmon Loaf

1 can (15½ ounces) red salmon
¾ cup fine saltine cracker
   crumbs
⅓ cup milk
2 eggs
¼ cup sliced pimiento-stuffed
   green olives
¼ cup chopped parsley
1 tablespoon chopped onion
   Hollandaise Sauce
   (see page 191)

1. Drain salmon; discard skin and bones, if desired. Flake salmon and put into a bowl. Add cracker crumbs, milk, eggs, olives, parsley and onion; mix thoroughly. Turn mixture into a 1-quart glass casserole; press lightly.

2. Cook uncovered in microwave oven **4 to 5 minutes at High**; rotate casserole one-quarter turn once.

3. Remove from oven; let stand 5 minutes. Serve with Hollandaise Sauce.

4 servings

Salmon Ring

1 can (15½ ounces) red
   salmon
½ cup chopped celery
½ cup chopped green pepper
2 tablespoons minced onion
1 cup fine dry bread crumbs
1 tablespoon lemon juice
1 cup undiluted evaporated
   milk
1 egg, beaten
1 package (10 ounces) frozen
   green peas, cooked
   (see chart on page 148)
1 cup Medium White Sauce
   (see page 188)

1. Drain salmon; discard skin and bones, if desired. Flake salmon and set aside.

2. Combine celery, green pepper and onion in a 2-quart glass casserole. Cook uncovered in microwave oven **2 minutes at High**, or until tender.

3. Add flaked salmon, bread crumbs, lemon juice and a mixture of evaporated milk and egg to cooked vegetables; mix well. Carefully spoon salmon mixture into a 5½- to 6-cup microwave-oven-safe ring mold. Cover with waxed paper.

4. Cook in microwave oven **8 to 9 minutes at High**; rotate ring mold one-quarter turn once.

5. Unmold salmon ring on a heated platter. Mix peas with white sauce. Spoon into center of ring.

6 servings

Hint: If a microwave-oven-safe ring mold is unavailable, form a ring mold by placing a glass custard cup right-side-up in an 8-inch round glass cake dish.

Trout Amandine with Pineapple

2 tablespoons butter or margarine
1 package (2¼ ounces) slivered almonds (about ⅓ cup)
¼ cup (½ stick) butter or margarine
1 tablespoon lemon juice
6 whole cleaned and boned trout (about 8 ounces each)
6 drained canned pineapple slices, halved

1. Put 2 tablespoons butter and almonds into a 9-inch glass pie plate. Cook uncovered in microwave oven **5 to 6 minutes at High**; stir every minute just until almonds are lightly toasted. Set aside.

2. Melt ¼ cup butter in a 2-cup glass measuring cup in microwave oven (**about 1 minute at High**). Add lemon juice; stir.

3. Brush whole trout inside and out with lemon-butter mixture. Arrange fish around edge of a microwave-oven-safe serving plate in a circular pattern. Fit a small piece of aluminum foil over each head to shield. Cover with plastic wrap. Cook in microwave oven **6 to 7 minutes at High**, or until fish flakes easily when tested with a fork. (Be certain to check for doneness under shielded area.) Remove from oven and let stand covered 2 minutes.

4. Meanwhile, arrange pineapple slices on toasted almonds. Cover with plastic wrap. Heat in microwave oven **2 minutes at High**. Garnish fish with almonds and pineapple.

6 servings

Crab-Stuffed Fillet of Sole

3 tablespoons butter or margarine
3 tablespoons all-purpose flour
½ teaspoon salt
1½ cups milk
⅓ cup dry white wine
1 cup (4 ounces) shredded Swiss cheese
⅓ cup minced onion
2 tablespoons butter or margarine
1 can (6½ ounces) crab meat, drained and flaked
1 can (4 ounces) mushrooms, drained and finely chopped
½ cup coarse cracker crumbs Salt
Freshly ground white pepper
2 pounds sole fillets Snipped parsley

1. Melt 3 tablespoons butter in a 1-quart glass measuring pitcher in microwave oven (**about 1 minute at High**). Stir in flour and ½ teaspoon salt. Add milk and wine gradually, stirring until smooth. Cook uncovered **4 minutes at High**, or until thickened; stir once. Stir in cheese; set aside.

2. Put onion and 2 tablespoons butter into a 1-quart glass casserole. Cook uncovered in microwave oven **2 minutes at High**, or until onion is tender; stir after 1 minute. Add crab, mushrooms and crumbs to onion; mix well. Season with salt and pepper.

3. Cut fillets into uniform serving-size pieces. Lay each fillet white-side-down and sprinkle with salt and pepper. Dividing the stuffing evenly, spread stuffing almost the full length of each fillet. Roll up and place seam-side-down in an 8-inch square glass baking dish. Cover with waxed paper.

4. Cook in microwave oven **5 minutes at High**; rotate dish one-half turn after 3 minutes and rearrange fish. With a bulb baster, draw off any juices in the baking dish and stir into the sauce. Cover and cook **4 to 5 minutes at High**, or until fish flakes easily when tested with a fork. Remove from oven. Cover with plastic wrap and let stand 5 minutes.

5. Meanwhile, heat sauce uncovered in microwave oven **5 minutes at High**, or until cheese is melted; stir once. Pour sauce into a sauce boat and garnish with parsley. Serve with fish.

8 servings

Fillet of Sole Amandine

1 package (16 ounces) frozen fillet of sole
1 tablespoon butter or margarine
¼ cup slivered almonds
¼ cup (½ stick) butter or margarine
¼ teaspoon salt
2 teaspoons lemon juice

1. Defrost fish in microwave oven following directions in Defrosting Chart on page 21.

2. Put 1 tablespoon butter and the almonds into a 9-inch glass pie plate. Cook uncovered in microwave oven **5 to 6 minutes at High**; stir every minute just until almonds are lightly toasted. Set aside.

3. Melt ¼ cup butter in a 2-cup glass measuring cup in microwave oven (**about 1 minute at High**).

4. Place fillets in an 8-inch square glass baking dish and lightly brush with melted butter. Cover with waxed paper. Cook in microwave oven **4 to 5 minutes at High**, or until fish flakes easily when tested with a fork.

5. Add almonds, salt and lemon juice to remaining melted butter; stir. Pour over fillets.

About 4 servings

Mississippi River Delight

2 skinned and dressed catfish or other fish (about 1 pound each), fresh or frozen
⅓ cup bottled French dressing
½ lemon, sliced (4 slices)
Paprika

1. If fish is frozen, defrost (see page 21). Wash and dry fish. Brush inside and out with some of the French dressing. Place fish, alternating thick and thin ends, in a 2-quart glass baking dish.

2. Cut 2 of the lemon slices in half and place 2 halves in each body cavity. Pour remaining dressing over fish and sprinkle with paprika. Place a lemon slice on top of each fish. Cover with waxed paper.

3. Cook in microwave oven **11 minutes at High**, or until fish flakes easily when tested with a fork; rotate dish one-half turn once.

4 servings

Hot Tuna Salad

1 package (10 ounces) frozen green peas
1 can (6½ or 7 ounces) tuna, drained
½ cup thinly sliced celery
½ cup chopped onion
Dash ground red pepper
½ cup bottled French dressing
Bread slices, toasted

1. Pierce package of frozen peas with a fork and place on a paper towel. Cook in microwave oven **4 minutes at High**. Drain.

2. Combine peas, tuna, celery, onion, red pepper and French dressing in a 1-quart glass measuring pitcher. Cook uncovered in microwave oven **3 to 4 minutes at High**, or until thoroughly heated. Serve on toast.

4 servings

Tuna-Macaroni Casserole

2 cups (7 ounces) uncooked elbow macaroni, cooked (see page 61)
1 package (10 ounces) frozen chopped broccoli
2 cans (6½ or 7 ounces each) tuna in vegetable oil
1 teaspoon salt
¼ cup chopped celery
1 can (11 ounces) condensed Cheddar cheese soup
1¼ cups milk

1. Prepare macaroni and set aside.

2. Pierce package of frozen broccoli with a fork. Heat in microwave oven just until defrosted (**about 3 minutes at High**); drain.

3. Put cooked macaroni, undrained tuna, salt, drained broccoli and the celery into a 3-quart glass casserole; mix well.

4. Blend condensed soup and milk; add to tuna mixture and mix well. Cover with an all-glass lid or plastic wrap. Cook in microwave oven **10 minutes at High**, or until thoroughly heated; stir twice.

About 6 servings

Tuna-Chip Casserole

2 cans (6½ or 7 ounces each) tuna, drained
1 can (10¾ ounces) condensed cream of mushroom soup
¾ cup (about 5 ounces) frozen green peas
⅓ cup chopped celery
1 tablespoon chopped onion
¼ cup milk
1 teaspoon Worcestershire sauce
2 cups potato chips, crushed slightly

1. Combine tuna, condensed soup, peas, celery, onion, milk and Worcestershire sauce in a bowl, mixing thoroughly. Spoon half of tuna into a 1-quart glass casserole. Sprinkle with half of crushed potato chips. Spoon remaining tuna mixture into casserole and sprinkle with remaining potato chips.

2. Cook uncovered in microwave oven **10 minutes at High**, or until thoroughly heated; rotate casserole one-quarter turn once.

About 6 servings

Seafood Casserole

2 frozen rock lobster tails
1 pound scrod fillets
¼ cup white wine
2 cans (6 ounces each) crab meat or 2 packages (6 ounces each) frozen crab, defrosted
1 can (10¾ ounces) condensed cream of shrimp soup
1 can (10¾ ounces) condensed cream of mushroom soup
½ cup whipping cream
2 tablespoons dry sherry
Dash pepper
2 tablespoons butter or margarine
¼ cup dry bread crumbs
¼ cup grated Parmesan or Romano cheese
Paprika

1. Defrost and cook lobster as directed on page 88. Remove lobster meat and cut into small pieces. Set aside.

2. Cut scrod into serving-size pieces. Place in a 1½-quart glass baking dish. Add wine. Cover with plastic wrap. Cook in microwave oven **5 minutes at High.**

3. Drain scrod and break up into small pieces. Combine lobster, scrod, crab, condensed soups, cream, sherry and pepper in a 1½-quart glass casserole. Heat uncovered in microwave oven to serving temperature (**about 15 minutes at High**, or if using Temperature Probe, set at **155°F and at High**).

4. Remove from oven and set aside.

5. Melt butter in a 2-cup glass measuring cup in microwave oven (**about 30 seconds at High**). Add crumbs and cheese; mix well. Sprinkle over seafood mixture. Sprinkle paprika over all.

6 servings

Whole Lobster

1 whole lobster (1½ pounds)
¼ cup hot water
1 teaspoon salt
2 tablespoons butter or
    margarine
    Salt and pepper
    Paprika

1. To kill the lobster, place lobster on a cutting board with back or smooth shell up. Hold a towel firmly over head and claws. Quickly insert the point of a sharp heavy knife into center of the small cross on the back of the head; this kills the lobster by severing the spinal cord. Before removing knife, bear down heavily, cutting through entire length of body and tail. Pull halves apart; remove and discard the stomach (a small sac which lies in the head) and the spongy lungs (which lie in upper body cavity between meat and shell). Remove and discard the dark red intestinal vein running through center of body.

2. Put hot water and 1 teaspoon salt into a 1½- or 2-quart glass baking dish. Put lobster into dish shell-side-up. Cover with plastic wrap. Cook in microwave oven **4 minutes at High**.

3. Remove from oven and turn lobster over. If using a 1½-quart dish, tips of tail and claws will extend over ends of dish.

4. Melt butter in a small glass container in microwave oven (**about 30 seconds at High**). Brush melted butter over lobster meat and sprinkle with salt, pepper and paprika. Continue cooking lobster covered in microwave oven **4 to 5 minutes at Medium-High**, or until flesh is opaque and shell is bright red.

1 serving

Lobster Tails

Frozen rock lobster tails,
about 6 ounces each
Melted butter or margarine
Paprika (optional)

1. To defrost lobster, put a tail or tails into a glass baking dish. Cover with plastic wrap. Defrost in microwave oven as directed on chart.

2. For "butterfly" style tails, cut hard shell down middle with sharp knife. Grasp tail in both hands and open flat. Place lobster tails flesh-side-up in dish, alternating tail end with fleshy end of tails. Brush with melted butter and, if desired, sprinkle with paprika. Cover with plastic wrap. Cook in microwave oven as directed; rearrange tails and rotate dish once.

Amount	Defrost at Medium-Low	Defrost—Standing Time	Cook at High	Cook—Standing Time
1	2 minutes	10 minutes	3 minutes	3 minutes
2	4 minutes	10 minutes	4½ to 5 minutes	5 minutes
4	6 minutes	10 minutes	5½ to 6 minutes	5 minutes

Hint: Cooking times are approximate. Color is the best indication of proper cooking; the flesh should be opaque and the shell red. If necessary, shield thinner parts of lobster tail with aluminum foil to prevent overcooking.

Deviled Crab

3 tablespoons butter or margarine
2 tablespoons chopped onion
2 tablespoons all-purpose flour
¾ cup milk
1 egg, beaten
½ teaspoon salt
Dash pepper
½ teaspoon dry mustard
½ teaspoon sage
Dash ground red pepper
1 teaspoon Worcestershire sauce
1 tablespoon lemon juice
1 tablespoon chopped parsley
12 ounces crab meat (bony tissue removed)
1 tablespoon butter or margarine
¼ cup dry bread crumbs

1. Put 3 tablespoons butter and onion into a 2-quart glass measuring pitcher. Cook uncovered in microwave oven **3 minutes at High**, or until tender; stir after 1 minute.

2. Stir flour into the butter. Add milk gradually, stirring constantly. Cook uncovered in microwave oven **2 minutes at High**, or until thickened; stir occasionally.

3. Stir a little of the hot sauce into beaten egg. Add to remaining sauce, stirring constantly. Add salt, pepper, mustard, sage, red pepper, Worcestershire sauce, lemon juice, parsley and crab; mix well.

4. Divide mixture into 6 individual microwave-oven-safe shells or glass custard cups.

5. Melt 1 tablespoon butter in a small glass dish in microwave oven (**about 30 seconds at High**). Mix bread crumbs with melted butter and sprinkle over top of each shell.

6. Cook uncovered in microwave oven **5 to 7 minutes at Medium-High**; rearrange shells once.

6 servings

Coquilles St. Jacques

2 tablespoons butter or margarine
3 tablespoons lemon juice
1 pound fresh mushrooms, cleaned and sliced lengthwise
1 cup dry white wine
¼ teaspoon ground thyme
1 bay leaf
½ teaspoon salt
⅛ teaspoon pepper
1 pound bay scallops
1½ tablespoons butter or margarine
1½ tablespoons all-purpose flour
½ cup milk
3 tablespoons butter or margarine
¾ cup dry bread crumbs

1. Put 2 tablespoons butter, lemon juice and mushrooms into an 8-inch square glass baking dish. Cook uncovered in microwave oven **5 minutes at High**; stir once. Drain mushrooms and set aside.

2. Combine wine, thyme, bay leaf, salt and pepper in the glass baking dish. Add scallops. Cover with plastic wrap. Cook in microwave oven **5 minutes at High**, or until tender; stir once. Drain, reserving ½ cup broth. Discard bay leaf. Add mushrooms to scallops in dish. Set aside.

3. Melt 1½ tablespoons butter in a 1-quart glass measuring pitcher in microwave oven (**about 30 seconds at High**). Add flour and blend to a smooth paste. Add milk and reserved broth gradually, stirring constantly. Cook uncovered **5 minutes at High**, or until thickened; stir after 3 minutes, then every 30 seconds.

4. Add white sauce to mushrooms and scallops; mix thoroughly.

5. Melt 3 tablespoons butter in a 2-cup glass measuring cup in microwave oven (**about 1 minute at High**). Add bread crumbs and mix well. Sprinkle over scallop mixture.

6. Cook uncovered in microwave oven **4 minutes at High**; rotate dish one-half turn once. Serve immediately.

6 servings

Scalloped Oysters

3 tablespoons butter or margarine
2 tablespoons chopped onion
3 tablespoons all-purpose flour
½ teaspoon salt
⅛ teaspoon pepper
Dash ground nutmeg
1 cup milk
1 pint oysters, drained
1 tablespoon snipped parsley
1 teaspoon grated lemon peel
1 teaspoon lemon juice
½ teaspoon Worcestershire sauce
1 cup cooked elbow macaroni
¼ cup dry bread crumbs

1. Put butter and onion into a 1-quart glass measuring pitcher. Cook uncovered in microwave oven **1½ minutes at High**, or until onion is tender.

2. Add flour, salt, pepper and nutmeg to onion and butter; mix well. Add milk gradually, stirring constantly until smooth. Cook uncovered in microwave oven **3 minutes at High**, or until thickened; stir after 2 minutes, then every 30 seconds.

3. Stir drained oysters, parsley, lemon peel, lemon juice and Worcestershire sauce into sauce.

4. Spread macaroni in a 1½-quart glass baking dish. Spoon oyster sauce over macaroni. Heat uncovered in microwave oven to serving temperature (**about 3 minutes at High**).

5. Sprinkle bread crumbs over top.

6 servings

Fresh Shrimp

1 pound uncooked fresh shrimp (or frozen, defrosted; see chart on page 21)

1. Shrimp can be shelled before or after cooking. Arrange shrimp in a layer on bottom of an 8-inch square glass baking dish.

2. Cook uncovered in microwave oven **5 to 6 minutes at High**, or until shrimp meat turns white and opaque; stir twice.

Shrimp in Sherry Sauce

3 tablespoons butter or margarine
1 cup dry bread crumbs
1 tablespoon dried parsley flakes
3 tablespoons butter or margarine
8 ounces fresh mushrooms, cleaned and sliced
¼ cup sliced green onion
¼ cup all-purpose flour
½ teaspoon salt
½ cup half-and-half
¼ cup dry sherry
2 cups cooked small shrimp, well drained

1. Melt 3 tablespoons butter in a small glass bowl in microwave oven (**about 1 minute at High**). Add bread crumbs and parsley; mix well and set aside.

2. Put 3 tablespoons butter, mushrooms and green onion into a 1-quart glass measuring pitcher. Cook uncovered in microwave oven **2 minutes at High**.

3. Stir flour and salt into mushroom mixture. Gradually add half-and-half and sherry, stirring until smooth. Cook uncovered in microwave oven **2 to 3 minutes at High**, or until thickened; stir once.

4. Stir shrimp into thickened sherry sauce. Pour into 8 microwave-oven-safe ramekins or glass custard cups. Top with reserved crumb mixture (about 2 tablespoons for each). Cook uncovered in microwave oven **3 to 4 minutes at High**, or until thoroughly heated.

8 servings

Shrimp Creole

1 pound fresh shrimp, cooked
(see page 90)
2 tablespoons vegetable oil
¾ cup finely chopped onion
¾ cup finely chopped green
pepper
2 tablespoons all-purpose flour
1 can (16 ounces) tomatoes,
sieved
1 teaspoon Worcestershire
sauce
1 bay leaf
1½ teaspoons salt
¼ teaspoon pepper
½ teaspoon sugar
½ teaspoon oregano leaves
Cooked rice (see page 59)

1. Reserve 8 whole shrimp for garnish and cut remainder into pieces. Refrigerate until ready to use.

2. Heat oil in a 2-quart casserole in microwave oven **30 seconds at High**. Mix in onion and green pepper. Cook uncovered **4 minutes at High**, or until tender; stir once.

3. Sprinkle flour over vegetables. Stir in remaining ingredients except cooked rice. Cook uncovered in microwave oven **6 minutes at High**; stir once or twice.

4. Stir in shrimp pieces. Heat uncovered in microwave oven to serving temperature (**3 minutes at High**).

5. Serve shrimp mixture on hot cooked rice and garnish with the whole shrimp.

About 4 servings

Shrimp in Patty Shells

2 tablespoons butter or
margarine
1 small onion, thinly sliced
1 small clove garlic, minced
1 can (10¾ ounces) condensed
cream of celery soup
½ cup milk
1 pound cooked shrimp
(see page 90), peeled and
deveined
½ cup cooked peas
6 frozen puff pastry patty
shells, baked conventionally

1. Put butter, onion and garlic into a 1½-quart glass casserole. Cook uncovered in microwave oven **4 minutes at High**, or until onion is tender; stir after 1 minute.

2. Add condensed soup, milk, cooked shrimp and peas; mix. Cover with waxed paper. Cook in microwave oven **3 to 4 minutes at High**, or until thoroughly heated; stir occasionally.

3. Serve shrimp mixture in patty shells.

6 servings

Beef Roast

Oriental
Pork Roast

Meats

Meat heads the menu in most homes, and it accounts for a major part of the food budget. Those are two good reasons to master meat cookery.

Contrary to common belief, meat does brown in the microwave oven. The amount of fat and length of cooking time will determine how brown. Properly prepared, meats cooked in the microwave oven are tender and flavorful. Many creative cooks brush on a brown or tomato-based sauce, sprinkle on dry onion soup mix, paprika or other spices to enhance the color of tender meat. Meats cooked with combination, of course, are browner due to the convection heat in addition to the microwave energy.

Tender Cuts of Meat

In meat cooking, tender cuts get different treatment than less-tender cuts. Tender cuts are steaks and roasts. The guide to doneness is internal temperature, just as it is for conventional cooking. The bonus of meat cooked in the microwave oven is that it only takes a fraction of the cooking time.

Uniformly shaped meat cooks the most evenly. Protruding parts of irregularly shaped roasts and steaks may cook too fast. Prevent overcooking those spots by tucking aluminum foil around to shield them. Roasts and steaks should be put in a microwave-oven-safe dish with a roast rack to hold the meat out of the juices. Save the juice for *au jus* or gravy. Cover loosely with waxed paper to help cooking by holding the heat around the meat and to prevent spattering.

Convection and combination roasting is easy and no special pans are required. Place the roast directly on the bottom metal rack so that the hot air can circulate around the meat and cook it evenly. No preheating is needed nor is it necessary to turn the roast over. The hot air quickly seals in the natural meat juices.

See the charts beginning on page 94 for timing, but consider the timing an estimate. Exact time will depend upon weight and shape of meat, doneness desired and starting temperature of the meat. The chart is based on the temperature of meat taken straight from the refrigerator. Frozen meat cuts, tender or less tender, should be fully defrosted before cooking. Insert the Temperature Probe in the meat, making sure it doesn't touch bone or fat.

Standing time is an important part of cooking time. Microwaves penetrate only the outer inch or so of thick roasts, and the heat generated moves to the center by conduction. Standing allows time for the temperature within the roast to rise and to equalize. Often it increases 10 degrees, so the meat must be taken from the microwave oven while internal temperature is accordingly lower than the finished temperature you wish. Cover the standing roast with a loose tent of foil to keep the surface warm, yet let moisture escape so the roast doesn't taste as though it were steamed.

Less-Tender Cuts

Less-tender cuts do need added liquid and a cover to trap the steam it generates. They benefit from longer cooking, too, so follow recipe directions. A marinade is useful for tenderizing less-tender cuts and adding color. Cutting the meat into evenly sized cubes, as for stew, exposes more surfaces to microwaves. Cubed meat can be stirred, promoting more even cooking.

Ground meat stars in microwave cooking. One meat patty can be cooked quickly. Remember to add more time as you add additional patties. Ground meat also can be combined with other ingredients for many exciting meals.

Microwave cooking makes it possible after a full day at work to prepare some dishes that formerly were reserved for weekend leisure. Whether it's meatloaf or an elegant roast, the microwave oven and meats were made for each other.

How to Cook Meats

Microwave

1. Place meat on a microwave-oven-safe roast rack set in a glass baking dish. Cover with waxed paper.

2. Determine the total cooking time by multiplying the actual pounds of meat by the approximate cooking minutes per pound. Divide by two to determine the first half of the cooking time. Set time and power for first half of the cooking time and cook without using the Temperature Probe.

3. After the first half of the cooking time has elapsed, turn the meat over. Shield parts that are cooking too fast with aluminum foil. Insert tip of Temperature Probe into the center of the meat. Set desired Temperature Probe and power setting. Cook for the second half of the cooking time.

4. When the meat interior reaches the preset temperature on the probe, the microwave oven will automatically turn off. Cover the meat with aluminum foil and let stand for 15 minutes before carving. During the standing time the internal temperature will rise 10 to 15 degrees.

Combination

1. Do not preheat convection oven.

2. Place meat fat-side-down directly on bottom metal rack.

3. Insert tip of Temperature Probe into the center of the meat. Set desired Temperature Probe and Combination setting.

4. When the meat interior reaches the preset temperature, the oven will automatically turn off. Remove meat to serving platter. Cover with aluminum foil and let stand 10 minutes before carving.

Microwave method

Combination method

Meat	Method	Oven Setting	Cooking Time per Pound	Internal Temperature	
				Probe Setting	After Standing
Beef					
Standing rib roast (5 to 7 pounds)					
Rare	Microwave	Medium-High	7 to 8 minutes	125°F	140°F
	Combination	Combination I	15 to 17 minutes	135°F	140°F
Medium	Microwave	Medium-High	8 to 9 minutes	145°F	160°F
	Combination	Combination I	18 to 20 minutes	155°F	160°F
Well	Microwave	Medium-High	10 to 11 minutes	155°F	170°F
	Combination	Combination I	23 to 25 minutes	165°F	170°F
Rolled rib roast (3 to 6 pounds)					
Rare	Microwave	Medium-High	8 to 9 minutes	125°F	140°F
	Combination	Combination I	10 to 12 minutes	130°F	140°F
Medium	Microwave	Medium-High	10 to 11 minutes	145°F	160°F
	Combination	Combination I	12 to 14 minutes	150°F	160°F
Well	Microwave	Medium-High	12 to 13 minutes	155°F	170°F
	Combination	Combination I	14 to 16 minutes	160°F	170°F
Sirloin tip roast (3 to 4 pounds)					
Rare	Microwave	Medium-High	8 to 9 minutes	125°F	140°F
	Combination	Combination I	17 to 19 minutes	130°F	140°F
Medium	Microwave	Medium-High	10 to 11½ minutes	145°F	160°F
	Combination	Combination I	21 to 23 minutes	150°F	160°F
Well	Microwave	Medium-High	12 to 13 minutes	155°F	170°F
	Combination	Combination I	23 to 25 minutes	160°F	170°F

Meats

Meat	Method	Oven Setting	Cooking Time per Pound	Internal Temperature Probe Setting	After Standing
Rolled rump roast, boneless (3 to 6 pounds)					
Medium-rare	Microwave Combination	Medium-High Combination I	8½ to 10 minutes 14 to 16 minutes	135°F 140°F	150°F 150°F
Medium	Microwave Combination	Medium-High Combination I	10 to 11 minutes 16 to 18 minutes	145°F 150°F	160°F 160°F
Well	Microwave Combination	Medium-High Combination I	11 to 12½ minutes 18 to 20 minutes	155°F 160°F	170°F 170°F
Tenderloin, half (2 to 3 pounds)					
Rare	Microwave Combination	High Combination I	2 to 3 minutes 12 to 15 minutes	125°F 130°F	140°F 140°F
Hamburgers					
Rare	Microwave	High	4 minutes		
Lamb					
Leg (4 to 8 pounds)					
Medium	Microwave Combination	Medium-High Combination I	8 to 9 minutes 14 to 17 minutes	145°F 150°F	160°F 160°F
Well	Microwave Combination	Medium-High Combination I	10 to 11 minutes 18 to 20 minutes	155°F 160°F	170°F 170°F
Boneless leg, rolled (3 to 6 pounds)					
Medium	Microwave Combination	Medium-High Combination I	10 to 11 minutes 17 to 19 minutes	145°F 150°F	160°F 160°F
Well	Microwave Combination	Medium-High Combination I	11 to 12½ minutes 20 to 22 minutes	155°F 160°F	170°F 170°F
Chops, loin					
Medium	Microwave	Medium-High	12 to 14 minutes		
Pork					
Loin roast (center) (3 to 5 pounds)					
Well	Microwave Combination	Medium-High Combination I	10 to 12 minutes 22 to 27 minutes	160°F 170°F	170°F 175°F
Shoulder roast, boneless (4 pounds)	Microwave	Medium-High	10 to 11 minutes	160°F	170°F
Chops, loin	Microwave	Medium-High	8 to 12 minutes		
Ham, canned (fully cooked) (2 to 5 pounds)	Microwave Combination	Medium-High Combination I	9 to 11 minutes 12 to 14 minutes	115°F 115°F	130°F 130°F
Ham, bone in half (fully cooked) (5 to 10 pounds)	Combination	Combination I	10 to 13 minutes	115°-120°F	130°-140°F
Veal					
Boneless shoulder roast (3 pounds)					
Well	Microwave	Medium-High	11 to 13 minutes	155°F	170°F

How to Cook Less-Tender Meat Cuts

Meat	Method	Oven Setting	Approximate Cooking Time
Beef brisket (3 to 3½ pounds; 2 cups water)	Microwave	High Medium	10 minutes 90 minutes or until fork tender
Beef short ribs (3 pounds)	Microwave	High Medium	10 minutes 40 to 50 minutes or until fork tender
Corned beef (3 pounds; 2 cups water)	Microwave	High Medium	10 minutes 90 minutes or until fork tender
Lamb stew (2 pounds lamb shoulder)	Microwave	High Medium	10 minutes 30 to 40 minutes or until fork tender
Pork spareribs (2 pounds)	Microwave	Medium	35 to 45 minutes or until fork tender
Pot roast (4 pounds beef chuck pot roast)	Microwave	Medium	65 to 75 minutes or until fork tender
Swiss steak (2 pounds beef round steak)	Microwave	Medium	50 to 60 minutes or until fork tender

Cooking Hints

Cut less-tender meat into even pieces and put into a casserole. Cover and cook at High to start, then at Medium until tender. Stir during cooking.	Begin meat on a microwave-oven-safe roast rack set in a glass dish to let fat run off. Or use a microwave-oven-safe roast rack that does not need an additional dish.	Place less-tender cuts of meat in a casserole. Cook covered. Turn over and rearrange in casserole to cook more evenly.

How to Broil Steaks

Meat	Method	Preheat Temperature	Oven Setting	Rack Position	Cooking Time
Beef steaks (¾ inch thick; 1½ to 2 pounds)					
Rare	Convection	450°F	450°F Broil	Bottom	10 to 15 minutes
Medium	Convection	450°F	450°F Broil	Bottom	15 to 20 minutes
Well	Convection	450°F	450°F Broil	Bottom	20 to 25 minutes

Yankee Pot Roast

1 beef arm chuck roast
(4 pounds)
1 package (¾ ounce) brown
gravy mix
4 small onions, peeled and cut
in half
Hot water
4 carrots, pared, halved and
cut in thirds
4 potatoes, pared and cut in
quarters

1. Put meat into a 4-quart microwave-oven-safe casserole. Sprinkle gravy mix over meat. Add onion and enough hot water to cover meat. Cover casserole with a microwave-oven-safe lid.

2. Cook in microwave oven **30 minutes at Medium**.

3. Turn meat over. Add carrots and potatoes to liquid. Cook covered in microwave oven **1 hour at Medium**, or until meat is tender.

4. Remove from oven and let stand covered 10 to 15 minutes.

5. If desired, thicken liquid as for Basic Gravy (see page 192).

6 to 8 servings

Sirloin Steak 'n' Blue Ribbon Sauce

1 beef sirloin steak (2 pounds),
cut about 1 inch thick
1 cup thinly sliced onion
1 medium lemon, thinly sliced
¼ cup (½ stick) butter or
margarine, softened
2 tablespoons prepared
mustard
1 cup chili sauce
1 tablespoon Worcestershire
sauce
1 teaspoon chili powder
1 can (6 ounces) cocktail
vegetable juice

1. Trim fat from steak. Cut steak into serving pieces and put into an 8-inch square glass baking dish. Arrange onion and lemon slices over meat.

2. Cream butter and prepared mustard; blend in chili sauce, Worcestershire sauce, chili powder and vegetable juice. Pour mixture over onion and lemon. Cover with plastic wrap.

3. Cook in microwave oven **15 minutes at High**, or until meat is done as desired; rotate dish one-quarter turn twice during cooking period.

4. Remove from oven. Let stand covered 5 minutes before serving.

About 6 servings

Caribbean Steak Kabobs

1¾ pounds boneless beef sirloin, cut 1¼ inches thick
1 cup soy sauce
⅓ cup honey
¼ cup finely chopped crystallized ginger
2 cloves garlic, minced
2 firm bananas with all-yellow peel
½ cup flaked coconut
Lime juice

1. Slice meat across grain into ¼-inch strips.

2. Combine soy sauce, honey, ginger and garlic in a large shallow dish; add meat strips and stir to coat with marinade. Refrigerate about 30 minutes, turning meat once.

3. Remove meat from marinade, reserving marinade. Thread meat onto 12 (8-inch) bamboo skewers, allowing space at end of each skewer for banana pieces.

4. Peel bananas and cut into 24 pieces; dip pieces into marinade, roll in coconut and drizzle with lime juice.

5. Put banana pieces on ends of skewers; brush meat and banana pieces with marinade.

6. Arrange 6 kabobs in an 8-inch square glass baking dish. Cover with waxed paper. Cook in microwave oven **4 to 5 minutes at High,** or until meat is done as desired; rotate dish, rearrange kabobs and brush with marinade twice during cooking period.

7. Put kabobs on a heated platter and keep warm.

8. Repeat procedure for remaining 6 kabobs.

6 servings

Beef Kabobs

¾ cup soy sauce
¼ cup honey
1 pound beef sirloin, cut in 1-inch pieces
24 pineapple chunks, fresh or canned
1 green pepper, cored and cut in squares
8 cherry tomatoes
Cooked rice (see page 59)

1. Combine soy sauce and honey in a bowl. Add meat; stir to coat. Marinate 1 hour.

2. Remove meat and reserve marinade.

3. Alternate beef, pineapple and green pepper on 8 skewers. (If using metal skewers, see page 10.) Arrange kabobs in an 8-inch square or a 2-quart glass baking dish and brush with marinade. Cover with waxed paper.

4. Cook in microwave oven **6 to 7 minutes at Medium-High,** or until meat is done as desired; turn and rearrange skewers and brush with marinade twice during cooking period.

5. Place a cherry tomato at the end of each skewer for garnish. Serve on a bed of cooked rice.

4 servings

Pepper Steak

2 pounds beef flank steak
¼ cup water
¼ cup soy sauce
1 teaspoon garlic salt
½ teaspoon sugar
¼ teaspoon ground ginger
⅛ teaspoon pepper
2 green peppers, cored and cut in 1-inch pieces
2 tomatoes, peeled and quartered
1 can (19 ounces) bean sprouts, drained and rinsed
1 tablespoon cornstarch
6 tablespoons cold water
Cooked rice (see page 59)

1. Slice flank steak across the grain into thin strips.

2. Mix ¼ cup water, the soy sauce, garlic salt, sugar, ginger and pepper in a 2½-quart microwave-oven-safe open oval casserole. Add meat and turn to coat. Cover with plastic wrap. Set in refrigerator to marinate 1 to 3 hours.

3. Add green pepper pieces to meat. Cook covered in microwave oven **5 minutes at Medium-High**; stir once.

4. Add tomatoes and bean sprouts; stir. Cook covered in microwave oven **5 to 10 minutes at Medium-High**, or until meat is fork-tender; stir once.

5. Mix cornstarch with cold water and stir into meat mixture. Cook uncovered in microwave oven **2 to 3 minutes at High**, or until thickened; stir once.

6. Serve with hot cooked rice.

6 to 8 servings

Microwave Sukiyaki

2 pounds beef tenderloin
½ cup soy sauce
¼ cup sherry or sake
¼ cup sugar
2 medium onions, peeled and sliced
1 can (8 ounces) mushroom stems and pieces, drained
5 green onions, diagonally sliced
½ pound spinach leaves, washed, drained and sliced
1 can (19 ounces) bean sprouts, drained and rinsed
1 can (8 ounces) bamboo shoots, drained and sliced
1 can (5 ounces) water chestnuts, drained and sliced
Cooked rice (see page 59)

1. Cut beef across the grain into ¾-inch strips. Put meat into a 3-quart glass casserole. Mix soy sauce, sherry and sugar; pour over meat. Set aside to marinate for 30 minutes.

2. Put sliced onion over meat. Cover with waxed paper. Cook in microwave oven **5 minutes at High**; stir 3 times.

3. Push meat into center of casserole. Put the remaining vegetables into casserole in separate piles around the edges. Spoon some of the marinade in casserole over each vegetable. Cook covered in microwave oven **6 minutes at High**; rotate casserole one-half turn once.

4. Serve with hot cooked rice.

6 to 8 servings

Microwave Stroganoff

1½ pounds boneless beef sirloin
⅓ cup all-purpose flour
¼ teaspoon salt
⅛ teaspoon pepper
⅓ cup butter or margarine
1 can (10½ ounces) condensed beef broth
1 can (10½ ounces) condensed french onion soup
1 can (4 ounces) sliced mushrooms, drained
1 cup dairy sour cream
5 drops liquid pepper sauce
Buttered cooked noodles or rice (see page 61 or 59)

1. Cut meat into 2x½x¼-inch strips. Coat with a mixture of flour, salt and pepper.

2. Melt butter in an 8-inch square glass baking dish in microwave oven (**about 1 minute at High**). Add the meat and stir to coat with butter. Cover with waxed paper. Cook **7 to 8 minutes at High**, or until meat is no longer pink; stir 3 times.

3. Pour beef broth and onion soup over meat in dish. Heat uncovered in microwave oven to boiling (**8 to 10 minutes at High**); stir once. Cook uncovered **3 minutes at High**; turn and rearrange strips once during cooking period.

4. Stir in mushrooms, sour cream and pepper sauce. Cover with waxed paper. Heat in microwave oven to serving temperature (**1 to 2 minutes at Medium-High**); stir once.

5. Serve over noodles or rice.

6 to 8 servings

Easy Beef Goulash

2 tablespoons beef drippings
2 medium onions, peeled and sliced
2 medium potatoes, pared and cubed
½ teaspoon paprika
2 cups cubed cooked roast beef
1 tablespoon Worcestershire sauce
¼ cup ketchup
½ teaspoon dry mustard
½ teaspoon salt
Dash pepper
2 cups water
2 tablespoons cornstarch

1. Heat drippings in a 2-quart glass casserole in microwave oven until hot (**20 to 30 seconds at High**). Add onion, potato and paprika. Cover with an all-glass lid or plastic wrap. Cook **8 minutes at High**; stir twice.

2. Add meat to casserole along with Worcestershire sauce, ketchup, dry mustard, salt and pepper; mix. Cook covered in microwave oven **3 minutes at High**.

3. Mix about 2 tablespoons of the water with cornstarch. Stir cornstarch mixture and remaining water into casserole mixture. Cook covered in microwave oven **10 to 12 minutes at High**, or until potatoes are tender; stir every 3 minutes.

4 servings

Beef Stew

2 tablespoons vegetable oil
1 clove garlic, minced
2 pounds beef for stew
3 cups hot tap water
½ cup all-purpose flour
2 teaspoons salt
¼ teaspoon pepper
2 teaspoons Worcestershire sauce
1 large onion, peeled and cut in eighths
2 medium carrots, pared and sliced on the diagonal
2 large potatoes, pared and cut in eighths
1 bay leaf

1. Put oil and garlic into a 4-quart microwave-oven-safe casserole. Cook uncovered in microwave oven **2 minutes at High**. Add meat; stir. Cook uncovered **10 minutes at High**; stir once.

2. Heat hot water in a 1-quart glass measuring cup in microwave oven to boiling (**about 7 minutes at High**).

3. Mix flour, salt and pepper with meat. Add boiling water, Worcestershire sauce, onion, carrot, potato and bay leaf; stir. Cover with a microwave-oven-safe lid.

4. Cook in microwave oven **70 to 85 minutes at Medium**, or until meat and vegetables are tender; stir 3 times. Let stand covered 5 minutes.

About 8 servings

Oven-Baked Beef Stew

3 pounds beef for stew, cut in 1-inch chunks
2 medium potatoes, pared and cut in cubes
3 carrots, pared and cut in ½-inch slices
1 medium onion, cut in pieces
1 cup sliced celery
1 can (16 ounces) tomatoes (undrained)
1 can (16 ounces) cut green beans, drained
½ cup soft bread crumbs
½ cup beef broth
½ cup red wine or beef broth
3 tablespoons cornstarch
1 tablespoon brown sugar
2 teaspoons salt
¼ teaspoon pepper
2 small bay leaves

1. Preheat convection oven to 325°F.

2. Combine beef, potatoes, carrots, onion, celery, undrained tomatoes, green beans and bread crumbs in a 4-quart casserole suitable for microwave and convection heat.

3. Combine beef broth, wine, cornstarch, brown sugar, salt and pepper; stir into meat mixture. Add bay leaves. Cover with casserole lid.

4. Place casserole on bottom metal rack. Cook in microwave/convection oven **90 minutes at Combination I**, or until meat is tender; stir once. Let stand covered 10 minutes; remove bay leaves and serve.

8 servings

Broiled Black Pepper Steak

1 tablespoon coarse-grind black pepper
1 beef sirloin steak (about 1¼ pounds)

1. Preheat convection oven to 450°F.

2. Sprinkle half of pepper on one side of steak and pound with a wooden mallet. Turn steak over and repeat with remaining pepper.

3. Place steak directly on bottom metal rack. Cook in convection oven **10 to 15 minutes at 450°F** for rare; **15 to 20 minutes at 450°F** for medium; **20 to 25 minutes at 450°F** for well done.

2 servings

Swiss-Style Steak

2 tablespoons vegetable oil
2 medium onions, peeled and sliced
¼ cup all-purpose flour
½ teaspoon salt
¼ teaspoon paprika
⅛ teaspoon pepper
2 pounds beef top round steak
1 can (28 ounces) Italian-style tomatoes (undrained)

1. Combine oil and onion in a 3-quart glass casserole. Cook uncovered in microwave oven **3 minutes at High**.

2. Preheat convection oven to 325°F.

3. Combine flour, salt, paprika and pepper. Cut round steak into serving pieces and coat with flour mixture. Put into casserole with onion. Break up tomatoes into chunks; add to casserole with liquid. Cover with an all-glass lid.

4. Place casserole on bottom metal rack. Cook in microwave/convection oven **70 to 75 minutes at Combination I**, or until meat is tender; stir once.

8 servings

Crown Roast with Apricot Stuffing

3 tablespoons butter or
  margarine
½ 8-ounce package
  herb-seasoned stuffing mix
¼ cup water
3 tablespoons chopped celery
3 tablespoons chopped dried
  apricots
1 lamb rib crown roast
  (5 to 6 pounds)

1. Melt butter in a 1-quart glass measuring pitcher in microwave oven
(**about 1 minute at High**). Add stuffing mix, water, celery and apricots;
mix well.

2. Place lamb crown roast on a microwave-oven-safe roast rack set in
a 2½-quart microwave-oven-safe open oval casserole. Fill center cavity
with stuffing. Cover with waxed paper. Cook in microwave oven
10 minutes at Medium-High.

3. Rotate casserole one-half turn. Shield meat and ribs as needed with
aluminum foil. Cover with waxed paper. Cook in microwave oven **45 to
55 minutes at Medium-High**. Or, if using Temperature Probe, insert
probe into meaty portion of roast and cook covered in microwave oven
set at **145°F and at Medium-High** for medium.

4. Remove from oven, cover with foil and let stand 10 minutes.

About 8 servings

Lamb Chops à l'Orange

4 lamb loin chops
Garlic salt
3 fresh orange slices, ½ inch thick
½ cup orange marmalade

1. Sprinkle chops lightly with garlic salt. Stand chops on bones fat-side-up alternately with orange slices in an 8-inch square glass baking dish. Spoon marmalade over all. Cover with waxed paper.

2. Cook in microwave oven **13 to 17 minutes at Medium-High**, or until done as desired; rotate dish one-half turn after 8 minutes.

4 servings

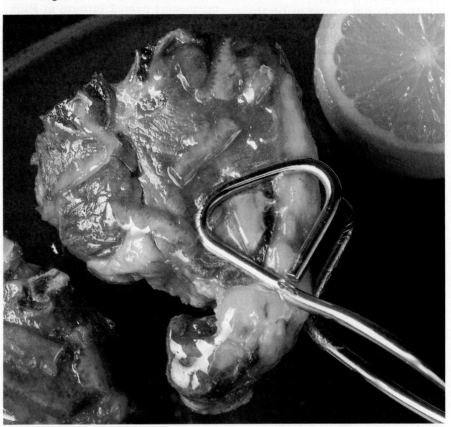

Lamb-Pineapple Kabobs

1½ pounds boneless lamb shoulder or leg, cut in 1¼-inch cubes
2 cans (8¼ ounces each) pineapple chunks in syrup, drained (reserve ½ cup syrup)
½ cup soy sauce
¼ cup lemon juice
2 cloves garlic, minced
½ teaspoon pepper
Cooked rice (see page 59)
Orange Barbecue Sauce (see page 191)

1. Put lamb cubes into a large shallow dish.

2. Reserve pineapple chunks. Mix ½ cup pineapple syrup, soy sauce, lemon juice, garlic and pepper. Pour over meat. Refrigerate covered several hours or overnight; turn meat occasionally.

3. Remove meat from marinade; reserve marinade for brushing kabobs during cooking.

4. Alternately arrange meat pieces and the reserved pineapple chunks on 8 (8-inch) bamboo skewers; brush with marinade. Arrange kabobs in an 8-inch square glass baking dish. Cover with waxed paper.

5. Cook in microwave oven **11 to 12 minutes at Medium-High**, or until meat is done as desired; rotate dish one-quarter turn twice and rearrange kabobs and brush with marinade twice.

6. Arrange kabobs on cooked rice and serve with Orange Barbecue Sauce.

4 servings

Quick Lamb Stew

1 cup chopped onion
2 tablespoons butter or margarine
2 cups cubed cooked lamb
3 tablespoons all-purpose flour
1 teaspoon salt
⅛ teaspoon pepper
1¼ cups liquid (water or broth)
1 cup cooked diced potato
½ cup diced cooked carrot
½ cup cooked green peas

1. Put onion into a 2-cup glass measuring cup. Cover with plastic wrap. Cook in microwave oven **2½ minutes at High**. Set aside.

2. Melt butter in a 1½-quart glass casserole in microwave oven (**about 30 seconds at High**). Add meat and stir to coat. Cook uncovered **2 minutes at High**.

3. Add flour, salt and pepper to meat; stir well. Cook uncovered in microwave oven **1 minute at High**.

4. Pour liquid into casserole; stir. Cook uncovered in microwave oven **2½ minutes at High**, or until thickened; stir once.

5. Add cooked onion and other cooked vegetables to meat mixture; stir. Cover with waxed paper. Heat in microwave oven to serving temperature (**9½ to 11 minutes at Medium-High**); stir once.

4 servings

Lamb Casserole

2 cups diced cooked roast lamb
2 cups Basic Gravy (see page 192; use roast lamb drippings)
2 cups cooked rice
½ cup cooked green peas
1 tablespoon chopped pimiento
½ teaspoon salt

1. Combine all ingredients in a 1½-quart glass baking dish. Cover with waxed paper.

2. Heat in microwave oven to serving temperature (**5 to 10 minutes at High**); stir.

4 servings

Lamb Shoulder with Rosemary

3½ to 5 pound lamb shoulder, boned, rolled and tied
2 cloves garlic, slivered in 6 pieces
½ teaspoon crushed rosemary leaves
¼ teaspoon pepper
⅛ teaspoon salt and dash pepper (optional)

1. Make six 1-inch slits halfway into lamb and insert 1 sliver of garlic in each.

2. Combine rosemary and pepper; rub over surface of lamb.

3. Place lamb on a microwave-oven-safe roast rack set in an 8-inch square or a 2-quart glass baking dish. Cover with waxed paper.

4. Cook in microwave oven **9 to 10 minutes at Medium-High** per pound for medium-rare, **10 to 11 minutes at Medium-High** per pound for medium or **11 to 12 minutes at Medium-High** per pound for well done. If using Temperature Probe, insert probe into center of meat. Cook in microwave oven set at **145°F and at Medium-High** for medium-rare, **160°F and at Medium-High** for medium or **170°F and at Medium-High** for well done.

5. Remove from oven. Cover with aluminum foil; let stand 10 minutes.

6. If desired, pour drippings into a 1-cup glass measuring cup; skim off fat. Add salt and dash pepper. Heat uncovered in microwave oven **2 minutes at High**.

8 servings

Pork Roast in Oriental Marinade

1 tablespoon all-purpose flour
1 boneless pork shoulder roast (about 4 pounds)
1 tablespoon sugar
½ teaspoon salt
½ teaspoon ground ginger
1 clove garlic, minced
½ cup dry sherry or orange juice
¼ cup lemon juice
¼ cup soy sauce
2 tablespoons ketchup

1. Shake 1 tablespoon flour in a medium-size plastic cooking bag. Place bag in a 1½-quart glass baking dish.

2. Trim excess fat from meat and place roast in the bag.

3. Mix remaining ingredients and pour over meat in the bag. Close bag securely with string (do not use metal twist tie). Refrigerate several hours.

4. Make six ½-inch slits in the top of the bag. Cook in microwave oven **40 minutes at Medium-High**, or until meat tests done. If using Temperature Probe, insert probe through plastic bag at an angle near center of meat; cook in microwave oven set at **160°F and at Medium-High**.

5. Let stand 20 minutes for heat to equalize; during this time internal temperature will rise to 170°F.

6. Pour cooking liquid into a 1-quart glass measuring cup. Cook uncovered in microwave oven **3 to 5 minutes at High**, or until thickened; stir twice. Serve with meat.

About 8 servings

Roast Pork and Sauerkraut

1 pound cooked roast pork
2 tablespoons pork drippings
1 can (27 ounces) sauerkraut (undrained)
1 teaspoon caraway seed
¼ teaspoon salt
Dash pepper

1. Slice and reserve meat. Heat drippings in a 2-quart glass casserole in microwave oven until hot (**15 to 30 seconds at High**).

2. Add undrained sauerkraut and caraway seed to drippings. Cover with waxed paper. Heat in microwave oven **7 minutes at High**; stir twice.

3. Place roast pork slices on top of sauerkraut. Sprinkle with salt and pepper. Heat covered in microwave oven to serving temperature (**4 to 5 minutes at Medium-High**).

4 servings

Stuffed Pork Shoulder Roast

Plum-Glazed Pork Ribs

Sweet-Sour Pork

Stuffed Pork Shoulder Roast

1 rolled pork shoulder roast
(about 4 pounds)
½ cup finely chopped celery
¼ cup chopped onion
2 tablespoons butter or
margarine
1 cup (4 ounces) shredded
Cheddar cheese
1 cup herb-seasoned croutons

1. Carefully untie roast and spread flat. Set aside.

2. Put celery, onion and butter into a 1-quart glass casserole. Cook uncovered in microwave oven **4 minutes at High**, or until onion and celery are crisp-tender; stir after 2 minutes.

3. Add cheese and croutons to vegetable mixture; stir. Spread stuffing over meat. Roll up meat and tie with clean string. Set on a microwave-oven-safe roast rack set in an 8-inch square or a 2-quart glass baking dish. Cover with waxed paper.

4. Cook in microwave oven **40 minutes at Medium-High**, or until meat tests done (see Meat Cooking Chart on page 95).

5. Remove from oven, cover with aluminum foil and let stand 20 minutes for heat to equalize; during this time internal temperature will rise to 170°F.

About 8 servings

Plum-Glazed Pork Ribs

3 pounds country-style pork
ribs
1 can (17 ounces) purple
plums, drained (reserve
½ cup syrup)
½ cup defrosted frozen orange
juice concentrate
½ teaspoon Worcestershire
sauce

1. Cut ribs into 1- or 2-rib portions. Place ribs on a microwave-oven-safe roast rack set in an 8-inch square or a 2-quart glass baking dish with thick part of ribs to the outside. Cover with plastic wrap.

2. Cook in microwave oven **12 minutes at Medium-High**. Drain off fat. Remove rack and turn ribs over in dish.

3. Pit plums and purée with reserved syrup. Put into a 1-quart glass measuring pitcher. Add orange juice concentrate and Worcestershire sauce; stir. Cook uncovered in microwave oven **5 to 6 minutes at High**, or until slightly thicker; stir once.

4. Pour sauce over ribs. Cover with waxed paper. Cook in microwave oven **10 to 12 minutes at Medium-High**, or until tender.

5. Remove from oven. Let stand covered 5 minutes. Serve ribs with sauce.

About 8 servings

Sweet-Sour Pork

1½ pounds boneless pork loin,
cut in thin strips
¼ cup packed brown sugar
¼ cup cornstarch
½ teaspoon salt
½ cup water
2 tablespoons soy sauce
1 tablespoon red wine vinegar
1 can (20 ounces) unsweetened
pineapple chunks
(undrained)
½ medium green pepper, thinly
sliced
½ medium onion, peeled and
thinly sliced
Cooked rice (see page 59)

1. Arrange pork strips in a 2½-quart microwave-oven-safe open oval casserole. Cover with plastic wrap. Cook in microwave oven **7 minutes at Medium-High**; rotate dish one-half turn once. Remove meat with a slotted spoon and set aside.

2. Combine brown sugar, cornstarch and salt. Stir in water, soy sauce and vinegar. Blend cornstarch mixture into meat juices in casserole. Add pineapple with juice, reserved meat, green pepper and onion; stir.

3. Cook covered in microwave oven **15 to 18 minutes at Medium-High**, or until pork is tender and sauce is thickened and bubbly; stir every 3 minutes.

4. Serve over hot cooked rice.

About 6 servings

Barbecued Ribs

2 pounds pork spareribs
2 cups ketchup
½ cup vinegar
½ cup water
1 tablespoon prepared horseradish
1 tablespoon Worcestershire sauce
½ cup chopped onion
¼ cup packed light brown sugar
1 tablespoon celery seed
⅛ teaspoon salt
⅛ teaspoon pepper

1. Cut spareribs into individual ribs and place in a 2½-quart microwave-oven-safe open oval casserole.

2. Combine remaining ingredients and pour over meat. Cover with waxed paper. Cook in microwave oven **40 to 45 minutes at Medium-High**, or until tender; turn ribs over and rearrange after 20 minutes.

4 servings

Hint: To reduce cooking time when grilling, ribs can be partially cooked in microwave oven approximately **20 to 25 minutes at Medium-High** before cooking on grill until well done.

Pork Stir-Fry

1 package (6 ounces) frozen pea pods, cooked (see page 149)
1 package (10 ounces) frozen Chinese mixed vegetables, cooked (see page 149)
1 pound pork tenderloin, trimmed of fat and cut in 1-inch strips
½ cup thinly sliced onion
1 tablespoon cornstarch
½ cup water
¼ cup soy sauce
½ teaspoon ground ginger

1. Prepare vegetables. Set aside.

2. Put pork into an 8-inch square glass baking dish. Cover with plastic wrap. Cook in microwave oven **10 minutes at Medium-High**; stir after 3 minutes and again after 6 minutes of cooking. Drain.

3. Add cooked pea pods, cooked Chinese vegetables and onion to meat; stir. Cook covered in microwave oven **3 minutes at High**; stir once.

4. Combine cornstarch, water, soy sauce and ginger until smooth. Add to pork-vegetable mixture; stir. Cook covered in microwave oven **3 to 4 minutes at High**, or until mixture thickens; stir once.

4 to 6 servings

Pork Chow Mein

1 pound lean pork, cut in small pieces
2 cups thinly sliced celery (on the diagonal)
1 cup chopped onion
2 tablespoons cornstarch
¼ cup water
1 can (19 ounces) Chinese mixed vegetables, drained and rinsed
1 cup beef broth (homemade, canned or from bouillon cube)
2 tablespoons soy sauce
1 tablespoon bottled brown sauce or molasses
¼ teaspoon ground ginger
1 tablespoon cornstarch

1. Put meat into a 2-quart glass casserole. Cover with an all-glass lid or plastic wrap. Cook in microwave oven **4 minutes at High**, or until meat begins to lose its pink color; stir once.

2. Add celery and onion to meat; mix. Cook covered in microwave oven **3 minutes at High**.

3. Blend 2 tablespoons cornstarch with the water; stir into meat mixture. Add Chinese vegetables, broth, soy sauce, brown sauce and ginger; mix well.

4. Cook covered in microwave oven **25 minutes at Medium**, or until meat is tender; stir twice. If sauce does not seem thick enough halfway through cooking period, remove ¼ cup of cooking liquid, cool slightly and mix in 1 tablespoon cornstarch. Stir into casserole mixture and continue cooking.

4 servings

Pork Cutlets on Prunes

2 packages (12 ounces each) pitted prunes
¾ cup water
2 pounds pork loin sirloin cutlets, trimmed of excess fat
Salt and pepper

1. Put prunes and water into a 2½-quart microwave-oven-safe open oval casserole. Arrange pork cutlets over top. Cover with plastic wrap.

2. Cook in microwave oven **25 to 30 minutes at Medium**, or until meat is fork-tender; rearrange and turn cutlets over and rotate dish one-half turn halfway through cooking period.

3. Season with salt and pepper. Let stand covered 5 minutes. Serve with prunes and sauce over cutlets.

4 to 6 servings

Stuffed Pork Chops

¼ cup apple jelly
1 tablespoon Worcestershire sauce
2 tablespoons butter or margarine
1 cup soft bread cubes
1 cup cubed pared apple
1 teaspoon salt
4 pork loin chops, 1¾ inches thick (have chops cut for stuffing)

1. For glaze, combine apple jelly and Worcestershire sauce in a 1-cup glass measuring cup. Heat uncovered in microwave oven **2 minutes at High**. Set aside.

2. Melt butter in a 1-quart glass casserole in microwave oven (**about 30 seconds at High**). Add bread, apple and salt; mix well.

3. Stuff chops with mixture and place in a single layer in a 1½-quart glass baking dish. Brush with glaze. Cover with waxed paper. Cook in microwave oven **11 minutes at Medium-High**.

4. Turn chops over and brush with glaze; rotate dish one-half turn. Cook covered **9 to 11 minutes at Medium-High**, or until well done.

5. Remove meat from oven and let stand covered 5 minutes.

4 servings

Pork Sausage Patties

1 pound bulk pork sausage

1. Make six 3x½-inch sausage patties. Put into a 2½-quart microwave-oven-safe open oval casserole. Cover with waxed paper.

2. Cook in microwave oven **6 to 8 minutes at High**, or until well done; rearrange patties halfway through the cooking period.

6 servings

Baked Ham Slice with Pineapple

1 smoked ham center slice, ¾ inch thick
1 teaspoon prepared mustard
¼ cup packed brown sugar
1 can (8¼ ounces) pineapple slices, drained and halved
2 tablespoons fine graham cracker crumbs

1. Put ham slice into a 1½-quart glass baking dish. Spread mustard over ham and sprinkle with brown sugar.

2. Coat pineapple half-slices with cracker crumbs. Arrange on ham. Cover with waxed paper.

3. Cook in microwave oven **4 minutes at High**. Rotate dish one-half turn. Cook covered **4 minutes at Medium-High**.

About 4 servings

Ham and Yams

3 tablespoons butter or margarine
3 tablespoons chopped onion
2 tablespoons all-purpose flour
1 can (8¼ ounces) unsweetened pineapple chunks, drained; reserve ½ cup juice
⅓ cup packed brown sugar
2 cups chopped cooked ham
2 cups cooked yam or sweet potato slices (½ inch)

1. Put butter and onion into a 1½-quart glass casserole. Cook uncovered in microwave oven **2 minutes at High**; stir after 1 minute.

2. Blend flour into onion and butter; stir in reserved pineapple juice. Cook uncovered in microwave oven **1 minute at High**, or until thick.

3. Stir brown sugar, pineapple chunks and ham into sauce. Pile in center of an 8-inch round glass cake dish. Put sliced yams around outer edge. Cover with waxed paper.

4. Heat in microwave oven to serving temperature (**6 to 8 minutes at Medium-High**).

4 servings

Baked Ham

3- to 10-pound fully cooked smoked ham (canned or half ham)
½ cup packed brown sugar
1½ teaspoons all-purpose flour
½ teaspoon dry mustard
1 tablespoon cider vinegar
1 can (8 ounces) sliced pineapple, drained
4 maraschino cherries

1. Set ham fat-side-down on a microwave-oven-safe roast rack set in an 8-inch square or a 2-quart glass baking dish. Cover with waxed paper. Cook in microwave oven for one-half of cooking time (see Meat Cooking Chart on page 95 for time and settings).

2. After one-half of cooking time is completed, turn ham over fat-side-up. Cook covered in microwave oven until 10 minutes before minimum recommended time is completed.

3. Mix brown sugar, flour and mustard in a small bowl. Stir in vinegar.

4. Remove ham from oven. Spread brown sugar mixture over ham. Arrange pineapple slices and cherries on ham and press firmly into glaze. Cook uncovered in microwave oven **10 minutes at Medium-High**, or if using Temperature Probe, set at **115°F and at Medium-High**.

5. Remove from oven. Cover meat with foil and let stand 20 minutes for heat to equalize; during this time internal temperature will rise.

Allow ¼ pound per serving

Hint: If shape of ham is uneven, cover small end with aluminum foil for the first half of cooking time.

Ham and Potatoes au Gratin

3 tablespoons butter or margarine
3 tablespoons all-purpose flour
½ teaspoon salt
⅛ teaspoon pepper
1½ cups milk
1½ cups (6 ounces) shredded Cheddar cheese
4 cups cooked potato slices (about 5 medium potatoes)
¼ cup chopped onion
3 cups cubed cooked ham (about 1 pound)

1. Melt butter in a glass measuring cup in microwave oven (**about 30 seconds at High**). Stir in flour, salt and pepper until smooth. Gradually add milk, stirring constantly.

2. Cook uncovered in microwave oven **3½ to 4 minutes at High**, or until thickened; stir twice.

3. Add 1 cup cheese; stir until melted.

4. Preheat convection oven to 450°F.

5. Layer potatoes, onion and ham in a 2-quart glass casserole. Pour cheese sauce over top. Sprinkle with remaining cheese.

6. Place casserole on bottom metal rack. Cook in convection oven **20 minutes at 450°F**, or until cheese is crusty and brown on top.

6 servings

Ham Roll-Ups with Broccoli

1½ pounds fresh broccoli, cooked (see page 145)
3 tablespoons butter or margarine
3 tablespoons all-purpose flour
1 teaspoon prepared horseradish
¾ cup chicken broth
¼ cup Madeira
¼ cup half-and-half
8 ounces fresh mushrooms, cleaned and sliced lengthwise
24 thin slices Swiss cheese (8 ounces)
12 slices (1½ pounds) cooked ham

1. Prepare broccoli. Drain. Let stand covered.

2. Melt butter in a 1-quart glass measuring pitcher in microwave oven (**about 1 minute at High**). Blend in flour. Add horseradish. Add broth and Madeira gradually, stirring until smooth. Cook uncovered **2½ to 3 minutes at Medium**, or until thickened; stir twice.

3. Stir in half-and-half and mushrooms. Cook uncovered in microwave oven **1 minute at Medium**.

4. Place 2 cheese slices and 2 broccoli spears on each ham slice. Roll up and place on a microwave-oven-safe platter. Pour sauce over all.

5. Heat uncovered in microwave oven to serving temperature (**6 to 8 minutes at Medium-Low**); rotate platter one-half turn once during cooking period.

6 servings

Ham and Asparagus

1 pound (about 16) asparagus
spears, cooked (see page 144)
or 1 package (10 ounces)
frozen asparagus spears,
cooked (see page 148)
2 tablespoons butter or
margarine
2 tablespoons all-purpose flour
1 cup milk
2 egg yolks
¼ teaspoon salt
¼ teaspoon dry mustard
4 slices (about 1¼ pounds)
boiled ham
¼ cup shredded Cheddar cheese
Bread slices, toasted

1. Prepare asparagus and set aside.

2. Melt butter in a 1-quart glass measuring pitcher in microwave oven (**about 30 seconds at High**). Stir in flour. Add milk gradually, stirring constantly. Cook uncovered **4 minutes at High**, or until thick; stir after each minute.

3. Beat egg yolks and stir into sauce. Add salt and dry mustard; stir.

4. Wrap 4 cooked asparagus spears in each slice of ham. Lay ham rolls in a 1½-quart glass baking dish and pour sauce over the top. Sprinkle with cheese. Cover with waxed paper.

5. Heat in microwave oven to serving temperature (**5 to 6 minutes at Medium-High**). Serve on toast.

4 servings

How to Cook Bacon

1. Arrange bacon slices on a microwave-oven-safe roast rack set in a 2-quart glass baking dish. Cover with paper towels. Cook in microwave oven.

2. Remove from microwave oven and let stand 1 to 2 minutes for crisp bacon.

3. If desired, when cooking 1 or 2 bacon slices at a time, use a paper-towel-lined paper plate.

4. Times are approximate, depending on thickness of bacon.

Amount of Slices	Cook at High
1	1½ minutes
2	2 minutes
4	4 minutes
8	7 minutes

How to Cook Bacon

Veal Parmesan

2 tablespoons butter or
   margarine
1 cup fine dry bread crumbs
½ cup grated Parmesan or
   Romano cheese
¼ teaspoon salt
⅛ teaspoon pepper
6 veal cutlets (about
   1½ pounds)
1 egg, beaten
   Italian Tomato Sauce
   (see page 189)
6 slices (3 ounces) mozzarella
   cheese

1. Melt butter in a 2½-quart microwave-oven-safe open oval casserole **(about 30 seconds at High)**.

2. Mix bread crumbs, Parmesan cheese, salt and pepper. Dip both sides of cutlets in egg, then coat with crumb mixture. Put breaded cutlets in butter in casserole and turn to coat with butter. Cover with waxed paper.

3. Cook in microwave oven **10 minutes at Medium-High**; rotate casserole one-half turn halfway through cooking period.

4. Pour tomato sauce over meat and top with cheese slices. Heat covered in microwave oven to serving temperature **(4 to 5 minutes at Medium-High)**.

6 servings

Veal Cutlets in Wine

¼ cup all-purpose flour
1 teaspoon salt
¼ teaspoon pepper
4 veal cutlets (about 1 pound)
2 tablespoons butter or
   margarine
¼ cup dry white wine
¼ cup sliced pimiento-stuffed
   green olives

1. Mix flour, salt and pepper. Coat meat with flour mixture.

2. Melt butter in an 8-inch square glass baking dish in microwave oven **(about 30 seconds at High)**. Arrange meat in dish; turn pieces over to coat. Cover with waxed paper. Cook **4 minutes at High**; turn meat over after 2 minutes.

3. Remove excess liquid from dish. Cook covered in microwave oven **12 minutes at Medium-High**, or until tender; rotate dish one-half turn after 7 minutes.

4. Turn meat over. Add wine and olives. Cook covered in microwave oven **1 minute at High**.

4 servings

Veal 'n' Tomato

2 tablespoons butter or margarine
2 tablespoons all-purpose flour
1½ cups beef broth (homemade, canned or from bouillon cubes)
1 tablespoon tomato paste
1 large tomato, diced
1 onion, peeled and minced
1 cup sliced fresh mushrooms
1 bay leaf
1½ pounds veal for stew, cut in 1-inch pieces
1 teaspoon salt
⅛ teaspoon pepper
Cooked rice (see page 59)

1. Melt butter in an 8-inch square glass baking dish in microwave oven (about 30 seconds at High). Blend in flour. Add broth gradually, stirring until smooth. Stir in tomato paste.

2. Cook uncovered in microwave oven 3 minutes at High; stir once. Add tomato, onion, mushrooms and bay leaf; stir. Cook uncovered 4 minutes at High; stir once.

3. Add meat, salt and pepper to sauce; stir. Cover with plastic wrap. Cook in microwave oven 25 to 30 minutes at Medium, or until meat is tender; stir occasionally and be sure meat is covered with sauce.

4. Remove from oven and let stand covered 5 to 10 minutes. Serve over rice.

4 to 6 servings

Corned Beef and Cabbage Dinner

1 quart hot tap water
3½ to 4 pounds corned beef
1 bay leaf
½ teaspoon peppercorns
1 clove garlic
3 potatoes, pared and quartered
3 medium carrots, pared and sliced ½ inch thick
1 medium head cabbage, cut in 8 wedges

1. Heat hot water in a 4-quart microwave-oven-safe casserole in microwave oven to boiling (7 to 9 minutes at High). Place corned beef in water. Add bay leaf, peppercorns and garlic. Cover with a microwave-oven-safe lid.

2. Cook in microwave oven 90 minutes at Medium; rotate casserole one-quarter turn twice during cooking period.

3. Add potato and carrot; arrange cabbage wedges on top. Cook covered in microwave oven 25 to 30 minutes at Medium, or until vegetables and meat are tender; rotate casserole one-quarter turn twice during cooking period. Let stand covered 10 minutes.

6 servings

Corned Beef Hash

1 tablespoon vegetable oil
1 medium onion, peeled and chopped
2 medium potatoes, baked (see page 147), pared and diced
2 cups diced cooked corned beef (about 8 ounces)
¼ cup half-and-half
¼ teaspoon salt
Dash pepper

1. Put oil and onion into a 1½-quart glass casserole. Cook uncovered in microwave oven 3 minutes at High.

2. Add potato and corned beef to onion; stir. Heat in microwave oven 5 minutes at High; stir once.

3. Add half-and-half; stir. Heat in microwave oven to serving temperature (about 2 minutes at High). Mix in salt and pepper.

4 servings

Liver and Onions

1 medium onion, peeled and
   thinly sliced
½ cup beef broth
½ teaspoon Worcestershire
   sauce
¼ teaspoon caraway seed
1 pound beef liver slices
   (about ½ inch thick)

1. Put onion, broth and seasonings into an 8-inch square glass baking dish. Cover with waxed paper. Cook in microwave oven **7 minutes at High**.

2. Meanwhile, cut away tubes and outer membrane from liver, if necessary. Rinse liver, pat dry and cut into serving pieces.

3. Remove the onion slices with slotted spoon. Add liver (thin ends to center of dish). Cook covered in microwave oven **2 minutes at High**.

4. Turn liver pieces over and put onion slices on top. Cook covered in microwave oven **6 to 7 minutes at Medium-High**, or until liver is done to taste; rotate dish one-half turn after 3½ minutes.

4 servings

Meatballs 'n' Potato-Mushroom Sauce

2 medium potatoes, pared and
   cut in small cubes
1 pound ground beef chuck
2 tablespoons chopped onion
1 tablespoon chopped parsley
2 tablespoons dry bread
   crumbs
½ teaspoon salt
1 egg
2 tablespoons water
1 can (10¾ ounces) condensed
   cream of mushroom soup
¾ cup milk

1. Put potato into a 1-quart glass casserole. Cover with an all-glass lid or plastic wrap. Cook in microwave oven **4½ minutes at High**, or until tender; stir once. Set aside.

2. Combine meat, onion, parsley, bread crumbs and salt. Mix egg and water. Stir into meat mixture.

3. Divide meat mixture into 12 portions. Shape each portion into a meatball, using 2 or 3 cooked potato cubes as the center. Put into a 1½-quart glass baking dish. Cover with waxed paper.

4. Cook in microwave oven **6 minutes at High**; rearrange after 3 minutes. Drain off fat.

5. Combine condensed mushroom soup and milk. Stir in remaining cooked potatoes. Pour over meatballs. Cook covered in microwave oven **5 minutes at Medium-High**; rotate dish one-quarter turn once during cooking period.

4 servings

Porcupine Meatballs

1 pound ground beef
1 can (10¾ ounces) condensed
   tomato soup
¼ cup finely chopped onion
1 teaspoon salt
1 cup packaged precooked rice
1 egg, slightly beaten
⅔ cup water
1 teaspoon prepared mustard

1. Put beef into a bowl. Add ¼ cup condensed soup, onion, salt, rice and egg; mix well. Shape meat mixture firmly into 20 balls. Put meatballs into an 8-inch square glass baking dish. Cover with waxed paper.

2. Cook in microwave oven **3 to 4 minutes at High**, or until meatballs are set; rotate dish one-quarter turn halfway through cooking period. Drain off fat. Turn meatballs over and rearrange.

3. Blend remaining condensed soup, water and prepared mustard. Pour over meatballs in dish. Cover with plastic wrap.

4. Cook in microwave oven **6 to 7 minutes at Medium-High**, or until rice is tender; rearrange meatballs and rotate dish one-quarter turn halfway through cooking period.

4 servings

Lattice-Top Beef Pot Pie

1 tablespoon butter or
margarine
½ cup chopped celery
⅓ cup chopped onion
¼ cup chopped green pepper
1½ pounds ground beef
¾ cup beef broth
¼ cup red wine
2 tablespoons cornstarch
1 teaspoon salt
¼ teaspoon pepper
⅛ teaspoon chili powder
¼ cup ketchup
1 medium potato, cooked,
peeled and cubed
1 package (16 ounces) frozen
mixed vegetables
Pastry for 1-crust pie
1 tablespoon milk

1. Put butter, celery, onion and green pepper into an 8-inch round glass cake dish. Cook uncovered in microwave oven **3 minutes at High**. Set aside.

2. Cook meat uncovered in a 2-quart glass measuring pitcher in microwave oven **5 minutes at High**, or until meat is no longer pink; stir and break meat apart with a wooden spoon once. Drain off fat from meat. Set aside.

3. Combine broth, wine, cornstarch, salt, pepper, chili powder and ketchup in a 1-quart glass measuring pitcher. Cook uncovered in microwave oven **2 to 3 minutes at High**, or until thickened; stir twice.

4. Preheat convection oven to 375°F.

5. Combine thickened broth, beef, potato and frozen mixed vegetables with onion mixture in glass dish; mix well.

6. Roll pastry to ¼-inch thickness. Cut into lattice strips (about ¾ inch wide). Arrange on beef mixture in crisscross woven fashion. Brush with milk.

7. Place dish on bottom metal rack. Cook in microwave/convection oven **40 to 45 minutes at Combination II**, or until lightly browned.

6 servings

Wine 'n' Cheese Burgers

1½ pounds ground beef
⅓ cup chopped parsley
⅓ cup chopped onion
1½ teaspoons salt
½ teaspoon pepper
1½ cups dry red wine, such as burgundy
6 blue cheese cubes

1. Mix ground beef, parsley, onion, salt and pepper. Shape into 6 patties. Place patties in a 2½-quart microwave-oven-safe open oval casserole.

2. Make a depression in top of each patty. Pour wine over the patties; cover and refrigerate 2 hours.

3. Discard wine marinade. Cover casserole with waxed paper. Cook in microwave oven **5 to 6 minutes at High**, or until done as desired; turn burgers over halfway through cooking period and rotate dish one-half turn once.

4. To serve, crumble a cube of blue cheese on each patty.

6 servings

Meatloaf

1½ pounds ground beef
½ cup fine dry bread crumbs
1 egg, beaten
¾ cup milk
¼ cup finely chopped onion
1½ teaspoons salt
¼ teaspoon pepper
½ cup ketchup

1. Mix ground beef lightly with bread crumbs, egg, milk, onion, salt and pepper in a bowl. Pack mixture lightly into a 2-quart glass loaf dish. Cover with waxed paper.

2. Cook in microwave oven **5 minutes at Medium-High**. Top with ketchup. Rotate dish one-half turn. Cook covered **15 minutes at High**, or until done. If using Temperature Probe, insert it through waxed paper at an angle near center of meat; cook in microwave oven set at **160°F and at Medium-High**.

3. Remove from oven, cover with aluminum foil and let stand 5 minutes.

6 servings

Stuffed Meatloaf

1½ **pounds ground beef**
½ **cup fine dry bread crumbs**
1 **egg**
¾ **cup milk**
¼ **cup finely chopped onion**
1½ **teaspoons salt**
¼ **teaspoon pepper**
1 **tablespoon butter or margarine**
¼ **cup chopped celery**
¼ **cup chopped red pepper**
¼ **cup chopped green pepper**
¼ **cup shredded Cheddar cheese**
½ **cup ketchup**

1. Mix ground beef lightly with bread crumbs, egg, milk, onion, salt and pepper in a bowl. Pack one-half of mixture lightly into a 2-quart glass loaf dish. Make a depression in the center of the meatloaf.

2. Put butter, celery, red pepper and green pepper into a 1-quart glass casserole. Cook uncovered in microwave oven **2 minutes at High**, or until vegetables are tender; stir once. Stir in cheese. Put vegetable mixture in depression of meat mixture. Place remaining meat mixture on top, pressing edges to seal. Cover with waxed paper.

3. Cook in microwave oven **10 minutes at Medium-High**. Top with ketchup. Rotate dish one-half turn. Cook covered **15 minutes at Medium-High**.

4. Remove from oven, cover with aluminum foil and let stand 5 minutes.

6 servings

Sauce-Crowned Meat Ring

¾ **cup coarse dry bread crumbs**
1 **cup lemon-lime carbonated beverage**
2 **pounds lean ground beef**
2 **eggs, slightly beaten**
1 **cup chopped onion**
1½ **teaspoons salt**
1½ **teaspoons dried dill weed**
⅓ **cup Worcestershire sauce**
½ **cup chili sauce**

1. Soak bread crumbs in lemon-lime carbonated beverage in a bowl until liquid is absorbed. Add ground beef and remaining ingredients except chili sauce; mix lightly but thoroughly.

2. Pack meat mixture lightly into a lightly oiled microwave-oven-safe 5½- to 6-cup ring mold. Unmold into a 10-inch glass pie plate. Cover with waxed paper. Cook in microwave oven **5 minutes at High**.

3. Remove excess liquid from meat ring with baster; rotate pie plate one-half turn. Cook covered in microwave oven **4 to 5 minutes at High**, or until meat is no longer pink on surface.

4. Again remove excess liquid with baster and rotate dish one-half turn. Spread chili sauce over meat ring. Cook covered in microwave oven **4 to 5 minutes at High**, or until set.

5. Remove from oven, cover with aluminum foil and let stand 5 minutes for heat to equalize. Remove any excess liquid with baster before serving.

About 8 servings

Chili Con Carne

1 pound ground beef
¼ cup chopped onion
1½ tablespoons all-purpose flour
1½ teaspoons chili powder
   (or more to taste)
1½ teaspoons salt
¼ teaspoon pepper
¼ teaspoon garlic salt
1 can (15½ ounces) kidney
   beans, drained
1½ cups tomato purée
1 cup water

1. Combine beef and onion in an 8-inch square glass baking dish. Cover with waxed paper. Cook in microwave oven **5 minutes at High**, or until meat is no longer pink; stir after each minute, breaking meat apart with a wooden spoon.

2. Drain off fat from meat. Stir flour and seasonings into meat mixture, then stir in remaining ingredients. Cook uncovered in microwave oven **16 to 18 minutes at Medium-High**; stir every 4 minutes.

About 6 servings

Stuffed Cabbage Rolls

8 cabbage leaves
1 pound ground beef
½ cup cooked rice
1 teaspoon instant minced
   onion
1 egg
½ teaspoon poultry seasoning
1 can (8 ounces) tomato sauce
1½ teaspoons light brown sugar
2 tablespoons lemon juice or
   vinegar
2 tablespoons water

1. Heat 6 cups hot tap water and 1 teaspoon salt in a 3-quart glass casserole in microwave oven to boiling (**about 10 minutes at High**). Add 4 cabbage leaves. Cook uncovered **2 minutes at High**, or until leaves are pliable. Drain on paper towels. Repeat procedure.

2. Put beef into a 1½-quart glass baking dish. Cook uncovered in microwave oven **4 minutes at High**, or until meat is no longer pink; stir and break meat apart with a wooden spoon once. Drain off fat from meat.

3. Add cooked rice, onion, egg and poultry seasoning to beef; mix. Divide meat mixture into 8 even portions.

4. Cut the core out of each cabbage leaf. Place ¼ cup of meat mixture in center of each cabbage leaf. Fold 2 sides of leaf over meat and roll up leaves from the end. Secure with wooden picks, if needed. Arrange cabbage rolls seam-side-down in a 2½-quart microwave-oven-safe open oval casserole.

5. Combine tomato sauce, brown sugar, lemon juice and water in a 2-cup glass measuring cup or small bowl. Pour over cabbage rolls. Cover with waxed paper. Cook in microwave oven **10 minutes at High**, or until heated; rotate casserole one-half turn and rearrange once during cooking period.

6. Remove from oven, cover with plastic wrap and let stand 10 minutes before serving.

8 servings

Stuffed Peppers

3 medium green peppers,
   cut in half lengthwise
¼ cup chopped onion
¾ pound ground beef
1 can (8 ounces) tomato sauce
¼ cup water
1 cup cooked rice
1 egg
½ teaspoon salt
⅛ teaspoon pepper

1. Remove cores from green peppers. Put pepper halves skin-side-up on paper towels. Cook uncovered in microwave oven **6 minutes at High**. Set aside.

2. Combine onion and beef in an 8-inch round glass cake dish. Cover with waxed paper. Cook in microwave oven **4 minutes at High**, or until meat is no longer pink; stir and break meat apart with a wooden spoon once. Drain off fat from meat.

3. Mix tomato sauce with water. Combine onion-beef mixture with cooked rice, half of tomato mixture, egg, salt and pepper. Stuff pepper halves and place in an 8-inch square glass baking dish. Pour remaining sauce over top. Cover with waxed paper.

4. Cook in microwave oven **12 to 14 minutes at Medium-High**, or until thoroughly heated; rotate dish one-half turn after 5 minutes.

6 servings

Taco Casserole

1 pound ground beef
1 package (1½ ounces) taco seasoning mix
¾ cup water
1 can (15 ounces) refried beans
2 cups shredded head lettuce (dried if necessary)
¼ cup chopped onion
1 tablespoon chopped green chilies
1 cup (4 ounces) shredded Cheddar cheese
  Nacho-flavored tortilla chips
  Chopped tomato
  Sliced ripe olives
  Dairy sour cream
  Taco sauce

1. Put meat into a 2-quart glass casserole. Cover with waxed paper. Cook in microwave oven **4 minutes at High**, or until meat is no longer pink; stir and break meat apart with a wooden spoon once. Drain off fat from meat.

2. Mix taco seasoning mix and water and add to ground beef; stir. Cover with waxed paper. Cook in microwave oven **5 minutes at Medium**; stir once.

3. Lightly grease bottom of a 2½-quart microwave-oven-safe open oval casserole. Spread refried beans evenly over the bottom. Sprinkle with shredded lettuce, onion and chilies; top with ground beef mixture. Cover with waxed paper.

4. Cook in microwave oven **3½ minutes at Medium-High**, or until bottom of casserole feels warm; rotate casserole one-half turn once during cooking period. Sprinkle cheese on top. Cook uncovered **3 minutes at Medium-High**, or until cheese melts.

5. Garnish with tortilla chips. Serve with chopped tomato, sliced olives, sour cream and taco sauce in separate dishes.

4 to 6 servings

Cheese-Tortilla Casserole

1 pound ground lean pork
½ pound smoked ham, ground
1 green pepper, cored and finely chopped
1 small onion, peeled and finely chopped
3 cloves garlic, minced
2 tablespoons snipped parsley
½ cup dark seedless raisins
¼ cup chopped pimiento-stuffed green olives
1 tablespoon capers
1 can (16 ounces) tomatoes, well drained; reserve 2 tablespoons juice
2 teaspoons sugar
½ teaspoon salt
¼ teaspoon pepper
2 cups shredded tortillas
1 egg, beaten
  Tortillas, cut in quarters
4 ounces sharp Cheddar cheese, thinly sliced
  Tortillas

1. Put pork and ham into a 1½-quart glass casserole. Cover with waxed paper. Cook in microwave oven **7 minutes at High**; stir once.

2. Add remaining ingredients except tortilla quarters, cheese and tortillas to meat; mix well. Cook uncovered in microwave oven **8 minutes at Medium-High**, or until thoroughly cooked.

3. Arrange tortilla quarters around edge of casserole and top with cheese. Heat uncovered in microwave oven **2½ minutes at Medium-High**, or until cheese melts and mixture bubbles.

4. Serve with warm tortillas (heat in microwave oven **15 to 30 seconds at High**).

8 servings

Mock Drumsticks

1½ pounds ground pork
1 egg, beaten
⅓ cup finely chopped onion
2 teaspoons prepared mustard
1 teaspoon Worcestershire sauce
1 teaspoon salt
Dash pepper
¾ cup fine dry bread crumbs

1. Put meat into a large bowl and add remaining ingredients except bread crumbs; mix lightly until well blended. Divide into 6 portions. Shape each portion evenly and firmly around a flat or round wooden stick. Roll meat in crumbs until well coated.

2. Arrange "drumsticks" on a microwave-oven-safe roast rack set in a 2½-quart microwave-oven-safe open oval casserole, alternating meat ends and stick ends. Cover with waxed paper.

3. Cook in microwave oven **15 minutes at Medium-High**, or until meat is done; rearrange and turn drumsticks over twice during cooking period.

6 servings

Marzetti

2 tablespoons butter or margarine
½ cup chopped onion
½ cup chopped green pepper
1 can (3 ounces) chopped mushrooms, drained
1 teaspoon salt
⅛ teaspoon pepper
½ teaspoon garlic salt (optional)
1 pound ground beef
3 cups cooked noodles
1 can (15 ounces) tomato sauce
1 cup soft bread crumbs
1 cup (4 ounces) shredded Cheddar cheese

1. Put butter, onion, green pepper and mushrooms into a 2-quart glass casserole. Cook uncovered in microwave oven **6 minutes at High**, or until onion is soft; stir after 1 minute. Add salt, pepper and garlic salt; mix well.

2. Put meat into a 1½-quart glass baking dish. Cover with waxed paper. Cook in microwave oven **5 minutes at High**, or until meat is no longer pink; stir and break meat apart with a wooden spoon once. Drain off fat from meat. Stir in vegetable mixture.

3. Alternate layers of noodles, meat mixture and tomato sauce in the glass casserole. Top with bread crumbs and cheese. Cover with an all-glass lid or plastic wrap.

4. Heat in microwave oven to serving temperature (**about 7 minutes at High**); rotate casserole one-half turn once. Let stand covered 5 minutes.

6 servings

Hamburger Stroganoff

1 pound lean ground beef
1 large onion, peeled and chopped
1 teaspoon salt
Dash pepper
1 can (10¾ ounces) condensed cream of chicken soup
1 cup dairy sour cream
Cooked noodles or baked potatoes (see page 61 or page 147)

1. Put ground beef and onion into an 8-inch square glass baking dish. Cover with waxed paper. Cook in microwave oven **6 minutes at High**, or until meat is no longer pink; stir twice, breaking meat apart with a wooden spoon.

2. Drain off fat from meat. Add salt, pepper and soup to meat; mix well. Cook covered in microwave oven **6 to 8 minutes at High**, or until thoroughly heated; stir occasionally.

3. Stir in sour cream. Cover with plastic wrap and let stand 2 minutes. Serve over noodles or baked potatoes.

About 4 servings

Bavarian Bratwurst Casserole

1 pound fresh bratwurst
¼ cup chopped onion
1 small head (about 2 pounds) red cabbage, thinly sliced
2 medium potatoes, pared and diced
2 small apples, cored and diced
1 tablespoon caraway seed
¼ cup packed brown sugar
2 tablespoons red wine vinegar
½ teaspoon salt

1. Remove bratwurst from casing and crumble into a 3-quart glass casserole. Add onion; stir. Cover with an all-glass lid or plastic wrap. Cook in microwave oven **4 to 5 minutes at High**, or until pink has disappeared from bratwurst; stir once. Drain.

2. Stir red cabbage, potato, apple, caraway seed, brown sugar, vinegar and salt into bratwurst mixture. Cook covered in microwave oven **18 to 20 minutes at High**; stir 3 times.

8 servings

Meat-Stuffed Acorn Squash

2 medium acorn squash
1 pound ground beef
¼ cup chopped onion
1 tablespoon butter or
    margarine
1 teaspoon salt
¼ cup packed brown sugar
⅛ teaspoon ground nutmeg
8 teaspoons butter or
    margarine
    Salt and pepper to taste
    Ground nutmeg (optional)

1. Cook squash (see Fresh Vegetable Cooking Chart on page 147). Cut squash in half; scoop out seedy centers. Cover with plastic wrap.

2. Put ground beef into a 9-inch glass pie plate. Cover with waxed paper. Cook in microwave oven **4 minutes at High**, or until meat is no longer pink; break meat apart and stir with a wooden spoon once. Drain and set aside.

3. Put onion and 1 tablespoon butter into a 1-cup glass measuring cup. Cook uncovered in microwave oven **2 minutes at High**. Add to ground beef along with 1 teaspoon salt, the brown sugar and nutmeg; stir.

4. Scoop out some of the cooked squash from each half, leaving a ¼-inch rim; add to beef mixture and mix with a fork. Set squash halves on a microwave-oven-safe platter.

5. Put 1 teaspoon butter into each squash half and sprinkle with salt and pepper. Spoon one-quarter of meat-and-squash mixture into each squash shell. Top with 1 teaspoon butter and sprinkle with nutmeg, if desired. Cover with plastic wrap. Cook in microwave oven **4 minutes at High**.

6. Let stand covered 5 minutes.

4 servings

Stuffed Franks

4 medium potatoes, pared and
    cut in half
½ cup milk
2 tablespoons butter or
    margarine
    Salt and pepper to taste
8 frankfurters
½ cup (2 ounces) shredded
    Cheddar cheese

1. Boil potatoes (see Fresh Vegetable Cooking Chart on page 147). Drain.

2. Heat milk in a 1-cup glass measuring cup in microwave oven until hot (**15 to 30 seconds at High**).

3. Mash or rice potatoes thoroughly. Whip in hot milk, butter, salt and pepper until fluffy.

4. Slit frankfurters down center to ¹⁄₁₆ inch from bottom. Open up and stuff each frankfurter with ¼ cup mashed potatoes. Sprinkle cheese on top. Arrange stuffed franks spoke-fashion on a microwave-oven-safe plate.

5. Heat uncovered in microwave oven **2 to 3 minutes at High**, or until cheese just begins to melt.

4 to 6 servings

Apricot-Almond Stuffing

Roast Turkey

Poultry

Out of the frying pan and into the microwave/convection oven! Chicken, turkey and all the rest of the culinary birds make the transition with flying colors.

Some birds, such as turkeys, geese, Cornish hens, and ducks, usually are purchased frozen. These, and any birds you may have frozen at home, should be defrosted before cooking in your microwave/convection oven. Defrosting can be done in the refrigerator or, for convenience, in the microwave oven, using the chart on page 21.

In the recipes and charts that follow you will find a variety of recipes using one of the three settings: microwave, convection or combination. In most cases, cut-up poultry works best with the speed of microwave. Those recipes that include pastry or biscuits need heat to brown and crisp. In the poultry charts, use microwave for fast results. If you prefer the skin crispy, use the other recommendations.

Cut-Up Poultry

Cut-up birds are so tasty that they have become the starting point for many recipes. By looking through the chapter you'll get an idea of how many variations of "fried" and "baked" chicken alone are possible. Then you can start applying your own creative touches. Some general principles apply.

Cooking dish: You can cook poultry pieces right in the serving dish, if the dish has passed the microwave-oven-safe test (page 9). For combination cooking, use a dish that is also heat resistant.

Arrange the pieces with thick parts toward the outside and thin parts in. When cooking drumsticks, for example, arrange spoke-fashion with the bony tips pointed in. Arrange so pieces don't touch and aren't stacked. A little space between each piece aids even cooking.

Cover with waxed paper before cooking in the microwave oven to prevent spattering and to help equalize heat.

Set the timer for the minimum time and the power setting as the recipe directs.

Rearrange and turn pieces over midway during microwave cooking, keeping the thickest portions to the outside.

Standing time is about 5 minutes for cut-up poultry. Let chicken stand covered as the recipe directs to complete the cooking process.

Test for doneness with a fork (it should feel tender and juices should run clear) or with a knife cut near the bone (the meat should not look pink).

Whole Birds

Turkeys, sixteen pounds or less, and other whole birds cook well with all three types of cooking. When preparing for microwave cooking omit the salt except for salting the cavity. Because salt has a special attraction for microwaves, it is better to sprinkle it on after cooking.

The Temperature Probe will monitor the internal temperature during cooking. If the temperature is below that recommended on the chart, return the bird to the oven for additional cooking. When the preset temperature is reached, remove from the oven and let stand, covered with foil, to complete cooking. Allow 20 minutes for standing time for a 16-pound turkey; less for smaller birds.

Use the doneness test given above for cut-up poultry to check whole birds after standing time. Don't be concerned if the "cooking gauges" that come in some turkeys pop out before the turkey tests done. They are not accurate for poultry cooked in the microwave oven.

Whole birds cooked with combination cooking are brown and crisp on the outer skin, but juicy and tender inside. Just place the bird directly on the bottom metal rack. You'll love the results and, especially, the time savings!

How to Cook Poultry

Microwave

1. Remove giblets and wash cavity. Stuff, if desired. Secure openings with wooden picks or poultry pins.

2. Place poultry breast-side-down on a microwave-oven-safe roast rack set in a 2-quart glass baking dish. Cover with waxed paper. Cook in microwave oven for half of time in chart below.

3. Turn poultry over halfway through cooking. Shield ends of wings and legs with aluminum foil. If using Temperature Probe, insert in thickest part of breast. Cover with waxed paper. Cook in microwave oven for remaining time (or if using Temperature Probe, set at 170°F).

4. Cover with foil and let stand 10 to 15 minutes for heat to equalize.

Combination and convection

1. Do not preheat oven.

2. Place poultry directly on bottom metal rack.

3. If using Temperature Probe, insert tip into inside thigh.

4. Cover with aluminum foil and let stand 10 to 20 minutes before serving.

Poultry	Method	Oven Setting	Cooking Time per Pound	Temperature Probe Setting
Turkey whole, unstuffed 5 to 9 pounds	Microwave	High, then Medium-High	9 to 9½ minutes	175°F
	Combination	Combination II	8 to 10 minutes	180°F
10 to 16 pounds	Microwave	High, then Medium-High	8 to 8½ minutes	175°F
	Combination	Combination I	9 to 11 minutes	180°-185°F
breast 2½ to 5 pounds	Combination	Combination I	16 to 18 minutes	170°F
Chicken 2 to 3 pounds	Microwave Convection	High 375°F	7 to 8 minutes 20 to 23 minutes	
Goose 8 to 10 pounds	Combination	Combination I	15 to 17 minutes	
Duckling 5 pounds	Combination	Combination II	13 to 15 minutes	
Cornish hen about 1 pound	Microwave	High	9 to 10 minutes	

How to Broil Chicken

1. Preheat oven at Broil.

2. Cut chicken into halves or quarters.

3. Place chicken on bottom metal rack.

4. Remove when desired degree of doneness is reached.

Type	Method	Oven Setting	Cooking Time
Chicken halves or quarters	Convection	450°F Broil	30 to 40 minutes

Microwave Oven-Fried Chicken

1 **broiler-fryer chicken (2½ to 3 pounds), cut in serving pieces, rinsed and patted dry**
Milk
1 **package seasoned coating mix for chicken**
Paprika

1. Dip chicken pieces in milk and then shake in a bag with coating mix. Place breaded pieces skin-side-up in a 1½-quart glass baking dish with thin end toward center and thicker end toward outside. Sprinkle with paprika. Cover with waxed paper.

2. Cook in microwave oven **9 minutes at High**. Rearrange chicken pieces. Cook covered **8 to 9 minutes at High**, or until done.

3. Remove from oven. Cover with aluminum foil and let stand 5 minutes before serving.

4 servings

Hint: For microwave/convection oven cooking, preheat convection oven to 375°F. Place dish filled with breaded chicken on bottom metal rack. Cook in microwave/convection oven **40 to 45 minutes at Combination II**, or until done.

Baked Chicken Pieces

2 tablespoons butter or margarine
2 pounds chicken pieces, rinsed and patted dry
Paprika

1. Melt butter in a 1-cup glass measuring cup in microwave oven (**about 30 seconds at High**).

2. Place chicken pieces skin-side-up in an 8-inch square glass baking dish with thin end toward center and thicker end toward outside. Brush pieces with melted butter and sprinkle with paprika. Cover with waxed paper.

3. Cook in microwave oven **12 minutes at High**. Turn chicken pieces over and rearrange.

4. Cook covered in microwave oven **3 to 4 minutes at High**, or until tender.

5. Remove from oven, cover with aluminum foil and let stand 5 minutes before serving.

4 servings

Greek-Style Chicken

1½ tablespoons olive oil
3 tablespoons fresh lemon juice
1½ teaspoons oregano leaves
1 broiler-fryer chicken (2½ to 3 pounds), cut in serving pieces, rinsed and patted dry
Salt and pepper to taste
Paprika
Cooked rice or noodles (see page 59 or 61)

1. Combine oil, lemon juice and oregano in an 8-inch square glass baking dish. Add chicken pieces and turn to coat. Arrange chicken pieces skin-side-up in a single layer with thin end toward center and thicker end toward outside. Sprinkle with salt and pepper. Cover with plastic wrap. Let marinate in refrigerator 1 hour; turn pieces over once.

2. Discard plastic wrap. Cover dish with waxed paper. Cook in microwave oven **9 minutes at High**.

3. Turn chicken pieces over and rearrange. Sprinkle with paprika. Cook covered in microwave oven **8 to 9 minutes at High**, or until thoroughly cooked.

4. Let stand 5 minutes. Serve with rice or noodles.

4 servings

Orange-Burgundy Chicken

1 broiler-fryer chicken (2½ to 3 pounds), cut in pieces, rinsed and patted dry
½ cup orange marmalade
½ cup orange juice
⅓ cup burgundy
2 tablespoons cornstarch
2 tablespoons brown sugar
2 tablespoons lemon juice
1 teaspoon salt

1. Arrange chicken pieces skin-side-down in an 8-inch square glass baking dish with thin end toward center and thicker end toward outside.

2. Mix marmalade, orange juice, burgundy, cornstarch, brown sugar, lemon juice and salt in a bowl. Pour sauce over chicken. Cover with waxed paper.

3. Cook in microwave oven **10 minutes at High**.

4. Turn chicken pieces over and rearrange. Cook covered in microwave oven **10 minutes at High**, or until tender.

4 to 6 servings

Fiesta Chicken Rolls

3 **whole chicken breasts (about 3 pounds), halved, boned and skinned**
3 **tablespoons butter or margarine**
3 **tablespoons pasteurized process sharp Cheddar cheese spread**
2 **teaspoons minced onion**
1 **teaspoon salt**
2 **tablespoons chopped green chilies**
3 **tablespoons butter or margarine**
1 **cup Cheddar cheese cracker crumbs**
1 **package (1¼ ounces) taco seasoning mix**
   Shredded lettuce
1 **tomato, diced**
   Sliced ripe olives

1. Pound each raw chicken piece with a meat hammer to flatten.

2. Mix 3 tablespoons butter and the cheese spread until well blended. Mix in onion, salt and chilies.

3. Divide mixture equally onto the 6 flattened chicken pieces, placing a portion at one end of each piece. Roll up, tucking in ends to completely enclose filling. Fasten rolls with wooden picks.

4. Melt 3 tablespoons butter in a 1½-quart glass baking dish in microwave oven (**about 1 minute at High**). Coat each roll with melted butter, then with a mixture of cheese cracker crumbs and taco seasoning mix.

5. Arrange rolls in the baking dish. Cover with waxed paper. Cook in microwave oven **10 to 12 minutes at High**; rotate dish one-quarter turn twice.

6. Serve chicken on a bed of lettuce, tomato and ripe olives.

6 servings

Chicken Hawaiian

¼ cup (½ stick) butter or margarine
1 can (20 ounces) unsweetened pineapple chunks
1 tablespoon cider vinegar
1 tablespoon brown sugar
1 tablespoon soy sauce
1 broiler-fryer chicken (2½ to 3 pounds), cut in serving pieces
3 tablespoons cornstarch
¼ cup cold water
2 green onions with stems, diagonally sliced

1. Melt butter in an 8-inch square glass baking dish in microwave oven (**about 1 minute at High**).

2. Drain pineapple, reserving juice. Set pineapple chunks aside. Add juice, vinegar, brown sugar and soy sauce to melted butter; stir. Place chicken pieces skin-side-down in mixture with thin end toward inside and thicker end toward outside. Cover with plastic wrap.

3. Cook in microwave oven **9 minutes at High**. Turn over and rearrange chicken pieces.

4. Cook covered in microwave oven **8 to 9 minutes at High**, or until chicken is thoroughly cooked. Keep chicken warm.

5. Pour cooking liquid into a 1-quart glass measuring pitcher. Add water to make 2 cups. Dissolve cornstarch in ¼ cup cold water and stir into cooking liquid. Cook uncovered in microwave oven **2 minutes at High**, or until thickened; stir after 1 minute.

6. Add pineapple chunks and green onion slices to sauce; stir. Heat in microwave oven **30 seconds at High**; stir. Pour sauce over chicken.

4 to 6 servings

Barbecued Chicken

1 broiler-fryer chicken (2½ to 3 pounds), cut in serving pieces, rinsed and patted dry
¾ cup bottled barbecue sauce (or use a favorite recipe) Parsley

1. Arrange chicken pieces in a single layer in an 8-inch square glass baking dish with thin end toward center and thicker end toward outside. Brush one-third of the sauce on the chicken. Cover with waxed paper.

2. Cook in microwave oven **6 minutes at High**.

3. Turn chicken pieces over and rearrange, then spread with one-third of the sauce. Cook covered in microwave oven **6 minutes at High**.

4. Again turn chicken over, rearrange pieces and spread with remaining sauce. Cook covered in microwave oven **6 minutes at High**, or until tender.

5. Remove from oven, cover with aluminum foil and let stand 5 minutes before serving.

6. Arrange chicken on a platter and garnish with parsley.

4 servings

Chicken à la King

¼ cup (½ stick) butter or
  margarine
3 tablespoons all-purpose flour
1 cup chicken broth
  (homemade, canned or from
  bouillon cube)
1 cup milk
½ teaspoon celery seed
½ teaspoon salt
¼ teaspoon pepper
2 cups diced cooked chicken
  (see page 133)
1 cup cooked green peas
¼ cup chopped pimiento
1 tablespoon finely shredded
  Cheddar cheese
  Toast, biscuits or patty shells

1. Melt butter in a 1½-quart glass casserole in microwave oven (**about 1 minute at High**). Blend in flour. Add chicken broth and milk gradually, stirring until smooth.

2. Cook uncovered in microwave oven **6 to 7 minutes at High**, or until sauce comes to boiling and thickens; stir after each minute.

3. Add seasonings, chicken, peas and pimiento to sauce; stir. Cook uncovered in microwave oven **5 minutes at High**, or until thoroughly heated; stir twice.

4. Stir cheese into chicken mixture. Serve over toast or biscuits or in patty shells.

About 6 servings

Chicken Cacciatore

1 broiler-fryer chicken (2½ to
  3 pounds), cut in serving
  pieces
1 can (15 ounces) tomato sauce
1 can (6 ounces) tomato paste
½ cup finely chopped onion
½ teaspoon garlic powder
1 teaspoon salt
¼ teaspoon pepper
¼ teaspoon ground thyme
1 cup water
½ cup red wine
1 can (4 ounces) sliced
  mushrooms, drained
  Cooked spaghetti or
  Homemade Pasta
  (see page 61)

1. Cut large pieces of chicken in half for uniform size. Rinse chicken pieces and pat dry. Set aside.

2. Combine tomato sauce, tomato paste, onion, dry seasonings, water and wine in a 3-quart glass casserole. Add chicken pieces and coat with sauce. Arrange pieces with thin end toward center and thicker end toward outside. Cover with waxed paper.

3. Cook in microwave oven **10 minutes at High**. Turn and rearrange chicken pieces. Cover and continue cooking **10 minutes at High**.

4. Add mushrooms to sauce; stir. Cook uncovered in microwave oven **5 minutes at High**, or until chicken is tender.

5. Serve with spaghetti garnished with parsley.

4 servings

Chicken Teriyaki

1 broiler-fryer chicken (2½ to 3 pounds), cut in serving pieces
¼ cup soy sauce
¼ cup sake or dry sherry
1 tablespoon vegetable oil
¾ teaspoon ground ginger
¼ cup sugar
¼ teaspoon salt

1. Cut large pieces of chicken in half for uniform size. Rinse chicken and pat dry. Put into a large shallow dish. Combine remaining ingredients and pour over chicken. Refrigerate several hours.

2. Arrange chicken pieces in an 8-inch square glass baking dish with thin end toward center and thicker end toward outside. Reserve marinade. Cover with waxed paper.

3. Cook in microwave oven **10 minutes at High**. Turn and rearrange chicken pieces. Cover and continue cooking **8 to 10 minutes at High**, or until chicken is tender; rotate dish one-quarter turn once and brush the chicken occasionally with the reserved marinade.

4 servings

Mushroom-Cream Chicken Breasts

2 whole chicken breasts (about 2 pounds), split lengthwise, rinsed and patted dry
1 pound fresh mushrooms, cleaned and sliced lengthwise
3 tablespoons butter or margarine
2 tablespoons all-purpose flour
1 teaspoon salt
1 cup half-and-half or cream
1 tablespoon dry sherry

1. Place chicken skin-side-down in an 8-inch square glass baking dish. Cover with waxed paper. Cook in microwave oven **8 minutes at High**.

2. Turn chicken over; cook covered in microwave oven **4 minutes at High**. Turn chicken right-side-up. Set aside covered.

3. Put mushrooms and butter into a 1½-quart glass casserole. Cook uncovered in microwave oven **4 minutes at High**; stir after 2 minutes.

4. Add flour and salt to mushrooms; mix well. Add half-and-half and sherry; stir. Cook uncovered in microwave oven **6 to 8 minutes at High**, or until sauce comes to boiling and is thickened; stir after 2 minutes, then stir every 30 seconds.

5. Pour off cooking liquid from chicken. Pour sauce over chicken. Cover with plastic wrap. Heat in microwave oven to serving temperature (**about 2 minutes at High**).

4 servings

Chicken Divan

1½ pounds fresh broccoli
 4 whole boneless chicken breasts (about 2 pounds)
 ¼ cup (½ stick) butter or margarine
 ¼ cup all-purpose flour
 ¼ teaspoon salt
 1 cup milk
 1 cup chicken broth (homemade, canned or from bouillon cube)
 1 teaspoon Worcestershire sauce
 ½ cup grated Parmesan or Romano cheese
 ½ cup crushed cereal flakes

1. Trim broccoli and cut into even pieces. Cook broccoli following directions in Fresh Vegetable Cooking Chart on page 144. Drain if necessary. Cover and keep warm.

2. Arrange chicken in an 8-inch square glass baking dish with thin end toward inside and thicker end toward outside. Cover with plastic wrap. Cook in microwave oven **7 minutes at High**, or until tender; rearrange pieces once.

3. Remove chicken from oven and remove cover. Let stand until cool enough to handle. Remove skin from chicken breasts and cut chicken pieces in half. Cover and keep warm.

4. Melt butter in a 1-quart glass measuring pitcher in microwave oven (**about 1 minute at High**). Add flour and salt; blend. Add milk and broth gradually, stirring constantly.

5. Cook uncovered in microwave oven **4 to 6 minutes at High**, or until thickened; stir after 2 minutes, then every 30 seconds.

6. Remove from oven. Stir Worcestershire sauce into sauce.

7. Arrange broccoli in a 1½-quart glass baking dish and cover with chicken pieces. Sprinkle half of cheese over chicken. Pour sauce over all. Mix remaining cheese and crushed cereal; sprinkle over sauce. Cover with waxed paper.

8. Heat in microwave oven to serving temperature (**3 to 5 minutes at High**).

6 servings

Stewed Chicken

 1 stewing chicken (about 5 pounds), cut in pieces and rinsed
 3 small onions, peeled and sliced
 3 stalks celery with leaves, sliced diagonally
 2 medium carrots, pared and thinly sliced
 1 tablespoon chopped parsley
 1 tablespoon salt
 ¼ teaspoon pepper
 6 cups boiling water, or enough to cover chicken

1. Combine all ingredients in a 4-quart microwave-oven-safe casserole. Cover with a microwave-oven-safe lid. Cook in microwave oven **2 hours (120 minutes) at Medium**, or until thickest pieces are tender; rearrange chicken pieces every 30 minutes. Add 1 cup boiling water, if needed, to keep chicken covered with broth. Remove chicken pieces from casserole. Strain broth.

2. If not serving immediately, let chicken cool in broth. When cool, remove skin and bones from chicken. Keep chicken in as large pieces as possible. Skim fat from broth. Refrigerate broth and chicken pieces separately in covered containers; use within several days. For longer storage, package chicken and broth together and freeze.

About 5 cups cubed cooked chicken and 6 to 7 cups broth

Chicken and Dumplings

2 tablespoons butter or margarine
¼ cup chopped onion
2 tablespoons chopped celery
1 tablespoon chopped celery leaves
1 small clove garlic, minced
2 tablespoons all-purpose flour
2 cups chicken broth (homemade, canned or from bouillon cubes)
½ teaspoon sugar
1 teaspoon salt
⅛ teaspoon pepper
½ teaspoon basil leaves
1 bay leaf
2 tablespoons chopped parsley
1 broiler-fryer chicken (2½ to 3 pounds), cut in serving pieces, rinsed and patted dry
1 package (10 ounces) frozen green peas
Basil Dumplings (see recipe)

1. Put butter, onion, celery, celery leaves and garlic into a 3-quart glass casserole. Cook uncovered in microwave oven **2½ to 3½ minutes at High**, or until crisp-tender; stir after 1 minute.

2. Sprinkle flour over vegetables and mix well. Add chicken broth, sugar, salt, pepper, basil, bay leaf and parsley; stir. Cook uncovered in microwave oven **8 to 10 minutes at High**, or until thickened; stir twice.

3. Arrange chicken pieces in casserole with sauce with thin end toward inside and thicker end toward outside. Spoon sauce over chicken. Cover with plastic wrap. Cook in microwave oven **8 minutes at High**.

4. Turn chicken pieces over in casserole. Cook covered in microwave oven **8 to 10 minutes at Medium-High**.

5. Remove chicken, cover with aluminum foil and keep warm. Add frozen peas to mixture in casserole and, if necessary, break apart with a fork. Cook uncovered in microwave oven **9 to 10 minutes at High**, or until boiling.

6. Meanwhile, prepare Basil Dumplings.

7. Return chicken to casserole. Drop dumpling mixture 1 tablespoon at a time next to chicken. Cover with plastic wrap. Cook in microwave oven **5 minutes at High**. Remove from oven and let stand covered 5 minutes before serving. (Dumplings when done should lose their moist look and spring back when touched.)

About 6 servings

Basil Dumplings: Combine 1 cup all-purpose biscuit mix and ½ teaspoon basil leaves in a bowl. Add ⅓ cup milk and stir with a fork until a dough is formed. Proceed as directed in recipe.

Chicken Casserole 'n' Cheese Biscuits

½ cup chopped onion
1 package (10 ounces) frozen mixed vegetables
3 cups cubed cooked chicken (see page 133)
1 can (10¾ ounces) condensed cream of chicken soup
1 can (10¾ ounces) condensed cream of mushroom soup
¼ cup half-and-half
¼ teaspoon Worcestershire sauce

Cheese biscuits:
1 cup all-purpose biscuit mix
1 tablespoon sugar
⅓ cup milk
½ cup (2 ounces) shredded Cheddar cheese

1. Cook onion uncovered in a 2-quart glass measuring pitcher in microwave oven **2 minutes at High**. Stir in frozen vegetables. Continue cooking **2 minutes at High**.

2. Preheat convection oven to 375°F.

3. Add chicken, condensed soups, half-and-half and Worcestershire sauce to vegetable mixture; mix well. Turn mixture into a 1½-quart glass baking dish.

4. Place on bottom metal rack. Cook in microwave/convection oven **5 minutes at Combination II**.

5. For cheese biscuits, combine biscuit mix and sugar in a bowl. Stir in milk just until moistened. Stir in Cheddar cheese. Drop cheese biscuit dough by tablespoonfuls onto hot chicken mixture (6 biscuits). Cook in microwave/convection oven **20 to 25 minutes at Combination II**, or until set.

6 servings

Chicken Turnovers

¼ cup chopped onion
2 tablespoons butter or margarine
1 tablespoon cornstarch
½ cup chicken broth
1½ cups chopped cooked chicken
1 can (4 ounces) mushroom pieces, drained
1 cup drained cooked mixed vegetables
1 teaspoon lemon juice
1 teaspoon dried parsley flakes
1 teaspoon salt
¼ teaspoon pepper
    Pastry for 2-crust pie

1. Put onion and butter into a 1-quart glass measuring pitcher. Cook uncovered in microwave oven **2 minutes at High**.

2. Stir in cornstarch. Slowly stir in chicken broth until smooth. Cook uncovered in microwave oven **1½ minutes at High**, or until thickened; stir once.

3. Add chicken, mushrooms, vegetables, lemon juice, parsley, salt and pepper to thickened broth. Set aside.

4. Preheat convection oven to 375°F.

5. Divide pastry into 8 portions. Roll each into a circle approximately 6½ inches in diameter and ⅛ inch thick. Divide chicken mixture evenly on 8 pastry circles (about ⅓ cup per circle). Fold each circle in half, pressing edges with fork to seal. Pierce with fork to make steam vents.

6. Arrange filled turnovers on two ungreased round metal trays. Place one tray on each metal rack. Cook in convection oven **40 to 50 minutes at 375°F**, or until light golden.

8 turnovers

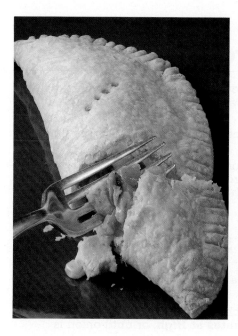

Chicken Pot Pies

3 tablespoons butter or margarine
¾ cup chopped onion
¾ cup coarsely chopped carrot
¾ cup coarsely chopped celery
⅓ cup all-purpose flour
¾ cup chicken broth
¾ cup half-and-half
½ teaspoon salt
⅛ teaspoon pepper
3 cups cubed cooked chicken (see page 133)
    Pastry for 1-crust pie
1 tablespoon milk

1. Put butter, onion, carrot and celery into a 1-quart glass measuring pitcher. Cook uncovered in microwave oven **3 to 4 minutes at High**, or until vegetables are tender. Stir in flour. Add broth and half-and-half gradually, stirring constantly. Stir in salt, pepper and chicken.

2. Divide mixture in four 10-ounce glass casseroles.

3. Preheat convection oven to 375°F.

4. Roll out pastry on a lightly floured surface. Cut out four pastry rounds ½ inch larger than tops of casseroles. Turn edge under and fit each to top of casserole. Cut steam vents in tops. Brush with milk.

5. Place casseroles on bottom metal rack. Cook in microwave/convection oven **38 to 40 minutes at Combination II**, or until pastry is lightly browned.

4 servings

Chicken Curry and Pineapple

¼ cup (½ stick) butter or margarine
½ cup slivered almonds
1 can (20 ounces) pineapple chunks, drained
2 to 3 tablespoons chutney
3 tablespoons butter or margarine
1 cup finely chopped onion
⅔ cup diagonally sliced celery
1 to 2 tablespoons curry powder
1 can (10¾ ounces) condensed cream of chicken soup
1 can (10¾ ounces) condensed cream of mushroom soup
2½ cups diced cooked chicken (see page 133)
½ cup dairy sour cream
Cooked rice (see page 59)

1. Put ¼ cup butter and the almonds into a 1-quart glass casserole. Cook uncovered in microwave oven **2 minutes at High**, or until almonds are golden brown; stir after 1 minute. Remove almonds with a slotted spoon and place on paper towels.

2. Add pineapple and chutney to butter in the casserole; mix well. Heat uncovered in microwave oven **2 minutes at High**, or until pineapple is glazed. Remove from oven and keep warm.

3. Put 3 tablespoons butter, the onion, celery and curry powder into a 3-quart glass casserole. Cook uncovered in microwave oven **6 to 8 minutes at High**, or until onion is tender; stir after 1 minute.

4. Put condensed soups and cooked chicken into casserole; mix well. Cover with an all-glass lid or plastic wrap. Heat in microwave oven to serving temperature (**6 to 8 minutes at High**); stir once.

5. Remove casserole from oven, stir in sour cream and let stand covered 1 minute.

6. Serve curry over rice and top with the pineapple and almonds.

6 to 8 servings

Chicken 'n' Mushroom Sauce

1 can (10¾ ounces) condensed cream of mushroom soup
1 cup (4 ounces) shredded Cheddar cheese
3 slices toast, cut in 1-inch pieces
2 cups diced cooked chicken (see page 133)

1. Combine condensed mushroom soup and cheese in a 1-quart glass casserole. Cook uncovered in microwave oven **2 minutes at High**, or until cheese is melted.

2. Put pieces of toast (reserve 6 pieces for top) in bottom of an 8-inch round glass cake dish.

3. Put chicken on toast and pour sauce over all. Garnish with remaining toast pieces. Heat uncovered in microwave oven to serving temperature (**8½ to 9½ minutes at Medium-High**).

About 6 servings

Chicken Livers in Sour Cream

1 pound chicken livers
3 tablespoons butter or margarine
½ cup chopped onion
¾ cup dairy sour cream
⅓ cup dry white wine
½ teaspoon salt
¼ teaspoon pepper
3 tablespoons chopped parsley
Cooked rice (see page 59)

1. Rinse chicken livers, pierce with a fork and drain on paper towels. Set aside.

2. Put butter and onion into an 8-inch square glass baking dish. Cook uncovered in microwave oven **3 minutes at High**, or until onion is tender; stir once.

3. Add chicken livers to onion-butter mixture; stir. Cover with waxed paper. Cook in microwave oven **9 to 10 minutes at High**, or until chicken livers are done; stir twice.

4. Blend sour cream, wine, salt and pepper. Add to chicken livers; stir. Sprinkle with parsley. Heat uncovered in microwave oven to serving temperature (**about 1 minute at High**).

5. Serve with rice.

6 servings

Chicken Livers and Mushrooms

1 pound chicken livers,
  cut in half if large
⅓ cup all-purpose flour
½ teaspoon salt
⅛ teaspoon white pepper
2½ tablespoons butter or
  margarine
½ medium onion, sliced
1 jar (4½ ounces) sliced
  mushrooms, drained
  Snipped parsley

1. Rinse chicken livers, pierce with a fork and drain on paper towels.

2. Mix flour, salt and pepper; coat chicken livers evenly.

3. Melt butter in an 8-inch square glass baking dish in microwave oven (**about 30 seconds at High**). Add livers and onion and coat with butter. Cover with waxed paper. Cook **9 to 10 minutes at High**; stir once.

4. Add mushrooms to livers. Heat uncovered in microwave oven to serving temperature (**about 1 minute at High**); or until chicken livers are done.

5. Sprinkle with parsley. Serve immediately.

About 4 servings

Chicken Fricassee

1 stewing chicken (4 to
  4½ pounds), cut in pieces
  and rinsed
1 medium onion, peeled and
  quartered
1½ cups diagonally sliced celery
¼ cup chopped parsley
1 bay leaf
1½ teaspoons salt
2 peppercorns
6 cups boiling water
¼ cup all-purpose flour
1 cup half-and-half
1 tablespoon lemon juice

1. Put chicken pieces, gizzard, heart and neck into a 4-quart microwave-oven-safe casserole. Add onion, celery, parsley, bay leaf, salt, peppercorns and boiling water. Cover with a microwave-oven-safe lid.

2. Cook in microwave oven **1½ hours at Medium**, or until thickest pieces are tender; rearrange chicken every 30 minutes. Add liver the last 3 minutes of cooking.

3. Remove chicken and giblets from broth. Strain broth and let cool slightly; skim off and reserve ¼ cup fat.

4. Heat the ¼ cup fat in the microwave-oven-safe casserole in microwave oven **1 minute at High**. Blend in flour. Cook uncovered **1 minute at High**, or until bubbly.

5. Add 2 cups chicken broth and the half-and-half gradually to butter-flour mixture, stirring constantly. Cook uncovered in microwave oven **10 to 12 minutes at High**, or until thickened and smooth; stir every 3 minutes.

6. Add lemon juice and chicken to sauce; stir. Heat in microwave oven to serving temperature (**about 5 minutes at High**).

About 6 servings

Hot Chicken Salad

½ cup chopped walnuts
3 cups cubed cooked chicken (see page 133) or turkey
1 cup sliced celery
1 can (20 ounces) pineapple chunks in heavy syrup, drained
¼ cup sliced green onion
1 cup (4 ounces) shredded sharp Cheddar cheese
¾ cup mayonnaise
1 tablespoon lemon juice
¼ teaspoon salt
¼ teaspoon ground ginger

1. Spread walnuts in a 9-inch glass pie plate. Cook uncovered in microwave oven **2½ to 3 minutes at High**, or until toasted; stir twice.

2. Combine chicken, celery, pineapple, green onion, cheese and toasted walnuts in a 2-quart glass casserole.

3. Combine mayonnaise, lemon juice, salt and ginger. Add to chicken mixture; mix well. Cover with waxed paper.

4. Cook in microwave oven to serving temperature (**6 to 7 minutes at High**).

5. Let stand covered 2 minutes before serving.

6 to 8 servings

Roast Duckling with Cherry Sauce

1 ready-to-cook duckling (5 pounds)
Cherry Sauce (see page 194)
Buttered rice (optional)

1. Remove giblets from duckling and wash duckling. (It is recommended that giblets be cooked conventionally.)

2. Secure openings with heavy round wooden picks. Tie legs and wings to body with string. Prick skin of duckling with a 2-tined fork. Cover ends of wings, legs and tail of duckling with small pieces of aluminum foil.

3. Place duckling breast-side-down on a microwave-oven-safe roast rack set in an 8-inch square or a 2-quart glass baking dish. Cook uncovered in microwave oven **10 minutes at High**.

4. Brush duck with drippings. Cook uncovered in microwave oven **14 minutes at Medium-High**. Brush bird with drippings. Cook uncovered **14 minutes at Medium-High**.

5. Turn duck breast-side-up, remove foil and brush with drippings. Cook uncovered in microwave oven **14 minutes at Medium-High**, or until drumstick feels very soft when pressed between protected fingers.

6. Remove from oven. Cover duckling with foil and let stand 15 to 20 minutes for heat to equalize. Serve duckling with Cherry Sauce and, if desired, buttered rice.

4 servings

Lime-Glazed Cornish Hens

2 frozen Cornish hens (about 1 pound each)
1 teaspoon salt
¼ cup (½ stick) butter or margarine
1 tablespoon brown sugar
1½ tablespoons lime juice
1 teaspoon soy sauce

1. Defrost Cornish hens following directions in Defrosting Chart on page 21.

2. Remove giblets from hens; rinse hens and pat dry. Rub cavities with salt.

3. Melt butter in a 1-cup glass measuring cup in microwave oven (**about 1 minute at High**). Mix in brown sugar, lime juice and soy sauce. Brush cavities with some of the butter mixture.

4. Tie legs and tail together with cotton thread. Cover ends of wings and legs with small pieces of aluminum foil.

5. Place hens breast-side-down on a microwave-oven-safe platter. Cover with waxed paper. Cook in microwave oven **8 minutes at High**.

6. Remove foil, turn hens over, brush with butter mixture and cover again with waxed paper. Cook in microwave oven **11 minutes at High**, or until tender.

7. Remove from oven. Cover hens with foil and let stand 15 to 20 minutes for heat to equalize.

2 servings

Cornish Hens Marsala

4 frozen Cornish hens
(about 1 pound each)
1 teaspoon salt
2 tablespoons butter or
margarine
¼ cup all-purpose flour
¼ cup honey
2 cups dry Marsala wine
½ cup chopped onion

1. Defrost Cornish hens as directed in Defrosting Chart on page 21.

2. Remove giblets from hens; rinse hens and pat dry. Rub cavities with salt.

3. Melt butter in a 1-quart glass measuring pitcher in microwave oven (**about 30 seconds at High**). Stir in flour, honey, Marsala and onion. Cook uncovered in microwave oven **4 minutes at High**, or until sauce comes to boiling and is thickened; stir after 2 minutes, then every minute.

4. Tie legs and tail together with cotton thread. Cover ends of wings and legs with aluminum foil.

5. Place hens breast-side-down on a microwave-oven-safe platter. Cover with waxed paper. Cook in microwave oven **8 minutes at High**.

6. Remove foil, turn hens over and brush with Marsala mixture. Cook covered in microwave oven **11 minutes at High**, or until tender.

7. Remove from oven. Cover with foil and let stand 15 to 20 minutes for heat to equalize.

4 servings

Turkey-Potato Casserole

3 tablespoons butter or margarine
¾ cup sliced fresh mushrooms
½ cup finely chopped onion
2 cups diced cooked turkey
2 cups diced cooked potatoes
2 tablespoons snipped parsley
1½ teaspoons seasoned salt
⅛ teaspoon pepper
⅔ cup (1 small can) undiluted evaporated milk

1. Put butter, mushrooms and onion into a 2-quart glass casserole. Cook uncovered in microwave oven **3 to 4 minutes at High**, or until mushrooms are tender; stir after 1 minute.

2. Put turkey, potatoes, parsley, seasoned salt and pepper into casserole. Add evaporated milk, stirring gently. Heat uncovered in microwave oven to serving temperature (**about 5 minutes at High**); stir once.

4 to 6 servings

Rice and Sausage Stuffing

½ pound bulk pork sausage
2 tablespoons butter or margarine
½ cup sliced fresh mushrooms
½ cup chopped celery
½ cup chopped onion
2 cups cooked rice
1½ cups dry bread crumbs
1 tablespoon snipped parsley
1 teaspoon poultry seasoning
¼ cup chicken broth

1. Crumble pork sausage into a 1-quart glass measuring pitcher. Cook uncovered in microwave oven **2 to 3 minutes at High**, or until meat is no longer pink; stir once. Drain and set aside.

2. Put butter, mushrooms, celery and onion into the glass pitcher. Cook uncovered in microwave oven **2 minutes at High**, or until tender. Add rice, bread crumbs, parsley, poultry seasoning and chicken broth; mix well.

Enough stuffing for an 11- to 12-pound turkey

Bread and Nut Stuffing

½ cup (1 stick) butter or margarine
1 cup chicken broth (homemade, canned or from bouillon cube)
½ cup chopped onion
4 stalks celery, thinly sliced
10 cups day-old bread crumbs or ½-inch cubes (about 16 bread slices)
½ cup finely chopped walnuts or pecans
¼ cup chopped fresh parsley
1 teaspoon poultry seasoning

1. Put butter, broth, onion and celery into a 3-quart glass casserole. Cover with an all-glass lid or plastic wrap. Cook in microwave oven **5 to 6 minutes at Medium**; stir once.

2. Add remaining ingredients; mix lightly.

Enough stuffing for an 11- to 12-pound turkey

Apricot-Almond Stuffing

6 tablespoons butter or margarine
1 package (8 ounces) herb-seasoned stuffing mix
½ cup water
6 tablespoons chopped celery
6 tablespoons chopped dried apricots
¼ cup chopped almonds

1. Melt butter in a 2-quart glass measuring pitcher in microwave oven (**about 1½ minutes at High**).

2. Add stuffing mix, water, celery, apricots and almonds; mix well.

Enough stuffing for an 11- to 12-pound turkey

Roast Turkey Drumsticks

1 tablespoon gravy browning
sauce
1 tablespoon vegetable oil
2 turkey drumsticks (about
2½ pounds), rinsed and
patted dry

1. Mix browning sauce and oil for brushing sauce.

2. Put turkey drumsticks on a microwave-oven-safe roast rack set in an 8-inch square or a 2-quart glass baking dish. Brush with sauce. Cover leg bones with small pieces of aluminum foil. Cover with waxed paper.

3. Cook in microwave oven **30 minutes at Medium-High**, or until tender; turn over twice and brush with sauce.

2 servings

Hint: If turkey drumsticks are frozen, defrost following directions in Defrosting Chart on page 21.

Turkey Tetrazzini

1 package (7 or 8 ounces)
thin spaghetti, cooked
(see page 61)
2 tablespoons butter or
margarine
½ pound fresh mushrooms,
cleaned and sliced
lengthwise
¼ cup chopped green pepper
¼ cup chopped red pepper or
drained pimiento
1 tablespoon finely chopped
onion
¼ cup (½ stick) butter or
margarine
¼ cup all-purpose flour
½ teaspoon salt
¼ teaspoon white pepper
1 cup chicken broth
1 cup milk
3 tablespoons dry sherry
¼ cup snipped parsley
3 cups diced cooked turkey
Grated Parmesan or Romano
cheese

1. Prepare spaghetti. Keep warm until ready to use.

2. Put 2 tablespoons butter, mushrooms, green pepper, red pepper and onion into a 2-quart glass measuring pitcher. Cook uncovered in microwave oven **3 minutes at High**, or until mushrooms are tender; stir after 1 minute.

3. Remove mushroom mixture with a slotted spoon; set aside. Melt ¼ cup butter in the glass pitcher in microwave oven (**about 1 minute at High**). Add flour, salt and pepper; blend well. Add broth and milk gradually, stirring constantly. Cook uncovered **4 to 5 minutes at High**, or until thickened; stir after 2 minutes, then every minute.

4. Add mushroom mixture, sherry, parsley and turkey to sauce; mix well. Mix in cooked spaghetti. Heat uncovered in microwave oven **3 minutes at High**.

5. Stir mixture well and sprinkle with Parmesan cheese. Heat uncovered in microwave oven to serving temperature (**3 to 5 minutes at High**).

6 to 8 servings

Ratatouille

Zucchini
Boats

Vegetables

Microwave cooking does a lot of things fast, and one of them is to convert vegetable haters into vegetable lovers. If there are any at your house, ease them into a new-found respect for vegetables with one of the recipes in this chapter. No special fanfare; just add, say, Eggplant Parmesan or Broccoli Casserole to the menu tonight. When they ask what makes it so good, you can answer "Vegetables!" And before you know it, they'll be eating the whole selection, from asparagus to zucchini, and loving it.

Vegetables cooked in the microwave oven retain nutrients as they keep all their lustrous color, crisp texture and good flavor.

They can be microwave-cooked in just a small amount of water. Greens, especially spinach, can be cooked in only water that clings to the leaves after washing. A glass lid or plastic wrap (vented) retains steam that cooks vegetables simultaneously with the microwave energy.

Frozen Vegetables

Frozen vegetables need no added water; the ice within provides sufficient liquid. For true convenience, they can be cooked right in the carton, merely pierce the box to prevent steam buildup. Or, empty the carton into a microwave-oven-safe serving dish and cover. Stir halfway through cooking to separate and spread into an even layer; cover and complete the cooking.

Frozen vegetables that come in plastic pouches can also be cooked in the microwave oven. Cut an "X" in the pouch and place cut-side-down in a cooking dish, or pierce the plastic so steam can escape. Midway through cooking, flex the pouch to mix the contents.

The cooking times in the chart starting on page 148 produce vegetables that are still crisp-tender. If you prefer them a little softer, add a bit more cooking time.

Fresh Vegetables

When preparing fresh vegetables, cut them into uniform-sized pieces for even cooking. The smaller the cut, the quicker the cooking.

Arrange large, uneven vegetable pieces such as asparagus and broccoli with the thickest parts turned to the outside of the cooking dish.

Large vegetables, such as potatoes and squash, should be arranged in a circle in the oven, with larger parts to the outside. Vegetables with a skin should be pierced with a fork so steam can escape during cooking. To prevent the bottoms from being soggy, place on a paper towel to absorb the extra moisture. Halfway through cooking, *turn* the vegetables over and *rearrange*. *Standing time* is an important part of cooking time, so allow a few minutes before ringing the dinner bell.

Take care when removing the lid or cover from a covered vegetable dish. Lift the lid away from you to avoid a painful steam burn.

New vegetable lovers will probably prefer to keep these new taste treats simple. But when you're in the mood to dazzle them, try vegetables in the recipes that follow, or take a look through the chapter on Sauces. Béchamel, Hollandaise and Mushroom Sauce are a few that would make vegetables special.

How to Cook Fresh Vegetables

1. When a cover is called for, cover with an all-glass lid or plastic wrap.

2. Stir, rotate or rearrange halfway through cooking. Slightly undercook vegetables; let stand covered 3 to 5 minutes before serving.

Vegetable	Amount	Cook at High	Cooking Directions
Artichokes (3 inches in diameter)	1	4 to 5 minutes	2 teaspoons lemon juice, 2 tablespoons water in a deep 1½-quart covered glass casserole. Rotate halfway through cooking.
	2	7 to 8 minutes	Same as above.
	4	12 to 14 minutes	2 teaspoons lemon juice, ½ cup boiling water in a 3-quart covered glass casserole. Rearrange halfway through cooking.
Asparagus pieces	16 (4-inch pieces)	5 to 7 minutes	¼ teaspoon salt, ¼ cup water in a 1½-quart covered glass casserole. Stir halfway through cooking.
spears	1 pound	7 to 8 minutes	¼ teaspoon salt, ¼ cup water in a 1-quart covered glass casserole. Rearrange halfway through cooking.
Beans Green or Wax	1 pound	9 to 11 minutes	¼ teaspoon salt, ¼ cup water in a 1½-quart covered glass casserole. Stir halfway through cooking.
	2 pounds	16 to 18 minutes	Same as above except use a 2-quart covered glass casserole. Stir halfway through cooking.
Lima or Butter (shelled)	1 pound	6 to 8 minutes	½ teaspoon salt, ½ cup water in a 1-quart covered glass casserole. Stir halfway through cooking.
	2 pounds	9 to 11 minutes	Same as above except use a 1½-quart covered glass casserole. Stir halfway through cooking.
Beets	4 medium size whole, trimmed	15 to 17 minutes	¼ teaspoon salt, ½ cup water in a 2-quart covered glass casserole. Rearrange halfway through cooking.
	4, sliced	11 to 13 minutes	¼ teaspoon salt, ½ cup water in a 1-quart covered glass casserole. Stir halfway through cooking.

How to Cook Small Whole Vegetables or Pieces

1. Place small whole vegetables or evenly cut pieces in specified casserole with amount of water given in chart.

2. Cover with an all-glass lid or plastic wrap; stir halfway through cooking time.

3. Slightly undercook vegetables; let stand covered 3 to 5 minutes before serving.

Vegetables

Vegetable	Amount	Cook at High	Cooking Directions
Broccoli	1 small bunch (1½ pounds), trimmed and split	8 to 10 minutes	½ teaspoon salt, ½ cup water in a 2-quart covered glass casserole. Stir halfway through cooking.
Brussels Sprouts	½ pound	4 to 6 minutes	2 tablespoons water in a 1-quart covered glass casserole. Stir halfway through cooking.
	1 pound	5 to 7 minutes	3 tablespoons water in a 1½-quart covered glass casserole. Stir halfway through cooking.
Cabbage	Small head, chopped or shredded	7 to 9 minutes	½ teaspoon salt, 2 tablespoons water in a 2-quart covered glass casserole. Stir halfway through cooking.
	Medium head, whole	12 to 14 minutes	½ teaspoon salt, 2 tablespoons water in a 2-quart covered glass casserole. Rotate halfway through cooking.
Carrots	4 peeled, cut in thin strips or diced	7 to 9 minutes	¼ teaspoon salt, ¼ cup water in a 1-quart covered glass casserole. Stir halfway through cooking.
	6 whole	10 to 12 minutes	Same as above except use a 1½-quart covered glass casserole. Rearrange halfway through cooking.
Cauliflower	1 medium head, cut in flowerets	7 to 9 minutes	¼ teaspoon salt, ¼ cup water in a 2-quart covered glass casserole. Stir halfway through cooking.
	1 medium head, whole	9 to 11 minutes	Same as above.
Celery	4 cups, cut in 1-inch pieces	8 to 10 minutes	½ teaspoon salt, ¼ cup water in a 1½-quart covered glass casserole. Stir halfway through cooking.
	6 cups, cut in 1-inch pieces	12 to 14 minutes	Same as above except use a 2-quart covered glass casserole. Stir halfway through cooking.

How to Arrange Whole Vegetables for Cooking

Corn husks provide a natural covering for the corn. Cook right on the microwave oven tray. Rearrange halfway through cooking time.

Arrange in a circle with thicker portions to the outside and lighter or thinner portions to the inside.

Alternate thick and thin portions in baking dish for even cooking. Cook covered. Rearrange halfway through cooking.

Vegetables

Vegetable	Amount	Cook at High	Cooking Directions
Corn on the cob	2 ears	4½ to 6½ minutes	Place corn in the husk on a microwave oven tray or place husked corn in a glass baking dish; cover dish with waxed paper. Rearrange halfway through cooking.
	4 ears	8 to 10 minutes	Same as above.
cut from the cob	1½ cups	4 to 6 minutes	½ teaspoon salt, ¼ cup water in a 1-quart covered glass casserole. Stir halfway through cooking.
Eggplant	1 small, peeled and diced (3 cups)	5 to 7 minutes	½ teaspoon salt, ¼ cup water in a 1½-quart covered glass casserole.
	1, whole (1¼ pounds)	6 to 8 minutes	Pierce skin of eggplant. Place on a paper towel. Cook. Let stand 5 minutes. Cut in half. Spoon out pulp.
Okra whole	½ pound	4 to 5 minutes	¼ teaspoon salt, ¼ cup water in a 1-quart covered glass casserole. Stir halfway through cooking.
sliced	½ pound	3 to 4 minutes	Same as above.
Onions	2 large, cut in eighths	6 to 8 minutes	½ teaspoon salt, ¼ cup water in a 1-quart covered glass casserole. Stir halfway through cooking.
	4 large, cut in eighths	8 to 10 minutes	Same as above except use a 2-quart covered glass casserole.
Parsnips	4 split, peel and core removed, if desired	7 to 9 minutes	½ teaspoon salt, ¼ cup water in a 1½-quart covered glass casserole. Rearrange halfway through cooking.
	8 split, peel and core removed, if desired	10 to 13 minutes	Same as above except use a 2-quart covered glass casserole.
Peas shelled	2 cups	4 to 6 minutes	¼ cup water in a 1-quart covered glass casserole.
	3 cups	6 to 8 minutes	Same as above except use a 1½-quart covered glass casserole.

How to Cook Whole Vegetables in Their Skins

Pierce skin and place on a paper towel on microwave oven tray. Turn over halfway through cooking.

Pierce skin and arrange on a paper towel on a rack to absorb excess moisture.

Pierce skin and place on a paper towel on microwave oven tray. Turn over halfway through cooking.

Vegetables

Vegetable	Amount	Cook at High	Cooking Directions
Potatoes baked	1 medium	4 to 6 minutes	Scrub and pierce potatoes. Place in a circle on a paper towel on microwave oven tray, leaving 1-inch space between each potato. Turn potatoes over and rearrange halfway through cooking.
	2 medium	7 to 8 minutes	
	3 medium	9 to 10 minutes	
	4 medium	11 to 13 minutes	
	5 medium	14 to 15 minutes	
	6 medium	16 to 18 minutes	
boiled	4 medium, whole	10 to 12 minutes	½ teaspoon salt, ¼ cup water in a 1½-quart covered glass casserole. Rearrange halfway through cooking.
	4 medium, pared and cut in half	8 to 10 minutes	Same as above.
	6 medium, pared and cut in half	12 to 14 minutes	Same as above except use a 2-quart covered glass casserole.
buttered	4 medium, sliced thin	10 to 12 minutes	2 tablespoons butter in a 1½-quart glass baking dish. Add potatoes, ½ teaspoon salt, and dot with butter. Cover with plastic wrap. Stir halfway through cooking.
	6 medium, sliced thin	15 to 17 minutes	Same as above.
Pumpkin	1, whole (2 pounds)	6 to 8 minutes per pound	Pierce skin of pumpkin. Place on a paper towel. Cook 7 minutes; turn over once. Cut in half; discard peel and seedy center. Cut pumpkin into chunks. Cook pumpkin in a 1-quart covered glass casserole 6 more minutes, or until tender. Stir halfway through cooking.
Rutabaga	1 pound	6 to 8 minutes	Pierce skin through waxy coating. Place on a paper towel. Cook. Let stand 5 minutes. Cut in quarters, peel and dice.
Spinach	1 pound	6 to 7 minutes	Wash. Cook in water that clings to the leaves in a 2-quart covered glass casserole.
Squash Acorn or Butternut	1, whole	6 to 8 minutes	Pierce skin of squash in several places. Place on a paper towel on microwave oven tray. Rotate halfway through cooking.
	2, whole	12 to 14 minutes	Same as above.
Hubbard	2 pounds, peeled and cut in 1-inch cubes	7 to 9 minutes	1 teaspoon salt, ¼ cup water in a 1½-quart covered glass casserole. Stir halfway through cooking.
Spaghetti Squash	1 medium, whole (about 4 pounds)	18 to 22 minutes	Pierce skin. Place on a paper towel on microwave oven tray. Turn over several times during cooking. Let stand 5 minutes. Cut in half, scoop out seeds and pull strands free with a fork.
Zucchini	2 medium, sliced	5 to 6 minutes	½ teaspoon salt, ¼ cup water in a 1½-quart covered glass casserole.
	4 medium, whole	7 to 9 minutes	Wash and pierce zucchini. Place on a paper-towel-covered microwave-oven-safe roast rack. Turn and rearrange twice during cooking period.
	6 medium, whole	10 to 12 minutes	Same as above.

Vegetables

Vegetable	Amount	Cook at High	Cooking Directions
Sweet Potatoes baked	whole: 1 medium	3 to 5 minutes	Scrub and pierce potatoes. Place in a circle on a paper towel on microwave oven tray, leaving 1-inch space between each potato. Turn potatoes over and rearrange halfway through cooking time.
	2 medium	5 to 7 minutes	
	4 medium	9 to 11 minutes	
	6 medium	13 to 15 minutes	
boiled	peeled, cut in half: 4 medium	7 to 9 minutes	½ teaspoon salt, ¼ cup water in a 1½-quart covered glass casserole. Stir halfway through cooking.
	6 medium	10 to 12 minutes	Same as above except use a 2-quart covered glass casserole.
Swiss Chard	1 pound	6 to 7 minutes	Wash; cook in water that clings to the leaves in a 3-quart covered glass casserole. Stir halfway through cooking.
Tomatoes	2, cut in half	2½ to 4 minutes	Place in a 1-quart covered glass casserole.
	4, cut in half	4 to 6 minutes	Place in a 1½-quart covered glass casserole and rearrange halfway through cooking.
Turnip Greens	1 pound, trimmed	12 to 14 minutes	½ cup water in a 3-quart covered glass casserole. Stir halfway through cooking.
Turnips	4 medium, cut in eighths	10 to 12 minutes	½ teaspoon salt, ¼ cup water in a 1½-quart covered glass casserole. Rearrange halfway through cooking.

How to Cook Frozen Vegetables

1. Slightly undercook vegetables.

2. Let stand covered 3 minutes before serving.

Hint: If any of these vegetables are in a pouch, cut a large "X" in the pouch with a knife to let steam escape and place the pouch, "X" side down, in a glass casserole; add *no* water. Reduce cooking time slightly from time shown in the chart for vegetables in a package.

Vegetable	Amount	Cook at High	Cooking Directions
Asparagus	10-ounce package	5 to 7 minutes	Place in a 1-quart covered glass casserole. Stir after 3 minutes to separate.
Beans Green or Wax	9-ounce package	6 to 7 minutes	Place in a 1-quart covered glass casserole. Add 2 teaspoons water. Stir after 3½ minutes to separate.
Broccoli	10-ounce package	7 to 8 minutes	Place in a 1-quart covered glass casserole. Stir after 4 minutes to separate.
Brussels Sprouts	10-ounce package	4 to 6 minutes	Place in a 1-quart covered glass casserole. Add 2 tablespoons water. Stir after 2 minutes to separate.
Carrots	10-ounce package	5 to 7 minutes	Place in a 1-quart covered glass casserole. Add 2 tablespoons water. Stir after 3 minutes to separate.
Cauliflower	10-ounce package	4 to 6 minutes	Place in a 1-quart covered glass casserole. Stir after 2 minutes to separate.

Vegetables

Vegetable	Amount	Cook at High	Cooking Directions
Chinese Mixed Vegetables	10-ounce package	4 to 5 minutes	Place in a 1-quart covered glass casserole. Stir after 3 minutes to separate.
Chinese Pea Pods	6-ounce package	3 to 4 minutes	Place in a 1-quart covered glass casserole. Stir after 2 minutes to separate.
Corn whole kernel	10-ounce package	4 to 6 minutes	Place in a 1-quart covered glass casserole. Add 2 tablespoons water. Stir after 2 minutes to separate.
on the cob	2 ears	4 to 6 minutes	Place ears of corn in a 1-quart covered glass casserole. Add ¼ cup hot water. Turn ears after 2 minutes.
Peas	10-ounce package	4 to 6 minutes	Place in a 1-quart covered glass casserole. Stir after 2 minutes to separate.
Black-eye	10-ounce package	8 to 10 minutes	Place in a 1-quart covered glass casserole. Add ¼ cup water. Stir after 4 minutes to separate.
Peas and Carrots	10-ounce package	5 to 7 minutes	Place in a 1-quart covered glass casserole. Stir after 3 minutes to separate.
Spinach	10-ounce package	4 to 6 minutes	Place in a 1-quart covered glass casserole. Stir after 2 minutes to separate.
Vegetables Mixed	10-ounce package	4 to 6 minutes	Place in a 1-quart covered glass casserole. Add 2 tablespoons water. Stir after 2 minutes to separate.

How to Cook Frozen Vegetables

To cook vegetables in a paper box: Pierce box with a fork. Place on a paper towel on microwave oven tray. Cook as directed.

To cook vegetables in a casserole or serving dish: Place in casserole. Cover and cook as directed.

To cook vegetables in a pouch: Cut an "X" in pouch. Place "X" side down in casserole. Do not add water. Cook as directed.

How to Cook Dried Beans

1. Rinse beans and put into indicated amount of water in a 4-quart glass casserole. Cover with an all-glass lid or plastic wrap and soak overnight.

2. The next day, cook covered following indicated cooking times; stir at the end of each cooking time.

Type of Bean	Amount	Water	Cook at High	Cook at Medium-High	Cook at Medium
Pinto	1 pound	1½ quarts	15 minutes	15 minutes	30 minutes
Navy	1 pound	1½ quarts	15 minutes	15 minutes	15 minutes
Black-eye pea	1 pound	3 quarts	15 minutes	15 minutes	none

Asparagus and Cheese

1 package (10 ounces) frozen asparagus spears or 1½ pounds fresh asparagus
2 tablespoons butter or margarine
4 fresh mushroom caps, cleaned
¼ cup all-purpose flour
1 teaspoon salt
1 cup milk
⅛ teaspoon dry mustard
2 tablespoons sherry
½ cup toasted slivered almonds
¼ cup shredded sharp Cheddar cheese

1. Cook asparagus following directions in Frozen or Fresh Vegetable Cooking Chart. Drain and keep warm.

2. Put butter and mushroom caps into a 1-quart glass measuring pitcher. Cook uncovered in microwave oven **3 minutes at High**.

3. Remove mushrooms and set aside. Stir flour and salt into butter in measuring pitcher. Cook uncovered in microwave oven **1½ minutes at High**; stir after 30 seconds.

4. Add milk gradually, stirring until smooth. Cook uncovered in microwave oven **2 minutes at High**, or until thickened; stir every 30 seconds.

5. Add dry mustard and sherry to sauce; mix well.

6. Place cooked asparagus in a 9-inch glass pie plate. Cover with almonds and top with mushroom caps. Pour sauce over all and sprinkle with cheese. Heat uncovered in microwave oven **1 minute at High**.

4 servings

Green Bean and Cheese Casserole

2 packages (9 ounces each) frozen cut green beans
1 can (10¾ ounces) condensed cream of mushroom soup
1 can (8 ounces) sliced water chestnuts, drained
½ cup (2 ounces) shredded Cheddar cheese
1 can (3 ounces) french-fried onion rings

1. Put beans into a 2-quart glass casserole. Cover with an all-glass lid or plastic wrap. Cook in microwave oven **9 minutes at High**, or until beans are tender; stir once. Drain.

2. Add mushroom soup, water chestnuts and cheese to beans; mix. Cover with an all-glass lid or plastic wrap. Cook in microwave oven **5½ to 6½ minutes at Medium-High**. Stir. Top with onion rings. Heat uncovered to serving temperature (**about 1½ minutes at Medium-High**).

About 6 servings

Green Bean and Bacon Casserole

1 package (9 ounces) frozen cut green beans
4 slices bacon, cut in small pieces
2 slices bread, cut in ½-inch cubes
⅓ cup condensed cream of mushroom soup

1. Cook green beans following directions in Frozen Vegetable Cooking Chart. Drain.

2. Put bacon into a 1½-quart glass baking dish. Cover with a paper towel. Cook in microwave oven **about 2½ minutes at High**, or until browned.

3. Remove bacon from dish. Add bread cubes to bacon fat in dish; mix well. Cook uncovered in microwave oven **2 minutes at High**; stir once.

4. Mix bacon with the beans in casserole, spoon undiluted soup over beans and top with the bread cubes. Cover with waxed paper. Heat in microwave oven to serving temperature (**3 to 4 minutes at High**).

4 servings

Baked Beans

4 slices bacon, chopped
1 can (16 ounces) pork and beans with tomato sauce
½ teaspoon dry mustard
1 small onion, peeled and finely chopped
¼ cup ketchup
2 tablespoons brown sugar

1. Put bacon into a 1-quart glass casserole. Cover with a paper towel. Cook in microwave oven **3 minutes at High**. Set bacon aside on paper towels. Discard fat in casserole.

2. Combine beans, dry mustard, onion, ketchup and brown sugar in the glass casserole. Cover with an all-glass lid or plastic wrap. Cook in microwave oven **8 minutes at High**; stir twice.

3. Top with cooked bacon. Cook covered in microwave oven **2 minutes at High**.

4 servings

Hot Three-Bean Salad

3 slices bacon, coarsely chopped
1 tablespoon all-purpose flour
⅔ cup sugar
⅔ cup cider vinegar
1 can (15½ ounces) cut green beans, drained
1 can (15½ ounces) cut wax beans, drained
1 can (15½ ounces) red kidney beans, drained
1 medium onion, peeled and thinly sliced

1. Put bacon into a 1-quart glass measuring pitcher. Cook uncovered in microwave oven **4 minutes at High**; stir once.

2. Stir flour, sugar and vinegar into bacon mixture. Cook uncovered in microwave oven **3 minutes at High**; stir once.

3. Combine green beans, wax beans, kidney beans and onion in a 1½-quart glass casserole. Heat uncovered in microwave oven until warm (**about 3 minutes at High**).

4. Pour bacon dressing over bean mixture; stir well.

10 servings

Old-Fashioned Baked Beans

1 pound dried Great Northern beans, rinsed
1½ quarts water
½ pound salt pork, rinsed and rind removed
½ cup chopped celery
½ cup chopped onion
1 cup ketchup
½ cup molasses
3 tablespoons brown sugar
1 teaspoon dry mustard
½ teaspoon pepper
¼ teaspoon ground ginger

1. Put beans and water into a 3-quart glass casserole. Cover and let soak overnight.

2. Cut salt pork into ¼-inch slices, then cut into pieces. Spread on a microwave-oven-safe roast rack set in a 1½-quart glass baking dish. Cover with a paper towel. Cook in microwave oven **5 minutes at High**. Reserve 1 teaspoon drippings and the salt pork.

3. Combine reserved drippings, celery and onion in a 2-cup glass measuring cup. Cook uncovered in microwave oven **2 minutes at High**.

4. Add the vegetables to beans; stir. Cover with an all-glass lid or plastic wrap. Cook in microwave oven **15 minutes at High**. Stir. Cook covered **30 minutes at Medium**; stir after 15 minutes.

5. Drain beans, reserving 1 cup liquid. Combine remaining ingredients, reserved salt pork and reserved bean liquid. Add to beans; mix well. Cook covered in microwave oven **1 hour at Medium**, or until beans are tender and sauce has thickened; stir every 15 minutes.

8 to 10 servings

Harvard Beets

⅓ cup sugar
1 tablespoon cornstarch
¼ teaspoon salt
¼ cup cider vinegar
1 can or jar (16 ounces) crinkle-cut-style or diced beets, drained; reserve ½ cup liquid
1 tablespoon butter or margarine

1. Combine sugar, cornstarch and salt in a 1-quart glass casserole. Stir in vinegar and reserved beet liquid. Cook in microwave oven **3 to 4 minutes at High**, or until mixture boils and thickens slightly; stir twice.

2. Add beets and butter to thickened sauce; stir. Cook in microwave oven **2 to 3 minutes at High**, or until thoroughly heated; stir once.

4 servings

Broccoli Casserole

1 small bunch broccoli (about 1½ pounds), trimmed and coarsely chopped
¼ cup (½ stick) butter or margarine
1 medium onion, peeled and chopped
2 tablespoons all-purpose flour
½ cup milk
1 jar (8 ounces) pasteurized process cheese spread
3 eggs, slightly beaten
¼ teaspoon salt
¼ teaspoon ground nutmeg
⅛ teaspoon pepper
½ cup finely crushed herbed croutons

1. Cook broccoli following directions in Fresh Vegetable Cooking Chart on page 144. Drain thoroughly.

2. Put butter and onion into a 2-quart glass casserole. Cook uncovered in microwave oven **2 to 3 minutes at High**, or until onion is tender; stir after 1 minute.

3. Stir flour into butter mixture. Cook uncovered in microwave oven **1 minute at High**.

4. Add milk gradually to flour mixture, stirring constantly. Cook uncovered in microwave oven **1 minute at High**, or until thickened.

5. Add cheese to sauce and stir until well blended. Mix in the drained cooked broccoli, eggs, salt, nutmeg and pepper. Cook uncovered in microwave oven **6 minutes at High**; stir after 3 minutes.

6. Stir mixture. Sprinkle crushed croutons over top. Cook uncovered in microwave oven **6 minutes at High**.

7. Remove casserole from oven; let stand uncovered 5 minutes before serving.

6 servings

Glazed Carrots and Pineapple

1 pound carrots, pared and cut in julienne strips
1 can (20 ounces) unsweetened pineapple chunks, drained; reserve ¼ cup juice
¼ cup packed dark brown sugar
¼ teaspoon salt
2 tablespoons cold water
1½ teaspoons cornstarch

1. Put carrot strips into an 8-inch square glass baking dish. Mix reserved pineapple juice, brown sugar and salt. Pour over carrots. Cover with plastic wrap. Cook in microwave oven **5 minutes at High**.

2. Add pineapple to carrots; mix well. Cook covered in microwave oven **10 to 15 minutes at High**, or until carrots are tender; stir 3 times.

3. Mix cold water and cornstarch until smooth. Stir into carrot mixture. Cook uncovered in microwave oven **3 minutes at High**, or until thickened; stir once.

6 servings

Sesame Seed Cauliflower

1 small head cauliflower (about 1 pound)
2 tablespoons sesame seed
2 tablespoons butter or margarine
⅓ cup sliced green onion
½ cup water
¼ cup snipped parsley
½ teaspoon salt
⅛ teaspoon pepper
Lemon juice (optional)

1. Trim cauliflower and break into flowerets. Cut flowerets lengthwise into ¼-inch slices. Set aside.

2. Put sesame seed and 1 tablespoon butter into a 1-cup glass measuring cup. Heat uncovered in microwave oven **3 to 4 minutes at High**; stir once. Set aside.

3. Put 1 tablespoon butter, sliced cauliflower, green onion and water into a 1-quart glass casserole. Cover with an all-glass lid or plastic wrap. Cook in microwave oven **4 to 5 minutes at High**, or until cauliflower is crisp-tender; stir after 1 minute.

4. Add parsley, salt, pepper and sesame seed to cauliflower; mix well. Heat uncovered in microwave oven **1 minute at High**.

5. If desired, drizzle lemon juice over top before serving.

About 4 servings

Creamed Cauliflower

1½ pounds fresh cauliflower
½ cup (1 stick) butter or margarine
½ cup all-purpose flour
½ teaspoon salt
1¾ cups milk
Paprika

1. Clean cauliflower and cut into flowerets. Cook following directions in Fresh Vegetable Cooking Chart on page 144; omit salt. Let stand covered while preparing sauce.

2. Melt butter in a 1-quart glass measuring pitcher in microwave oven (**about 1 minute and 15 seconds at High**). Add flour and salt and blend well. Gradually add milk, stirring constantly. Cook uncovered **4 minutes at High**, or until sauce bubbles and thickens; stir after 2 minutes, then every 30 seconds.

3. Drain cauliflower and add sauce; mix. Sprinkle lightly with paprika.

About 6 servings

Celery and Almonds au Gratin

4 cups 1-inch celery pieces
¼ cup chicken broth
½ cup coarsely chopped blanched almonds
3 tablespoons butter or margarine
3 tablespoons all-purpose flour
¼ teaspoon salt
Dash pepper
1 cup chicken broth (homemade, canned or from bouillon cube)
½ cup half-and-half
1 cup (4 ounces) shredded sharp Cheddar cheese
1 tablespoon butter or margarine
¼ cup dry bread crumbs

1. Put celery and ¼ cup chicken broth into a 1½-quart glass casserole. Cover with an all-glass lid or plastic wrap. Cook in microwave oven **7 to 8 minutes at High**; stir twice. Drain celery. Stir in almonds and set aside uncovered.

2. Melt 3 tablespoons butter in a 1-quart glass measuring pitcher in microwave oven (**about 1 minute at High**). Add flour, salt and pepper; mix well. Add 1 cup broth and half-and-half gradually, stirring constantly. Cook uncovered **4 minutes at High**, or until thickened; stir after 2 minutes, then every 30 seconds.

3. Add ½ cup cheese to sauce and stir until melted. Pour over celery and almonds in casserole. Sprinkle with remaining cheese.

4. Melt 2 tablespoons butter in a small glass dish in microwave oven (**about 30 seconds at High**). Combine melted butter and bread crumbs; sprinkle over cheese. Cover with waxed paper. Cook **1 to 2 minutes at High**, or until cheese melts.

About 4 servings

Braised Cucumber Sticks

2 medium cucumbers
2 tablespoons butter or margarine
1 teaspoon instant chicken bouillon granules
2 tablespoons boiling water
Salt and pepper to taste
Snipped parsley

1. Wash cucumbers, score peel with a fork and cut off ends. Cut cucumbers in half crosswise, then cut into narrow sticks.

2. Melt butter in a 1½-quart glass baking dish in microwave oven (**about 30 seconds at High**).

3. Dissolve instant bouillon in water. Add to melted butter and mix well. Add cucumber sticks and turn to coat with butter mixture. Cover with plastic wrap.

4. Cook in microwave oven **5 to 6 minutes at High**, or until cucumber is crisp-tender. Season with salt and pepper to taste. Garnish with parsley.

6 servings

Eggplant Parmesan

1 eggplant (1 pound)
2 eggs, beaten
¼ cup undiluted evaporated milk
⅔ cup fine dry bread crumbs
2 tablespoons finely chopped onion
1 small clove garlic, minced
1 tablespoon olive oil
3 cups chopped fresh tomatoes
½ teaspoon salt
⅛ teaspoon pepper
1 cup grated Parmesan cheese
6 slices mozzarella cheese

1. Remove peel from eggplant; cut into ½-inch slices. Coat with a mixture of beaten egg and evaporated milk, then coat with crumbs.

2. For tomato sauce, mix onion, garlic and olive oil in a 1-quart glass measuring pitcher. Cook uncovered in microwave oven **3 minutes at High**; stir once. Add tomatoes, salt and pepper; stir. Cook uncovered **15 minutes at High**; stir once.

3. Layer one-third of the eggplant slices, ⅓ cup Parmesan cheese and ⅓ cup sauce in a 2-quart glass casserole. Repeat twice. Cover with waxed paper.

4. Cook in microwave oven **12 minutes at High**, or until eggplant is fork-tender; rotate dish one-half turn once.

5. Top eggplant mixture with cheese slices. Heat uncovered in microwave oven **45 seconds at High**, or until cheese melts.

6 servings

Wilted Lettuce

1 large head leaf lettuce (about 10 ounces)
6 slices bacon
½ cup cider vinegar
¼ cup water
3 tablespoons sugar
½ teaspoon salt

1. Wash lettuce, drain and pat dry. Tear lettuce into large pieces; put into a bowl and set aside.

2. Arrange bacon on a microwave-oven-safe roast rack set in a glass baking dish. Cover with a paper towel. Cook in microwave oven **6 to 7 minutes at High**, or until crisp. Reserve 2 tablespoons bacon drippings. Crumble bacon and add to lettuce.

3. Combine reserved bacon drippings and remaining ingredients in a 1-quart glass measuring pitcher. Cook uncovered in microwave oven **3 to 5 minutes at High**, or until mixture boils. Pour over lettuce and bacon; toss lightly. Serve immediately.

About 6 servings

Sautéed Mushrooms

8 ounces fresh mushrooms, cleaned and sliced lengthwise
1 tablespoon butter or margarine

1. Put mushrooms and butter into a 1-quart glass casserole. Cover with an all-glass lid or plastic wrap.

2. Cook in microwave oven **3 to 4 minutes at High**, or until tender; stir after 1 minute.

1 cup

Sautéed Onion

1 medium onion, peeled and sliced
1 tablespoon butter or margarine

1. Put onion slices and butter into a 1-quart glass casserole. Cover with an all-glass lid or plastic wrap.

2. Cook in microwave oven **4 to 6 minutes at High**, or until tender; stir after 1 minute.

About ⅓ cup

Creamed Onions

1 cup Medium White Sauce (see page 188)
1 pound creaming onions, peeled and trimmed
¼ cup water

1. Prepare white sauce and set aside.

2. Put onions and water into a 1-quart glass casserole. Cover with an all-glass lid or plastic wrap. Cook in microwave oven **4 minutes at High**.

3. Drain onions and add white sauce; stir well. Cover and cook in microwave oven **3 minutes at High**, or until thoroughly heated.

4 servings

Stuffed Onions with Cheese Sauce

4 large yellow onions (about
   4 pounds)
6 tablespoons butter or
   margarine
2 cups cornbread stuffing mix
⅛ teaspoon oregano leaves
¼ cup water
1 cup Cheese Sauce
   (see page 188)

1. Peel onions and hollow out centers, leaving ½-inch-thick shells. Invert on a paper towel. Set aside.

2. Melt butter in a 1-cup glass measuring cup in microwave oven **(about 1 minute at High)**.

3. Combine stuffing mix, melted butter, oregano and water. Spoon stuffing into onion shells. Place in an 8-inch square glass baking dish. Cover with waxed paper.

4. Cook in microwave oven **16 to 18 minutes at High**; rotate dish one-quarter turn every 4 minutes.

5. Let stand covered 5 minutes. Serve with sauce.

4 servings

Tiffany Chips

2 medium-large Idaho potatoes
   (about 1½ pounds)
½ cup corn flake or wheat flake
   crumbs
1½ tablespoons grated Parmesan
   cheese
1½ teaspoons sesame seed
¼ cup (½ stick) butter or
   margarine

1. Scrub but do not pare potatoes. Cut in half lengthwise, then cut each half lengthwise into 4 or 5 wedges.

2. Combine half of crumbs with cheese and half with sesame seed.

3. Melt butter in a 1½-quart glass baking dish in microwave oven **(about 1 minute at High)**.

4. Dip potato wedges in melted butter and generously coat half with each crumb mixture. Arrange in a 1½-quart glass baking dish. Cover with waxed paper. Cook in microwave oven **11 minutes at High**, or until potato is tender.

4 servings

Scalloped Potatoes

6 medium potatoes (about
   2 pounds)
¼ cup water
3 tablespoons butter or
   margarine
3 tablespoons all-purpose flour
1 teaspoon salt
¼ teaspoon pepper
2½ cups milk
¼ cup chopped onion
   Paprika

1. Pare potatoes and cut in half. Place potato halves cut-side-down in an 8-inch round glass cake dish. Add water to dish. Cover with plastic wrap. Cook in microwave oven **8 minutes at High**. Uncover to cool slightly.

2. Melt butter in a 1-quart glass measuring pitcher in microwave oven **(about 1 minute at High)**. Add flour, salt and pepper; mix well. Add milk gradually, stirring constantly. Cook uncovered **6 to 7 minutes at High**, or until thickened; stir after 2 minutes, then every minute.

3. Thinly slice potatoes. Put half the potatoes into a buttered 2-quart glass casserole. Cover with half the onion and half the sauce. Repeat layers. Cover with an all-glass lid or plastic wrap.

4. Cook in microwave oven **about 15 minutes at High**, or until potatoes are tender.

5. Remove from oven and sprinkle with paprika.

About 8 servings

Au Gratin Potatoes: Follow recipe for Scalloped Potatoes and add 1 cup (4 ounces) shredded Cheddar cheese (¾ cup for layering and ¼ cup for top).

Mashed Potatoes

6 medium potatoes (about
  2 pounds), pared
½ cup milk
¼ cup (½ stick) butter or
  margarine
  Salt and pepper to taste

1. Cook potatoes in a covered 1½-quart glass casserole following directions in Fresh Vegetable Cooking Chart. Drain.

2. Heat milk in a 1-cup glass measuring cup in microwave oven until hot (**15 to 30 seconds at High**).

3. Mash or rice potatoes thoroughly. Whip in hot milk, butter, salt and pepper until fluffy.

6 to 8 servings

Hint: Mashed potatoes can be prepared in advance and reheated in the glass casserole. Cover with an all-glass lid or plastic wrap. Heat in microwave oven **3 minutes at High**; stir once.

German Potato Salad

4 medium potatoes
6 slices bacon
½ cup finely diced celery
½ cup finely diced onion
½ teaspoon salt
¼ teaspoon hickory salt
½ cup white vinegar
2½ tablespoons sugar

1. Cook potatoes following directions in Fresh Vegetable Cooking Chart. Cool slightly, peel and thinly slice. Set aside.

2. Arrange bacon on a microwave-oven-safe roast rack set in a glass baking dish. Cover with a paper towel. Cook in microwave oven **4 to 6 minutes at High**, or until crisp. Reserve 2 tablespoons drippings. Crumble bacon and set aside.

3. Alternate layers of potatoes, celery and onion in a 2-quart glass casserole, sprinkling each layer with salt or hickory salt.

4. Mix vinegar and sugar. Pour over potatoes; mix carefully. Sprinkle crumbled bacon over top and drizzle with reserved bacon drippings; mix carefully.

5. Heat uncovered in microwave oven to serving temperature (**about 5 minutes at High**); mix carefully once.

4 to 6 servings

Candied Sweet Potatoes

6 medium sweet potatoes
  (about 2 pounds)
¼ cup (½ stick) butter or
  margarine
½ cup packed brown sugar
1½ teaspoons lemon juice

1. Cook sweet potatoes following directions in Fresh Vegetable Cooking Chart. Peel cooked potatoes and cut into 1-inch slices.

2. Put butter and brown sugar into a 1½-quart glass casserole. Cook uncovered in microwave oven **1 minute at High**, or until butter and brown sugar are melted.

3. Stir in lemon juice. Add potatoes and toss lightly to coat. Cover with an all-glass lid or waxed paper. Heat in microwave oven to serving temperature (**about 6 minutes at High**); stir occasionally.

8 servings

**Baked
Stuffed Potatoes**

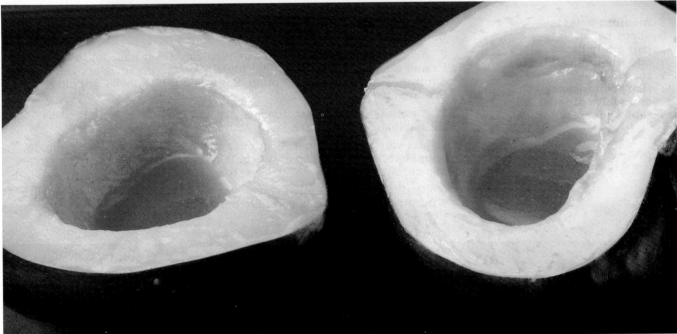

**Baked
Acorn Squash**

Zucchini Boats

158

Baked Stuffed Potatoes

4 medium potatoes, scrubbed
1 tablespoon butter or margarine
¼ cup chopped onion
½ to ¾ cup milk
2 tablespoons butter or margarine
Salt and pepper to taste
½ cup (2 ounces) shredded pasteurized process American cheese

1. Bake potatoes following directions in Fresh Vegetable Cooking Chart on page 147. Remove potatoes from oven and let stand 5 minutes.

2. Meanwhile, put 1 tablespoon butter and the onion into a glass dish. Cook uncovered in microwave oven **4 to 5 minutes at High,** or until tender; stir twice.

3. Cut a thin slice from top of each potato. Scoop potato from shells, being careful to keep shells intact. Mash or rice potato thoroughly.

4. Heat milk in a 1-cup glass measuring cup in microwave oven until hot (**about 30 seconds at High**).

5. Add milk, 2 tablespoons butter, salt, pepper and cooked onion to potato. Whip until fluffy. Spoon into potato shells. Top with cheese. Arrange on a microwave-oven-safe serving plate. Heat uncovered in microwave oven **2 to 3 minutes at High,** or until cheese melts.

4 servings

Hint: Potatoes can be prepared in advance and reheated just before serving. Heat uncovered in microwave oven to serving temperature (**3 to 4 minutes at High**).

Baked Acorn Squash

1 acorn squash
1½ tablespoons butter or margarine
1½ teaspoons brown sugar
¼ teaspoon salt
⅛ teaspoon ground ginger

1. Cook squash following directions in Fresh Vegetable Cooking Chart on page 147.

2. Cut squash in half. Scoop out seedy center. Divide butter, brown sugar, salt and ginger in squash cavities. Cover with plastic wrap.

3. Cook in microwave oven **2 minutes at High.** Let stand 5 minutes before serving.

2 servings

Dilly Squash

2 tablespoons butter or margarine
1 pound yellow summer squash (2 small), sliced
1 tablespoon dried parsley flakes
¼ teaspoon dried dill weed
¼ teaspoon salt
Dash onion powder

1. Melt butter in a 1½-quart glass casserole in microwave oven (**about 30 seconds at High**). Add remaining ingredients; stir well. Cover with an all-glass lid or plastic wrap.

2. Cook in microwave oven **4 to 5 minutes at High,** or until tender; stir after 2 minutes. Let stand 2 minutes before serving.

4 servings

Zucchini Boats

6 medium zucchini, 5 to 6 inches in length, washed and ends removed
1 medium tomato, cut in small pieces
¼ cup chopped salted almonds
1 tablespoon chopped parsley
1 teaspoon finely chopped onion
½ teaspoon seasoned salt
2 tablespoons butter or margarine
¼ cup cracker crumbs

1. Cook zucchini following directions in Fresh Vegetable Cooking Chart on page 147. Let cool until easy to handle.

2. Remove top third of each zucchini and chop coarsely. Scoop out and discard centers. Set zucchini aside in a 1½-quart glass baking dish or on a microwave-oven-safe serving platter. Put chopped zucchini and tomato into a bowl. Add almonds, parsley, onion and seasoned salt; mix well.

3. Melt butter in a small glass dish in microwave oven (**about 30 seconds at High**). Brush zucchini with half of melted butter. Spoon filling into zucchini shells. Mix remaining melted butter and cracker crumbs. Sprinkle over filling.

4. Heat uncovered in microwave oven to serving temperature (**2 to 3 minutes at High**).

6 servings

Zucchini Provençale

2 cans (6 ounces each) tomato paste
1 tomato paste can water
1 clove garlic, minced
1 teaspoon salt
⅛ teaspoon pepper
8 to 10 small zucchini, sliced
⅔ cup coarsely chopped onion
8 ounces fresh mushrooms, cleaned and sliced lengthwise
3 tablespoons olive oil
⅔ cup grated Parmesan cheese

1. Combine tomato paste, water, garlic, salt and pepper in a bowl; set aside.

2. Combine zucchini, onion, mushrooms and oil in a 3-quart glass casserole. Cover with an all-glass lid or plastic wrap. Cook in microwave oven **6 to 7 minutes at High**, or until zucchini is tender; stir once.

3. Stir half of cheese into zucchini mixture. Pour tomato mixture over zucchini and top with remaining cheese. Cook covered in microwave oven **3 minutes at Medium-High**.

About 8 servings

Scalloped Corn

1 can (16 ounces) whole kernel golden corn, drained
½ cup chopped onion
2 tablespoons chopped green pepper
½ cup soda cracker crumbs
½ teaspoon salt
Dash pepper
½ cup milk
1 egg

1. Combine all ingredients thoroughly and turn into a greased 1-quart glass casserole. Cover with an all-glass lid or plastic wrap.

2. Cook in microwave oven **6 to 8 minutes at High**; stir occasionally.

4 to 6 servings

Sweet-Sour Red Cabbage

1 head red cabbage (about 2 pounds), coarsely shredded
½ teaspoon salt
3 tablespoons water
6 tablespoons white vinegar
3 tablespoons sugar

1. Combine cabbage, salt and water in a 3-quart glass casserole. Cover with an all-glass lid or plastic wrap. Cook in microwave oven **10 to 12 minutes at High**, or until crisp-tender; stir once.

2. Add a mixture of vinegar and sugar to crisp-tender cabbage; mix well. Cook covered in microwave oven **1 to 2 minutes at High**, or until tender.

About 8 servings

Sweet-Sour Spinach

1 pound fresh spinach, washed and chopped
2 slices bacon, cut in small pieces
1 teaspoon all-purpose flour
1 teaspoon sugar
¼ cup half-and-half
1 tablespoon cider vinegar

1. Cook spinach following directions in Fresh Vegetable Cooking Chart on page 147. Drain.

2. Put bacon into a 1½-quart glass casserole. Cover with a paper towel. Cook in microwave oven **1½ minutes at High**, or until bacon is crisp.

3. Pour off all but 1 tablespoon fat. Add flour to fat and blend. Stir in sugar and half-and-half. Cook uncovered in microwave oven **1½ minutes at High**, or until thickened; stir once.

4. Add vinegar to mixture in casserole; stir. Add chopped spinach and mix well. Cover with waxed paper. Heat in microwave oven to serving temperature (**about 2 minutes at High**).

4 servings

Creamed Spinach

1 **package (10 ounces) frozen chopped spinach**
1 **package (3 ounces) cream cheese**
¼ **cup milk**
1 **teaspoon grated lemon peel**
¼ **teaspoon ground ginger**
¼ **teaspoon salt**

1. Cook spinach following directions in Frozen Vegetable Cooking Chart on page 149; drain.

2. Soften cream cheese in a 2-cup glass measuring cup in microwave oven (**about 15 seconds at Medium-High**). Blend with a fork until smooth. Stir in milk, lemon peel, ginger and salt. Heat uncovered to serving temperature (**1 to 2 minutes at Medium-High**); stir once.

3. Put drained spinach into a serving dish. Stir sauce and mix with spinach.

4 servings

Ratatouille

1 **cup sliced onion**
2 **tablespoons butter or margarine**
1 **medium eggplant, pared and cut in ½-inch pieces (about 2 cups cubes)**
2 **medium zucchini, cut lengthwise, then in ¼-inch pieces**
1 **medium green pepper, cut in strips**
½ **teaspoon salt**
½ **teaspoon marjoram leaves**
¼ **teaspoon oregano leaves**
¼ **teaspoon garlic salt**
⅛ **teaspoon pepper**
2 **large tomatoes, peeled and cut in wedges**

1. Put onion and butter into a 2-quart glass casserole. Cook uncovered in microwave oven **1½ minutes at High**; stir after 1 minute.

2. Add eggplant, zucchini and green pepper to onion and butter. Cover with an all-glass lid or plastic wrap. Cook in microwave oven **3 minutes at High**.

3. Add seasonings to vegetables and stir well. Cook covered in microwave oven **2 minutes at High**.

4. Add tomatoes and mix well. Cook covered in microwave oven **5 to 6 minutes at High**, or until vegetables are tender.

6 to 8 servings

Hint: To remove peel from tomatoes, heat tomatoes uncovered in microwave oven **30 to 45 seconds at High**. Let stand 2 minutes, then peel. Time will vary according to ripeness of tomatoes.

Hominy and Tomatoes

1 cup (4 ounces) shredded
    sharp Cheddar cheese
1 can (15 ounces) whole
    hominy, drained
1 can (16 ounces) tomatoes,
    drained and cut in pieces
¼ cup chopped onion
1 teaspoon chili powder
½ teaspoon salt

1. Reserve ½ cup cheese for topping. Combine remaining ingredients in a 1-quart glass casserole. Cook uncovered in microwave oven **6 minutes at High**; stir once.

2. Stir vegetable mixture. Sprinkle ½ cup cheese over top. Cover with plastic wrap. Cook in microwave oven **1 to 1½ minutes at Medium-High**, or until cheese melts.

About 6 servings

Stewed Tomatoes

2 large tomatoes
2 tablespoons sugar
½ teaspoon seasoned salt
    Dash pepper
1 tablespoon butter or
    margarine
1 tablespoon cornstarch
¼ cup water
¼ cup snipped parsley

1. Peel and quarter tomatoes. Put into a 1-quart glass casserole. Add sugar, seasoned salt, pepper and butter. Cover with an all-glass lid or plastic wrap.

2. Cook in microwave oven **5 minutes at High**, or until tender; stir halfway through cooking time.

3. Blend cornstarch and water; gradually add to the cooked tomatoes, stirring constantly. Cook covered in microwave oven **1 minute at High**.

4. Stir parsley into tomatoes before serving.

4 servings

Stuffed Tomatoes

4 firm ripe tomatoes
3 tablespoons butter or
    margarine
¼ cup finely chopped green
    onion
2 cups soft bread crumbs
¼ teaspoon poultry seasoning
    or dash sage
1 teaspoon sugar
¾ teaspoon salt
    Dash pepper
    Paprika

1. Wash tomatoes, cut a ¼-inch slice off top of each and cut out stems. Scoop out and reserve ½ cup of pulp; chop any large pieces.

2. Put butter and onion into a 1-quart glass casserole. Cook uncovered in microwave oven **2 to 3 minutes at High**, or until tender; stir after 1 minute.

3. Add bread crumbs, poultry seasoning, sugar, salt, pepper and reserved tomato pulp to cooked onion; toss lightly. Fill tomatoes with stuffing and put into an 8-inch round glass cake dish. Sprinkle with paprika. Cover with waxed paper.

4. Cook in microwave oven **3 to 4 minutes at High**, or until tomatoes are tender.

4 servings

Tomatoes Stuffed with Peas

6 firm ripe tomatoes (2½ to
    2¾ inches in diameter)
1 cup Cheese Sauce
    (see page 188)
1 package (10 ounces)
    frozen green peas, cooked
    (see page 149)
½ teaspoon salt

1. Cut a ¼-inch slice from top of each tomato. Scoop out center of each tomato leaving ¼-inch shell. Place upside-down on paper towels to drain.

2. Prepare cheese sauce and peas; mix.

3. Sprinkle insides of tomatoes with salt. Spoon sauced peas into tomato shells.

4. Place tomato shells in an 8-inch square glass baking dish. Cover with waxed paper.

5. Cook in microwave oven **3 to 4 minutes at High**, or until tomatoes are hot; rotate each tomato one-quarter turn after 2 minutes.

6 servings

Tomato Casserole

3 tablespoons butter or
   margarine
2 tablespoons chopped green
   pepper
2 tablespoons chopped onion
1 can (16 ounces) tomatoes
   (undrained)
1 tablespoon all-purpose flour
1 teaspoon sugar
½ teaspoon salt
1 cup seasoned croutons

1. Put butter, green pepper and onion into a 1-quart glass casserole. Cook uncovered in microwave oven **3 to 4 minutes at High**, or until tender; stir after 1 minute.

2. Add tomatoes and liquid to casserole; mix well. Cover with an all-glass lid or plastic wrap. Bring to boiling in microwave oven (**2½ to 3½ minutes at High**); stir once.

3. Add flour, sugar and salt to tomatoes; mix. Cook uncovered in microwave oven **2 to 3 minutes at High**; stir once. Top with croutons.

4 servings

Vegetable Stir-Fry

2 tablespoons vegetable oil
1 slice fresh ginger (¼ inch),
   peeled
1 clove garlic, peeled and
   crushed
½ cup sliced onion
1 cup fresh broccoli flowerets
1 cup cauliflower slices
1 cup red or green pepper
   strips
½ teaspoon salt
1 package (6 ounces) frozen
   pea pods
1 cup sliced fresh mushrooms

1. Put oil, ginger and garlic into a 2-quart glass casserole. Cook uncovered in microwave oven **2 minutes at High**.

2. Add onion, broccoli, cauliflower and pepper to casserole; stir. Cover with an all-glass lid or plastic wrap. Cook in microwave oven **3 to 4 minutes at High**, or until vegetables are crisp.

3. Sprinkle mixture with salt. Add pea pods and mushrooms; stir. Cook covered in microwave oven **3 minutes at High**, or until mixture is hot.

8 servings

Fruit
Pound Cake

Peanut Butter
Cookies

Lemon Meltaway
Cookies

Chocolate Drop
Cookies

Lemon Meringue
Pie

Desserts

If desserts were "treats only for weekends" in pre-microwave oven days, welcome them now to your midweek menu! Cakes baked in your microwave oven save about a third of conventional baking time. Baked as cupcakes they take only half the time, or much less, depending on the total number.

Cakes

The most common microwave cake mistake is in the eye of the beholder. Microwave-cooked cakes look moist when done, but beginners often overcook them, striving for a dry, "done" look. The *doneness test* for microwave cakes is the same as for conventional cakes; insert a wooden pick near the center. If it comes out clean the cake is done. It will be fluffier and loftier than conventional cake, because the crustless top permits high rise.

Microwave cake pans are actually round dishes, or fluted tube shapes in plastic or ceramic. Round shapes have no corners that could overcook, and the center post in tube pans exposes more surfaces to microwave energy for even baking.

Planning to serve the cake right from the baking dish? When cooking in the microwave oven, lightly grease, but do not flour before adding batter. If you plan to remove the cake before serving, line the cake dish with two layers of paper towels cut to fit. They will absorb extra moisture and help the cake to slip easily from the dish. Fill the cake dish only half full as cakes rise higher than conventional cakes.

Set the timer for the minumum cooking time. *Rotate* the cake dish for a more even top. *Standing time* continues the microwave baking, so let the cake rest on the counter a minute or two before making the wooden pick doneness test.

For a more traditional looking cake, convection or combination cooking is the way to do it. Preheat the convection oven and follow the recipe or package directions. Two layers bake easily and evenly on both metal racks. Baking pans will be hot from convection heat so use pot holders.

Cupcakes in the microwave oven should be baked in microwave-oven-safe ring-shaped pans or custard cups arranged in a circle. Line cups with two paper baking cups each. There is usually leftover batter from cake mixes, as cake dishes are filled only half full. Bake leftover batter as single layers or cupcakes and freeze. You can enjoy them later on a moment's notice. Cupcakes can be baked with convection heat to create a crusty brown top. You will find the best results using metal muffin pans.

Bar Cookies

Bar cookies from the microwave are another success story. You may find it helpful to shield corners with foil if you notice any overcooking. Test cake-type bars with a wooden pick. Fudge-like brownies remain moist inside, however, so the recipe time is a better guide. Because of the short cooking time, bars won't brown with microwave cooking, however, if you use a dark batter (chocolate or spice) or add a frosting, everyone will be happy. Or, try our convection or combination directions for baking bar cookies.

Cookies

Two metal trays of cookies will cook quite conveniently in the preheated convection oven. Cook your family's favorites using your recipe or package for suggested temperatures and times. Watch out for Cookie Snitchers!

Pies

Pie crusts are cooked quickly in the microwave oven. Crumb crusts can be mixed and shaped right in the cooking dish. A one-crust pastry shell is baked in a glass pie dish for microwave and combination. Check after the minimum cooking time for any raw spots and return for a little more cooking, if needed.

For a brown appearance preheat the convection oven and cook with convection heat. Follow your own recipe for temperatures and times. Two-crust pies can be cooked beautifully in combination cooking with a nice time savings!

Other Desserts

Candy can easily be made in the microwave oven. To make candy-making easier, use a candy thermometer you can leave in the microwave oven during cooking; conventional candy thermometers should be used only after removing the syrup from the microwave oven.

Fruit desserts are at their all-time best when made in the microwave oven. Most need little or no water. Don't forget to allow for *standing time*.

Custards and puddings, your own or mixes, are fast and convenient. They do bubble up, so cook them in a dish twice the size of the recipe. Or make them right in your serving dishes, and have even fewer dishes to wash.

Prepared Cake Mix — Layer Cake

1 package (18½ ounces) cake mix

1. Line two 8-inch round glass cake dishes with 2 layers of paper towels cut to fit. Set aside.

2. Prepare cake mix following directions on the package.

3. Fill each of the lined cake dishes half full with batter. Tap the bottom of the dish to remove large air bubbles. Cover with a paper towel.

4. Cook one layer at a time in microwave oven **6 to 7 minutes at Medium-High,** or until a wooden pick inserted near center comes out clean; rotate dish one-quarter turn once.

5. Cool on a flat surface 5 minutes. Run a knife around edge of dish, then remove cake from dish and peel off paper.

Two 8-inch round cake layers

Hint: For convection oven cooking, preheat oven to 350°F. Grease two 8-inch round metal cake pans; line with greased waxed paper circles. Divide batter evenly in pans. Place one cake pan on each metal rack. Cook in convection oven **35 to 40 minutes at 350°F,** or until done.

Old-Fashioned Fudge Cake

4 ounces (4 squares) unsweetened chocolate
⅔ cup butter or margarine
1 teaspoon vanilla extract
1¾ cups sugar
2 eggs
2½ cups all-purpose flour
1¼ teaspoons baking soda
½ teaspoon salt
1¼ cups ice water

1. Line two 8-inch round glass cake dishes with 2 layers of paper towels cut to fit. Set aside.

2. Melt chocolate in a small glass bowl in microwave oven (**about 3 minutes at High**). Cool.

3. Cream butter, vanilla extract and sugar thoroughly in a bowl. Add eggs, one at a time, beating well after each addition. Beat in melted chocolate.

4. Blend flour, baking soda and salt. Add flour mixture alternately with ice water to creamed mixture, beating until blended after each addition.

5. Divide batter evenly in the lined dishes. Tap the bottom of each dish to remove large air bubbles.

6. Cook one layer at a time uncovered in microwave oven **9 to 10 minutes at Medium-High,** or until cake pulls away from edges of dish; rotate dish one-quarter turn halfway through cooking period.

7. Cool on flat surface 5 minutes. Loosen cake from dish, trimming away any cake on edge of dish. Invert on a rack and peel off paper.

Two 8-inch round cake layers

Hint: For convection oven cooking, preheat oven to 350°F. Grease two 8-inch round metal cake pans; line with greased waxed paper circles. Divide batter evenly in pans. Place one cake pan on each metal rack. Cook in convection oven **30 to 35 minutes at 350°F,** or until done.

Fruit Pound Cake

1 tablespoon sugar
1½ cups chopped dried mixed fruit (apricots, prunes, raisins, peaches)
½ cup chopped pecans
1 package (3¾ ounces) instant banana cream pudding mix
1 package (18½ ounces) regular yellow cake mix (not pudding style)
4 eggs, beaten
1 cup dairy sour cream
½ cup vegetable oil

1. Preheat convection oven to 325°F.

2. Grease a 12-cup fluted tube pan suitable for microwave and convection heat; sprinkle with sugar. Set aside.

3. Combine mixed fruit, nuts and pudding mix; set aside.

4. Combine cake mix, eggs, sour cream and oil; beat 2 minutes at medium speed of electric mixer to mix well. Fold in fruit-nut mixture until well distributed. Spread in prepared cake pan.

5. Place pan on bottom metal rack. Cook in microwave/convection oven **40 to 45 minutes at Combination I,** or until a wooden pick inserted near center comes out clean. Let cool in pan 10 minutes. Invert onto serving plate; cool. Sprinkle with confectioners' sugar before serving.

One fluted tube cake

Pineapple Upside-Down Cake

2 tablespoons butter or
  margarine
½ cup packed brown sugar
6 slices pineapple
6 maraschino cherries
½ 18½-ounce package yellow
  cake mix
⅓ cup unsweetened pineapple
  juice
  Water

1. Melt butter in an 8-inch round glass cake dish in microwave oven (**about 30 seconds at High**). Mix brown sugar into melted butter. Cook uncovered until brown sugar melts (**about 2 minutes at High**).

2. Arrange pineapple slices and maraschino cherries in dish.

3. Prepare cake batter following directions on package, using half of ingredient amounts; use pineapple juice and water instead of water called for on package. Fill cake dish half full with batter. (Use any remaining batter for cupcakes.) Cover with a paper towel.

4. Cook in microwave oven **9 to 11 minutes at Medium-High**, or until a wooden pick inserted near center comes out clean; rotate dish one-quarter turn once. Immediately invert cake onto serving plate.

6 servings

Strawberry Shortcake

2 cups all-purpose flour
¼ cup sugar
1 tablespoon baking powder
½ teaspoon salt
½ cup (1 stick) butter or
  margarine, softened
¾ cup milk
  Sweetened strawberries or
  other fresh fruit
  Sweetened whipped cream

1. Line two 8-inch round glass cake dishes with 2 layers of paper towels cut to fit dish. Set aside.

2. Combine flour, sugar, baking powder and salt in a bowl. Cut in butter with pastry blender until mixture resembles coarse crumbs. Add milk and mix only until the dry ingredients are moistened. Dough will be thick and lumpy.

3. Divide dough into 2 portions. Drop one-half of dough by teaspoonfuls into each lined cake dish. Spread evenly with moistened fingers.

4. Cook one dish at a time uncovered in microwave oven **3 to 3½ minutes at High**, or until top springs back when touched with finger; rotate dish one-quarter turn once.

5. Remove shortcake from dishes and peel off paper.

6. Serve shortcake warm, filled and topped with fruit and whipped cream.

6 to 8 servings

Carrot Cupcakes

1 cup sugar
¾ cup vegetable oil
2 eggs
1 cup grated pared raw carrot
1½ cups all-purpose flour
1 teaspoon baking powder
1 teaspoon baking soda
½ teaspoon salt
½ teaspoon ground cinnamon
½ cup chopped walnuts
Cream Cheese Frosting
(see page 171)

1. Beat sugar and oil together in a large mixer bowl. Add eggs, one at a time, beating thoroughly after each addition. Mix in grated carrot.

2. Blend flour, baking powder, baking soda, salt and cinnamon. Add carrot mixture gradually, stirring until blended. Stir in chopped walnuts.

3. Line microwave-oven-safe muffin-ring cups with 2 paper baking cups each. Fill each cup half full with batter, using 2 tablespoons batter for each.

4. Cook uncovered in microwave oven **2½ to 3 minutes at Medium-High**; rotate ring one-quarter turn halfway through cooking period. Tops will appear slightly moist and a wooden pick inserted near center will come out clean.

5. Immediately remove cupcakes from muffin ring, discard extra baking cups and let cupcakes cool on racks. Frost with Cream Cheese Frosting.

24 cupcakes

How to Cook Cupcakes

1. Prepare cake mix according to package directions.

2. Put two paper liners into each well of a microwave-oven-safe muffin ring. Fill liners half full with batter.

3. Cook 6 cupcakes at a time in microwave oven **2 to 3 minutes at Medium-High**; rotate muffin ring after 1 minute. Cupcakes will be moist at edges. Remove from muffin ring and discard outer paper liner. Let cool on rack before frosting as desired.

4. Repeat with remaining batter.

About 2 dozen cupcakes

Hint: For convection oven cooking, preheat oven to 375°F. Spoon batter into 24 paper baking cups set in two metal muffin pans. Place one pan on each metal rack. Cook in convection oven **20 to 25 minutes at 375°F**, or until a cake tester comes out clean.

How to Bake Cakes

Type	Method	Preheat and Oven Temperatures	Rack Position	Time
Angel food				
packaged	Convection	Follow package directions	Bottom	Follow package
Layer cake (round)				
recipe	Convection	Follow recipe directions	Both	Follow recipe
packaged	Convection	Follow package directions	Both	Follow package
Pound cake				
packaged	Convection	Follow package directions	Bottom	Follow package
	Combination	325°F—Combination I	Bottom	35 minutes
Sponge cake				
recipe	Convection	Follow recipe directions	Both	Follow recipe
Tube cake				
recipe	Convection	Follow recipe directions	Bottom	Follow recipe
	Combination	325°F—Combination I	Bottom	40 to 45 minutes
packaged	Convection	Follow package directions	Bottom	Follow package
	Combination	325°F—Combination I	Bottom	35 to 40 minutes

Gingerbread

½ cup water
1 cup molasses
¼ cup vegetable oil
2 tablespoons sugar
1 teaspoon baking soda
¼ teaspoon salt
1½ teaspoons ground ginger
¼ teaspoon ground nutmeg
2 cups all-purpose flour
Lemon Sauce (see page 194)

1. Line an 8-inch square glass baking dish with 2 layers of paper towels cut to fit. Set aside.

2. Combine water, molasses and oil in a 2-quart glass measuring pitcher. Cook uncovered in microwave oven **3 minutes at High**, or until boiling.

3. Blend sugar, baking soda, salt, ginger and nutmeg; stir into molasses mixture. Blend in flour, ½ cup at a time, stirring until smooth after each addition. Pour into the lined dish and spread evenly. Shield each corner of dish with a small piece of aluminum foil.

4. Cook uncovered in microwave oven **7 to 9 minutes at Medium-High**; rotate dish one-quarter turn halfway through cooking period.

5. Remove foil. Let stand 10 minutes. Loosen edges of cake from dish. Invert onto a rack; discard paper. Serve warm with Lemon Sauce.

9 servings

Chocolate-Zucchini Cake

1½ cups all-purpose flour
¼ cup unsweetened cocoa
½ teaspoon baking soda
½ teaspoon baking powder
½ teaspoon salt
2 eggs
1 cup sugar
1 cup vegetable oil
1 teaspoon vanilla extract
1 cup grated unpeeled raw zucchini (2 small)
Penuche Glaze (see recipe)

1. Blend flour, cocoa, baking soda, baking powder and salt; set aside.

2. Beat eggs in a mixer bowl for 1 minute at medium speed. Beat in sugar gradually, then pour in oil and vanilla extract. At lowest speed, mix in zucchini, then flour mixture. Pour batter into an ungreased 12-cup microwave-oven-safe fluted tube pan.

3. Cook in microwave oven **10 to 12 minutes at Medium-High**; rotate pan one-quarter turn halfway through cooking period. Cake will appear slightly moist and pull away from edges of pan.

4. Cover pan with plastic wrap; let stand 5 minutes. Loosen edges and invert onto a rack. Cool. Spread with Penuche Glaze.

12 to 16 servings

Penuche Glaze

2 tablespoons butter or margarine
¼ cup packed brown sugar
1½ cups confectioners' sugar
2 tablespoons milk

1. Melt butter and brown sugar in a 1-quart glass casserole in microwave oven (**about 1 minute at High**).

2. Remove from oven. Stir in confectioners' sugar and milk. Mix until smooth.

About ¾ cup

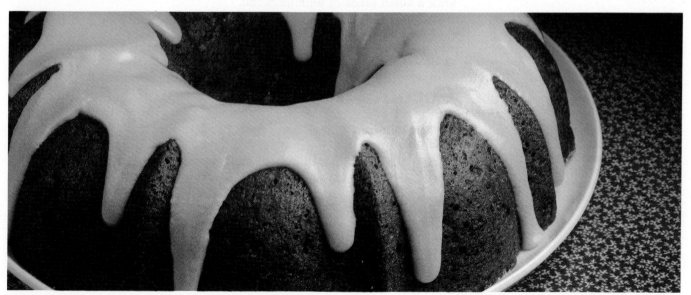

Fudge-Frosted Cake

1 package (6 ounces)
  semisweet chocolate pieces
2 tablespoons water
⅔ cup sweetened condensed
  milk
1 teaspoon vanilla extract
1 cup all-purpose biscuit mix
½ cup sugar
2 tablespoons vegetable
  shortening
1 egg
½ cup milk
1 teaspoon vanilla extract
½ cup chopped walnuts

1. Line an 8-inch round glass cake dish with waxed paper cut to fit. Set aside.

2. Melt semisweet chocolate in a 1-quart glass measuring pitcher in microwave oven (**about 2½ minutes at High**); stir once. Add water, sweetened condensed milk and 1 teaspoon vanilla extract; stir with a spoon until smooth. Pour into lined dish.

3. Combine biscuit mix, sugar, shortening, egg and ¼ cup milk in a small bowl; beat 1 minute. Add remaining ¼ cup milk and the vanilla extract; beat 1 minute. Pour batter over chocolate mixture. Cover with waxed paper.

4. Cook in microwave oven **8 to 8½ minutes at Medium-High**, or until a wooden pick inserted near center comes out clean; rotate dish one-quarter turn once.

5. Immediately invert cake on a serving plate, peel off paper and sprinkle with chopped walnuts. Serve warm.

6 servings

Oatmeal Cake with Coconut Topping

1¼ cups boiling water
1 cup quick-cooking oats
1⅓ cups all-purpose flour
1 teaspoon baking soda
1 teaspoon ground cinnamon
½ teaspoon salt
½ cup (1 stick) butter or
  margarine
1 cup sugar
1 cup packed dark brown sugar
2 eggs, well beaten
1 teaspoon vanilla extract
  Coconut Topping (see recipe)

1. Pour boiling water over oats in a bowl; let stand 20 minutes.

2. Line an 8-inch square glass baking dish with 2 layers of paper towels cut to fit. Set aside.

3. Blend flour, baking soda, cinnamon and salt; set aside.

4. Cream butter and sugars in a large mixer bowl at medium speed of electric mixer until light and fluffy. Add oat mixture and beat for 1 minute.

5. Add beaten eggs, vanilla extract and dry ingredients; beat 2 minutes. Turn batter into the lined dish.

6. Cook uncovered in microwave oven **11 to 12½ minutes at Medium-High**, or until a wooden pick inserted near center comes out clean; rotate dish one-half turn every 4 minutes.

7. Turn cake onto a serving platter. Peel off paper.

8. Prepare topping. Cook uncovered in microwave oven **1½ minutes at High**, or until bubbly. Spread topping over baked cake.

12 servings

Hint: If the corners of cake are cooking too fast, cover each corner with a small piece of aluminum foil.

Hint: If your microwave oven has a browning element, prepare topping and spread over baked cake. Place cake on the microwave oven tray on the shelf position under browning element. Cook **5 minutes at Brown**, or until bubbly and browned.

Coconut Topping

¼ cup (½ stick) butter or
  margarine
½ cup packed brown sugar
¼ cup half-and-half
1 cup flaked coconut
½ cup chopped nuts

1. Melt butter in a small glass bowl in microwave oven (**about 1 minute at High**).

2. Add remaining ingredients to melted butter and mix well.

3. Use as directed above or spread as a frosting on cupcakes or cake.

About 1½ cups

Caramel Frosting

½ cup (1 stick) butter or
  margarine
1 cup packed brown sugar
¼ teaspoon salt
¼ cup milk
2½ cups sifted confectioners'
  sugar
½ teaspoon maple flavoring
1 tablespoon half-and-half or
  milk (optional)

1. Melt butter in a 1-quart glass measuring cup in microwave oven (**about 1 minute and 15 seconds at High**).

2. Stir in brown sugar and salt. Cook uncovered in microwave oven **1 minute at High**.

3. Stir in milk gradually. Cook uncovered in microwave oven **1½ minutes at High**; stir every 30 seconds.

4. Blend in confectioners' sugar and maple flavoring. Add half-and-half if a thinner consistency is desired.

Enough frosting for two 8-inch round cake layers

Easy Fudge Frosting

3 ounces (3 squares)
  unsweetened chocolate
2 tablespoons butter or
  margarine
2¾ cups sifted confectioners'
  sugar
5 to 7 tablespoons half-and-half
  Dash salt
1 teaspoon vanilla extract

1. Melt chocolate and butter in a 2-quart glass bowl in microwave oven (**about 1 minute at High**). Stir.

2. Add 1½ cups confectioners' sugar, 5 tablespoons half-and-half and the salt; beat until smooth. Cook uncovered in microwave oven **1½ minutes at High**, or until bubbly.

3. Remove from oven. Add vanilla extract, then remaining 1¼ cups confectioners' sugar in thirds, beating after each addition until smooth. Beat in additional half-and-half, if necessary.

Enough frosting for two 8-inch round cake layers

Caramel Frosting

Coconut Topping

Easy Fudge Frosting

Confectioners' Sugar Frosting

1 tablespoon milk
1 teaspoon butter or margarine
½ cup confectioners' sugar
¼ teaspoon vanilla extract

1. Put milk and butter into a small glass mixer bowl. Heat uncovered in microwave oven only until butter melts (**about 15 seconds at High**).

2. Remove from oven. Add confectioners' sugar and vanilla extract to milk; beat thoroughly. Spread thinly on cookies.

About ¼ cup

Cream Cheese Frosting

1 package (3 ounces)
  cream cheese
1 tablespoon lemon juice
2½ cups confectioners' sugar

1. Soften cream cheese in a small glass bowl in microwave oven (**about 30 seconds at Medium**).

2. Add lemon juice and beat until smooth.

3. Add confectioners' sugar gradually, beating until smooth.

Enough frosting for one 10x6-inch cake layer or 24 cupcakes

Brownies

Chocolate Chip Squares

Oatmeal-Date Squares

Brownies

2 ounces (2 squares)
  unsweetened chocolate
⅓ cup vegetable shortening
1 cup sugar
2 eggs
¼ teaspoon vanilla extract
1 cup all-purpose flour
¼ teaspoon baking powder
¼ teaspoon salt
1 cup chopped nuts
  Confectioners' sugar

1. Melt chocolate in a glass custard cup in microwave oven (1½ to 2 minutes at High). Cool.

2. Cream shortening and sugar. Add eggs, one at a time, and beat well after each addition. Add vanilla extract and cooled chocolate; mix well.

3. Blend flour, baking powder and salt; stir into creamed mixture. Mix in nuts.

4. Turn batter into a greased 1½-quart glass baking dish. Cook uncovered in microwave oven **7 to 8 minutes at Medium-High**, or until a wooden pick inserted near center comes out clean; rotate dish one-quarter turn once.

5. Set dish on flat surface; cool, then cut into bars. Sprinkle with confectioners' sugar.

About 2 dozen

Hint: For microwave/convection oven cooking, preheat convection oven to 375°F. Place filled dish on bottom metal rack. Cook in microwave/convection oven **12 to 13 minutes at Combination II**, or until done.

Chocolate Chip Squares

½ cup (1 stick) butter or
  margarine
1 teaspoon vanilla extract
⅔ cup packed dark brown sugar
1 egg
1¼ cups all-purpose flour
1 teaspoon baking powder
¼ teaspoon salt
1 package (6 ounces)
  semisweet chocolate pieces

1. Cream butter and vanilla extract in a bowl. Add brown sugar gradually, creaming until fluffy. Add egg and beat thoroughly.

2. Blend flour, baking powder and salt thoroughly; stir into creamed mixture. Stir in half of chocolate pieces. Turn into an ungreased 1½-quart glass baking dish. Top with remaining chocolate pieces.

3. Cook uncovered in microwave oven **7 to 8 minutes at Medium-High**, or until edges begin to pull away from the sides of the dish; rotate dish one-quarter turn once.

4. Set dish on a flat surface; cool, then cut into squares.

About 1 dozen

Hint: For convection oven cooking, preheat oven to 375°F. Spread mixture in a lightly greased 10¾x7x1½-inch metal baking pan; sprinkle remaining chocolate pieces over top. Place pan on bottom metal rack. Cook in convection oven **15 to 20 minutes at 375°F**, or until done.

Oatmeal-Date Squares

1 package (8 ounces) pitted
  dates, chopped
½ cup chopped walnuts
¼ cup sugar
1 cup water
1 teaspoon lemon juice
1¾ cups all-purpose flour
1 cup packed dark brown sugar
1½ cups quick-cooking oats
1 teaspoon salt
½ teaspoon ground cinnamon
1 cup (2 sticks) butter or
  margarine

1. Combine dates, walnuts, sugar, water and lemon juice in a 1-quart glass measuring pitcher. Cook uncovered in microwave oven **8 minutes at High**. Set aside.

2. Preheat convection oven to 375°F.

3. Combine flour, brown sugar, oats, salt and cinnamon in a large bowl. Cut in butter with a pastry blender or two knives until well mixed and crumbly.

4. Pat two-thirds of crumb mixture in bottom of a greased 8-inch square glass baking dish. Spread on date mixture. Top with remaining crumb mixture.

5. Place dish on bottom metal rack. Cook in microwave/convection oven **20 to 25 minutes at Combination II**, or until set in center. Cool and cut into squares.

16 squares

How to Bake Cookies

Type	Method	Preheat and Oven Temperatures	Rack Position	Time
Refrigerator cookies				
recipe	Convection	Follow recipe directions	Both	Follow recipe
packaged	Convection	Follow package directions	Both	Follow package
Molded cookies				
recipe	Convection	Follow recipe directions	Both	Follow recipe
Drop cookies				
recipe	Convection	Follow recipe directions	Both	Follow recipe
Bar type cookies				
recipe	Convection	Follow recipe directions	Bottom	Follow recipe
	Combination	375° F—Combination II	Bottom	15 to 25 minutes
packaged	Convection	Follow package directions	Bottom	Follow package
	Combination	325° F—Combination I	Bottom	25 to 30 minutes

Lemon Meltaway Cookies

½ cup (1 stick) butter or margarine, softened
½ cup confectioners' sugar
1 teaspoon grated lemon peel
2 teaspoons lemon juice
½ teaspoon vanilla extract
1 cup all-purpose flour
¼ cup cornstarch
¼ teaspoon salt
4 teaspoons water
24 pecan halves

1. Preheat convection oven to 375°F.

2. Combine butter, confectioners' sugar, lemon peel, lemon juice and vanilla extract in a small mixer bowl. Beat until fluffy. Combine flour, cornstarch and salt; add alternately with water and beat until well mixed. Drop mixture by rounded teaspoonfuls onto two ungreased round metal trays. Press pecan half on each cookie.

3. Place one tray on each metal rack. Cook in convection oven **12 to 14 minutes at 375°F**, or until light golden brown. Remove cookies to cooling racks.

2 dozen

Chocolate Drop Cookies

2 ounces (2 squares) unsweetened chocolate
½ cup (1 stick) butter or margarine
½ cup sugar
½ cup packed dark brown sugar
1 egg
2 cups all-purpose flour
½ teaspoon baking soda
½ cup milk
1 teaspoon vanilla extract

1. Melt chocolate and butter in a 2-quart glass measuring pitcher in microwave oven (**about 2 minutes at High**); stir.

2. Preheat convection oven to 375°F.

3. Add sugars and egg to melted butter and chocolate; beat well. Combine flour and baking soda; stir in alternately with milk. Stir in vanilla extract. Drop by tablespoonfuls onto two ungreased round metal trays. Place one tray on each metal rack. Cook in convection oven **12 to 15 minutes at 375°F**, or until set. Remove cookies to cooling racks.

4. Preheat oven to 375°F. Repeat using remaining batter; cook on bottom metal rack.

2½ dozen

Peanut Butter Cookies

½ cup (1 stick) butter or margarine
½ cup crunchy peanut butter
½ teaspoon vanilla extract
1 cup packed brown sugar
1 egg
1 cup all-purpose flour
¾ teaspoon baking soda
¼ teaspoon salt

1. Preheat convection oven to 375°F.

2. Cream butter, peanut butter, vanilla extract, and brown sugar in a bowl. Add egg and beat well. Blend flour, baking soda and salt. Add flour mixture gradually to creamed mixture, mixing until blended. Drop by teaspoonfuls onto ungreased round metal trays. Flatten each with a floured fork, making a crisscross pattern.

3. Put one tray on each metal rack. Cook in convection oven **9 to 10 minutes at 375°F**, or until edges are lightly browned. Let cookies cool slightly on trays, then transfer to cooling racks.

4. Preheat oven to 375°F. Repeat, using remaining cookie mixture.

About 4 dozen

Desserts

Ting-a-Lings

1 cup salted peanuts
2 cups chow mein noodles
1 package (12 ounces) butterscotch-flavored pieces

1. Toss peanuts and noodles together in a 2-quart glass casserole.

2. Melt butterscotch pieces in a 1-quart glass measuring pitcher in microwave oven (**about 3 minutes at High**). Stir until smooth. Add to peanut mixture and toss gently until coated.

3. Drop from a teaspoon onto waxed paper. Chill to harden.

36 pieces

Rocky Road Clusters

2 cups sugar
5 tablespoons unsweetened cocoa
½ cup milk
½ cup (1 stick) butter or margarine
½ teaspoon vanilla extract
3 cups quick-cooking oats
½ cup chopped walnuts
1 cup raisins
1 cup miniature marshmallows

1. Combine sugar and cocoa in a 2-quart glass measuring pitcher. Stir in milk and add butter. Cook uncovered in microwave oven **4 minutes at High**, or until mixture comes to a rolling boil. Stir well. Continue cooking **1 minute at High**.

2. Remove from oven and stir in vanilla extract. Add oats and walnuts; stir. Let cool for 5 minutes. Add raisins and marshmallows; stir.

3. Drop mixture by teaspoonfuls onto waxed paper. Refrigerate to set.

About 5 dozen

Marshmallow-Cereal Bars

¼ cup (½ stick) butter or margarine
½ cup peanut butter
1 package (10 ounces) regular marshmallows or 5 cups miniature marshmallows
5 cups ready-to-eat crisp rice cereal
1 package (6 ounces) semisweet chocolate pieces
1 package (6 ounces) peanut butter pieces

1. Put butter, peanut butter and marshmallows into a 2-quart glass measuring pitcher. Cook uncovered in microwave oven **1½ to 2 minutes at Medium-High**, or until melted and smooth; stir once.

2. Mix cereal into marshmallow mixture and press into a lightly buttered 1½-quart baking dish.

3. Combine semisweet chocolate pieces and peanut butter pieces in a 1-quart glass measuring pitcher. Melt in microwave oven (**2 to 2½ minutes at High**). Stir until smooth. Spread over cereal mixture. Cool until set. Cut into bars.

12 bars

Chocolate Wafer Crust

⅓ cup butter or margarine
1½ cups chocolate wafer crumbs
(about 40 wafers)

1. Melt butter in a 9-inch glass pie plate in microwave oven (**about 45 seconds at High**). Mix in wafer crumbs. Press evenly over bottom and sides of pie plate.

2. Cook uncovered in microwave oven **2 minutes at High**; rotate pie plate one-quarter turn after 1 minute. Cool shell before filling.

One 9-inch crumb crust

Vanilla Wafer Crust: Substitute vanilla wafer crumbs for chocolate wafer crumbs.

Baked Pastry Shell

1 pie crust stick or mix
(enough for a 9-inch
pie shell)

1. Prepare pie crust dough following directions on package.

2. Roll out ⅛ inch thick and place in a 9-inch glass pie plate; be careful not to stretch pastry.

3. Trim and flute edge. Prick bottom and sides of pie shell with a fork.

4. Cook uncovered in microwave oven **4 to 5½ minutes at Medium-High**, or until crust appears flaky; rotate pie plate one-quarter turn twice. Cool.

One 9-inch pastry shell

Hint: You can also use your favorite homemade pastry recipe with one addition; add 4 drops yellow food coloring to the water before sprinkling water over flour mixture. Proceed as directed above. A brown appearance can also be obtained by brushing prepared pie shell with vanilla extract before cooking.

Hint: For convection oven cooking, preheat oven at 375°F. Use a metal pie pan. Place pastry-lined pie pan on bottom metal rack. Cook in convection oven **12 to 15 minutes at 375°F**, or until pastry is light golden brown.

Graham Cracker Crust

⅓ cup butter or margarine
¼ cup sugar
1½ cups graham cracker crumbs
(about 18 graham crackers)

1. Melt butter in a 9-inch glass pie plate in microwave oven (**about 45 seconds at High**). Mix in sugar and cracker crumbs. Press evenly onto bottom and sides.

2. Cook uncovered in microwave oven **2 minutes at High**; rotate pie plate one-quarter turn after 1 minute. Cool crust before filling.

One 9-inch crumb crust

Cherry Pie

Pastry for 2-crust pie
2 cans (16 ounces each) red tart pitted cherries packed in water
¾ cup sugar
¼ cup cornstarch
Dash salt

1. Prepare pastry for one crust; fit into a 9-inch glass pie plate.

2. Drain cherries; reserve ¾ cup liquid.

3. Combine sugar, cornstarch and salt in a 1-quart glass measuring pitcher. Add liquid gradually, stirring constantly. Cook in microwave oven **3 minutes at High**, or until thickened; stir once. Mix in cherries.

4. Preheat convection oven to 375°F.

5. Fill pastry-lined pie plate with cherry mixture; spread evenly. Prepare pastry for second crust. Cut into lattice strips and arrange in crisscross woven fashion on top of pie. Trim and seal edges.

6. Place pie plate on bottom metal rack. Cook in microwave/convection oven **40 to 45 minutes at Combination II**, or until lightly browned. Cool on cooling rack.

One 9-inch pie

Apple Pie

Pastry for 2-crust pie
6 large cooking apples
½ cup sugar
2 tablespoons all-purpose flour
½ teaspoon ground cinnamon
1 tablespoon milk

1. Preheat convection oven to 375°F.

2. Prepare pastry for one crust; fit into a 9-inch glass pie plate.

3. Wash, core, pare and thinly slice apples. Combine apple slices with sugar, flour and cinnamon. Turn into pastry shell.

4. Prepare pastry for second crust; arrange on top of apples. Cut vents for steam; trim excess dough and flute edges to seal. Brush top with milk.

5. Place pie plate on bottom metal rack. Cook in microwave/convection oven **40 minutes at Combination II**, or until golden brown and apples are tender. Cool on cooling rack.

One 9-inch pie

Lemon Meringue Pie

1 baked 9-inch pastry shell
  (see page 176)
1½ cups sugar
⅓ cup cornstarch
1½ cups boiling water
3 egg yolks, slightly beaten
3 tablespoons butter or
  margarine
¼ cup lemon juice
1 teaspoon grated lemon peel
  Meringue (see recipe)

1. Prepare pastry shell in a 9-inch glass pie plate. Set aside.

2. Mix sugar and cornstarch thoroughly in a 1-quart glass measuring pitcher. Stir in water. Cook uncovered in microwave oven **2½ minutes at High**; stir. Continue cooking **1 minute at High**, or until thick; stir after 30 seconds.

3. Beat a small amount of the hot mixture into egg yolks, then return to mixture in the glass pitcher. Cook uncovered in microwave oven **30 seconds at High**.

4. Add butter, lemon juice and lemon peel to hot mixture; stir. Cool filling slightly. Pour into baked pastry shell. Cover with Meringue and cook as directed.

One 9-inch pie

Meringue

3 egg whites
⅛ teaspoon salt
6 tablespoons sugar

1. Beat egg whites and salt in a bowl until frothy. Add sugar gradually, beating until soft peaks form.

2. Pile meringue lightly over pie filling. Swirl with back of a spoon; seal to edges of crust.

3. Cook uncovered in microwave oven **3 minutes at High**.

Hint: For convection oven cooking, preheat oven to 375°F. Set on bottom metal rack. Cook in convection oven **10 minutes at 375°F**, or until meringue is lightly browned.

How to Bake Pies

Type	Method	Preheat and Oven Temperatures	Rack Position	Time
Pastry shell				
recipe	Convection	Follow recipe directions	Bottom	Follow recipe
frozen, packaged	Convection	Follow package directions	Bottom	Follow package
Two-crust fruit pie				
recipe	Convection	Follow recipe directions	Bottom	Follow recipe
	Combination	375°F—Combination II	Bottom	40 minutes
frozen, packaged	Convection	Follow package directions	Bottom	Follow package
Baked custard				
recipe	Convection	Follow recipe directions	Bottom	Follow recipe
	Combination	325°F—Combination I	Bottom	45 minutes
frozen, packaged	Convection	Follow package directions	Bottom	Follow package
Meringue-covered pie				
recipe	Convection	375°—375°F	Bottom	10 minutes

Baked Alaska Loaf

1 baked pound cake
(10¾ ounces)
1 pint chocolate ice cream
3 egg whites
¼ teaspoon cream of tartar
3 tablespoons sugar

1. Slice pound cake lengthwise in three layers. Slice pint of ice cream lengthwise into 4 slices. Place one cake layer on aluminum foil. Alternate ice cream slices and remaining cake layer, ending with cake.

2. Wrap and freeze for several hours.

3. To bake, preheat convection oven to 450°F.

4. Beat egg whites with cream of tartar until foamy. Gradually add sugar, continuing to beat until stiff, not dry, peaks form.

5. Place frozen loaf on an oven-proof platter or round metal tray. Spread meringue on all surfaces. (Be sure to seal edges next to platter.)

6. Place platter on bottom metal rack. Cook in convection oven **2½ to 3 minutes at 450°F**, or until peaks are golden brown.

1 loaf

Cream Puffs

½ cup (1 stick) butter or
margarine
1 cup hot water
1 cup all-purpose flour
½ teaspoon salt
4 eggs
Vanilla Pudding
(see page 184)

1. Put butter and water into a 2-quart glass measuring pitcher. Cook uncovered in microwave oven **2 to 3 minutes at High**, or until butter melts.

2. Stir in flour and salt. Cook uncovered in microwave oven **1 minute at High**. Remove from oven.

3. Preheat convection oven to 375°F.

4. Add eggs, one at a time, beating well after each addition.

5. Drop dough by tablespoonfuls onto two ungreased round metal trays.

6. Place one tray on each metal rack. Cook in convection oven **35 to 45 minutes at 375°F**, or until golden brown. Cool on cooling rack. Cut off tops, remove moist dough from inside and fill with Vanilla Pudding (about 2 tablespoons for each). Replace tops.

About 20 cream puffs

Cheese Cake

¼ cup (½ stick) butter or margarine
1¼ cups fine graham cracker crumbs (18 to 20 crackers)
½ teaspoon ground cinnamon
1 package (8 ounces) cream cheese
¼ cup sugar
½ teaspoon vanilla extract
1 egg
1 cup dairy sour cream
2 tablespoons sugar
½ teaspoon vanilla extract

1. For crust, melt butter in a 9-inch glass pie plate in microwave oven (**about 45 seconds at High**). Add cracker crumbs and cinnamon; mix well with a fork. Press crumb mixture evenly onto bottom and sides of pie plate. Cook uncovered in microwave oven **2 minutes at High**; rotate pie plate one-quarter turn halfway through cooking period. Remove from oven and set aside.

2. For filling, soften cream cheese in a small glass bowl in microwave oven (**about 1 minute at High**). Add ¼ cup sugar, ½ teaspoon vanilla extract and the egg to cream cheese; mix until well blended. Pour filling into crust.

3. Cook uncovered in microwave oven **3 minutes at Medium-High**, or until bubbles appear on surface; rotate pie plate one-quarter turn once. Remove from oven and cool slightly.

4. Blend sour cream, 2 tablespoons sugar and ½ teaspoon vanilla extract. Spoon sour cream mixture over filling. Cook uncovered in microwave oven **2½ minutes at Medium-High**, or until set. Cool, then chill thoroughly.

One 9-inch pie

Baked Apple

1 medium baking apple
1 tablespoon brown sugar
2 teaspoons butter or margarine
  Ground cinnamon

1. Wash and core apple. Pare a thin section of skin from top of apple. Place apple in a glass custard cup.

2. Fill center of apple with brown sugar and top with butter. Sprinkle with cinnamon.

3. Cook uncovered in microwave oven **2 to 2½ minutes at High**, or until almost tender. Let stand 5 minutes before serving.

1 serving

Hint: For more than 1 apple, rearrange apples once during cooking.

Amount of Apples	Cook at High
2	3 to 3½ minutes
3	4 to 4½ minutes
4	5 to 5½ minutes

Cinnamon-Spiced Pear

¼ cup water
3 tablespoons sugar
2 drops anise extract
1 cinnamon stick (1½ inches long)
½ slice lemon
1 ripe Bosc pear (½ pound)

1. Combine all ingredients except pear in a 10-ounce glass dish. Cover with plastic wrap.

2. Cook in microwave oven **2 to 3 minutes at High**, or until sugar is dissolved; stir once.

3. Remove the core from the blossom end of pear. Slit skin from stem to bottom 4 times. Stand pear in syrup.

4. Cook covered **2½ to 3½ minutes at High**, or until pear is tender but still retains shape. Let stand 3 minutes before serving.

1 serving

Hint: For more than 1 pear, increase recipe; follow chart below.

Amount of Pears	Utensil	Syrup—Cook at High	Pears—Cook at High
2	1-quart glass casserole	2 to 3 minutes	2½ to 3½ minutes
3	1½-quart glass casserole	4 to 5 minutes	3½ to 4 minutes
4	2-quart glass casserole	4 to 5 minutes	4 to 6 minutes

Peach Crisp

3 cans (16 ounces each) peach halves, drained and cut in half
⅓ cup butter or margarine
⅓ cup all-purpose flour
1 cup uncooked oats, quick or old-fashioned
½ cup packed brown sugar
½ teaspoon salt
¼ teaspoon ground cinnamon
¼ teaspoon ground nutmeg

1. Arrange peaches in an 8-inch square glass baking dish.

2. Melt butter in a small glass bowl in microwave oven (**45 to 60 seconds at High**).

3. Mix flour, oats, brown sugar, salt, cinnamon and nutmeg in a bowl. Add melted butter and mix until crumbly. Sprinkle crumb mixture over peaches.

4. Cook uncovered in microwave oven **7 to 8 minutes at High**; rotate dish one-quarter turn once.

8 servings

Peaches Flambée

⅓ cup packed brown sugar
2 tablespoons butter or margarine
2 tablespoons orange-flavored liqueur
1 package (16 ounces) frozen unsweetened sliced peaches, defrosted
¼ cup kirsch
Vanilla ice cream (optional)

1. Put brown sugar and butter into a 1-quart glass casserole. Cook uncovered in microwave oven **30 seconds at High**. Stir in orange liqueur until blended. Cook uncovered **30 seconds at High**.

2. Add peaches to brown sugar mixture; stir. Cover with an all-glass lid or plastic wrap. Cook in microwave oven **1 minute at Medium-High**.

3. Measure kirsch in a 1-cup glass measuring cup. Heat uncovered in microwave oven until warm (**about 20 seconds at High**). Pour over peaches and ignite.

4. Serve plain or over vanilla ice cream.

6 servings

How to Cook Syrup and Candies

Use a candy thermometer especially designed for use in the microwave oven.

Stage	Temperature	Test
Thread	230° to 234°F	The syrup spins a 2-inch thread when allowed to drop from fork or spoon.
Soft Ball	234° to 240°F	The syrup forms a soft ball in very cold water; it flattens when removed from water.
Firm Ball	244° to 248°F	The syrup forms a firm ball in very cold water; it does not flatten when removed from water.
Hard Ball	250° to 266°F	The syrup forms a ball which is pliable yet hard enough to hold its shape in very cold water.
Soft Crack	270° to 290°F	The syrup separates into threads which are hard but not brittle in very cold water.
Hard Crack	300° to 310°F	The syrup separates into threads which are hard and brittle in very cold water.

Chocolate-Covered Treats

½ **16-ounce package chocolate-flavored confectionery coating**

55 **mini-size pretzels (about 2 cups), 55 dried apricot halves (8 ounces) or 1½ cups raisins or peanuts**

1. Melt chocolate coating in a 1-quart glass measuring pitcher in microwave oven (**3 to 3½ minutes at Medium**); stir once. Stir until smooth.

2. If using pretzels or apricots, dip each piece in coating to cover completely and set on waxed paper. (If coating begins to thicken, heat in microwave oven **30 seconds at Medium**; stir.) If using raisins or peanuts, stir into coating and drop by teaspoonfuls onto waxed paper. Cool until set.

Chocolate-coated treats
(55 pretzels or 55 apricots or 30 raisin or nut clusters)

Hint: Semisweet chocolate can be substituted, if desired. Melt 1 package (6 ounces) semisweet chocolate pieces and 1 tablespoon vegetable shortening in a 1-quart glass measuring pitcher in microwave oven (**about 2½ minutes at High**); stir once. Stir until smooth before using. (If chocolate begins to thicken, heat in microwave oven **30 seconds at Medium**; stir.)

Divinity

3 **cups sugar**
¾ **cup light corn syrup**
¾ **cup water**
2 **egg whites**
1 **package (3 ounces) strawberry-flavored gelatin**
1 **cup chopped nuts or candied red cherries**
1 **teaspoon vanilla extract**

1. Mix sugar, corn syrup and water in a 2-quart glass casserole.

2. Cook uncovered in microwave oven to hard-ball stage (**19 to 22 minutes at High**).

3. Beat egg whites in the small bowl of an electric mixer until stiff, but not dry, peaks form. Beat in dry gelatin.

4. When syrup reaches hard-ball stage, pour in a thin stream over egg whites while beating constantly. Add vanilla extract and continue beating until mixture loses its gloss (about 8 minutes).

5. Spread in a lightly buttered 8-inch square dish or pan and cool until firm. Cut into 36 pieces.

About 2 pounds

Microwave Chocolate Fudge

4 ounces (4 squares) unsweetened chocolate
2 packages (3 ounces each) cream cheese
4 cups confectioners' sugar
1 tablespoon vanilla extract
¾ cup coarsely chopped nuts

1. Melt chocolate in a small glass bowl in microwave oven (**about 3 minutes at High**). Set aside to cool.

2. Soften cream cheese in a 1½-quart glass bowl in microwave oven (**30 to 60 seconds at Medium**). Beat cheese until fluffy. Add confectioners' sugar gradually, beating until fluffy. Blend in the cooled chocolate and vanilla extract. Stir in chopped nuts.

3. Turn fudge into a buttered 8-inch square dish or pan. Chill in refrigerator until firm. Cut into squares.

36 pieces

Crackle Peanut Brittle

2 cups sugar
1 cup light corn syrup
½ cup water
2 cups salted peanuts
2 teaspoons butter or margarine
2 teaspoons baking soda
1 teaspoon vanilla extract

1. Combine sugar, corn syrup and water in a 2-quart glass measuring pitcher. Cook uncovered in microwave oven **6 minutes at High**, or until sugar is dissolved.

2. Stir peanuts into syrup. Cook uncovered in microwave oven **8 minutes at High**; stir twice.

3. Stir butter into mixture. Cook uncovered in microwave oven to hard-crack stage (**8 to 10 minutes at High**); stir twice.

4. Add baking soda and vanilla extract to mixture; mix well. Pour onto 2 lightly buttered large baking sheets, spreading as thinly as possible.

5. As soon as candy is cool enough to handle, wet hands with water and stretch as thin as desired. Turn candy over and cool completely.

6. When firm and cool, break into medium-size pieces. Store in a tightly covered container.

About 2 pounds

Year-Round Fruit Compote

1 cup dried apricots
1 cup golden raisins
1 package (12 ounces) pitted prunes
1 can (20 ounces) unsweetened pineapple chunks (undrained)
Lemon peel from ¼ lemon
1 cinnamon stick, broken in half

1. Put fruits, lemon peel and cinnamon sticks into a 1½-quart glass casserole; stir. Cover with an all-glass lid or plastic wrap.

2. Cook in microwave oven **8 minutes at High**; rotate dish one-quarter turn once.

3. Remove lemon peel and cinnamon before serving.

8 to 10 servings

Frozen Chocolate Bananas

6 firm ripe medium bananas
1 package (12 ounces)
semisweet chocolate pieces

1. Peel bananas and cut crosswise into halves. Insert a wooden stick into the end of each banana piece. Place in a 13x9x2-inch pan; set in freezer 2 to 3 hours or overnight.

2. Melt semisweet chocolate in a small glass bowl in microwave oven (**about 3 minutes at High**); stir once.

3. Stir chocolate until smooth. With a spatula generously spread chocolate over frozen bananas, using lengthwise strokes. Chocolate will become firm as it is spread.

4. Wrap each piece in aluminum foil and store in freezer. Serve frozen.

12 servings

Chocolate Fondue

12 ounces (12 squares)
semisweet chocolate
1 cup whipping cream
3 tablespoons brandy or rum
Assorted dippers
(marshmallows, strawberries
with hulls, apple slices,
banana chunks, pineapple
chunks, mandarin orange
segments, cherries with
stems, cake cubes, melon
balls)

1. Melt semisweet chocolate in a 1-quart glass measuring pitcher in microwave oven (**about 5 minutes at Medium-High**). Stir to blend. Add cream and stir until well blended. Heat uncovered 1½ minutes at **Medium-High**.

2. Add brandy to chocolate mixture and stir well.

3. Serve in fondue pot and keep warm. Accompany with desired dippers.

About 2⅓ cups

Vanilla Pudding

⅓ cup sugar
¼ teaspoon salt
3 tablespoons cornstarch
2 cups milk
1 egg, separated
½ teaspoon vanilla extract

1. Combine sugar, salt and cornstarch in a 1-quart glass casserole. Add milk gradually, blending well. Cook uncovered in microwave oven **6 to 8 minutes at Medium-High**; stir 3 times.

2. Beat egg yolk and stir a little of hot mixture into yolk. Return to casserole. Cook uncovered in microwave oven **1 to 1½ minutes at Medium-High**, or until mixture coats a metal spoon; do not leave spoon in mixture.

3. Beat egg white in a medium bowl until stiff, but not dry, peaks form. Fold hot mixture into beaten egg white. Mix in vanilla extract. Pour into individual serving dishes or a large bowl to cool.

4 servings

Steamed Chocolate Puddings

3 ounces (3 squares) unsweetened chocolate
1⅓ cups all-purpose flour
1½ teaspoons baking powder
½ teaspoon salt
⅔ cup butter or margarine
1½ teaspoons vanilla extract
¾ cup packed brown sugar
2 eggs
¾ cup milk
½ cup chopped walnuts
2 cups water for steaming
  Whipped cream

1. Melt chocolate in a small glass dish in microwave oven (**about 2½ minutes at High**). Set aside to cool.

2. Blend flour, baking powder and salt. Set aside.

3. Cream butter and vanilla extract in a mixer bowl. Add brown sugar gradually, beating until blended. Add eggs, one at a time, beating until fluffy after each addition. Blend in cooled chocolate.

4. Add dry ingredients alternately with milk to creamed mixture, beating just until blended after each addition. Stir in chopped walnuts. Spoon ½ cup batter into each of 8 ungreased 6-ounce glass custard cups; spread evenly. Cover each cup with plastic wrap.

5. Meanwhile, pour water into an 8-inch square glass baking dish. Cover with plastic wrap. Heat in microwave oven to boiling (**about 6 minutes at High**). Remove plastic wrap.

6. Set 4 cups at a time in the dish with boiling water. Cook covered in microwave oven **7 to 9 minutes at Medium-High**, or until a wooden pick inserted near center comes out clean; rotate and rearrange cups after 3 minutes of cooking and again after 6 minutes.

7. Remove from oven. Let stand covered 5 minutes. Repeat with remaining 4 cups. Loosen edges and invert onto individual serving plates.

8. Serve warm with whipped cream.

8 servings

Bread Pudding

2 cups milk
1 tablespoon butter or margarine
3 eggs
½ cup sugar
1 teaspoon vanilla extract
¾ teaspoon ground cinnamon
¼ teaspoon salt
⅓ cup chopped walnuts
3 cups white bread cubes
⅓ cup raisins
  Meringue (see page 179)

1. Put milk and butter into a 1-quart glass measuring cup. Cook uncovered in microwave oven **4½ minutes at High**.

2. Beat eggs slightly in a 1-quart glass measuring pitcher, then beat in sugar. Add hot milk to eggs gradually, stirring until well blended. Add vanilla extract, cinnamon, salt and nuts; stir.

3. Put bread cubes and raisins into a 1½-quart glass casserole. Pour egg mixture over bread and raisins.

4. Cook uncovered in microwave oven **12 minutes at Medium-High**, or until set in center; rotate casserole one-half turn every 4 minutes.

5. Cover with Meringue and cook as directed.

6 to 8 servings

Baked Custard

1⅔ cups milk
3 eggs
¼ cup sugar
¼ teaspoon salt
½ teaspoon vanilla extract
  Ground nutmeg (optional)

1. Scald milk in a 2-cup glass measuring cup in microwave oven (**3 to 4 minutes at High**).

2. Meanwhile, put eggs into a 1-quart glass casserole and beat slightly. Add sugar, salt and vanilla extract; mix well.

3. Add the scalded milk gradually to egg mixture, stirring constantly. Sprinkle with nutmeg, if desired. Cover with an all-glass lid or plastic wrap.

4. Heat 1½ cups water in a 2-quart glass casserole in microwave oven to boiling (**3 to 4 minutes at High**).

5. Place the casserole with custard in the hot water. Cook in microwave oven **7 minutes at Medium-High**, or until almost set (center of custard will become firm on cooling).

6. Remove the casserole of custard from water and set on a rack to cool.

6 servings

Mushroom Sauce

Melba Sauce

Sauces and Gravies

Cooks who approach microwave cooking with awe are always pleasantly surprised with the wonderful sauces they can make so effortlessly, and in less time, with less stirring!

You are familiar with range-top cooking, in which sauce cooks by heat conducted from the bottom of the pan. Microwave energy cooks sauces from the top and sides as well as bottom, so the sauces cook more evenly. Stir to equalize the temperature throughout. You can leave a wooden or plastic stirring spoon right in the sauce in the microwave oven; you can't beat that for convenience!

Use a microwave-oven-safe serving dish for cooking, if you wish, to save on clean up. Use a bowl of generous size; double the size of the recipe if the sauce contains milk or sugar, or it may bubble over.

White Sauce

Now, for an easy lesson on making a white sauce. Notice in the recipe on page 188 that the flour is blended to a paste with other ingredients. Liquid is stirred in until smooth (a whisk works wonderfully!). The sauce is cooked uncovered for a few minutes. The microwave oven is stopped several times and the sauce stirred. This may seem like "intensive care" for the sauce, but remember that conventional cooking requires that the sauce be stirred constantly. And for a longer time! The finished sauce from the microwave oven never scorches and it is virtually impossible to make it lumpy.

Thin white sauce can become soup or a flavored sauce, depending upon additions. Medium white sauce is used in "creamed" vegetables and some casseroles. Thick white sauce goes into soufflés, and some main dish casseroles.

Other Sauces

Egg-thickened sauces work equally well. So well that it has led some hollandaise sauce lovers to claim that this one recipe (page 191) justifies the purchase of a microwave oven. But again, practice makes perfect. Notice that the half-and-half goes into the melted butter before the egg yolks. This is to reduce the temperature, since too much heat could curdle the eggs. The lower power setting when the egg mixture goes back into the oven, and frequent stirring, will produce a reputation-making sauce. It's great over vegetables and cooked fish, and without it, Eggs would not be Benedict.

Our Italian Meat and Italian Tomato Sauce (page 189) are always at home on rice or pasta. Any gravy becomes an everyday, not a holidays-only treat, using our method on page 192.

Dessert Sauces

Guests coming? You can set up a whole ice-cream sundae bar, using the dessert sauce recipes starting on page 194. But they are so easy you don't have to wait for company to enjoy them. Make them right in the glass measuring pitchers, and they are easy to pour too. They store well, so you can keep a supply of dessert toppers at all times.

Thin White Sauce

1 tablespoon butter or
  margarine
1 tablespoon all-purpose flour
1 cup milk
¼ teaspoon salt

1. Melt butter in a 1-quart glass measuring pitcher in microwave oven (**about 30 seconds at High**). Add flour and blend to a smooth paste. Add milk gradually, stirring constantly.

2. Cook uncovered in microwave oven **4 minutes at High**, or until thickened; stir vigorously after 2 minutes, then every 30 seconds. Stir in salt.

About 1 cup

Medium White Sauce: Use 2 tablespoons butter and 2 tablespoons flour with 1 cup milk and the salt.

Thick White Sauce: Use 3 tablespoons butter and 3 tablespoons flour with 1 cup milk and the salt.

Sour Cream Sauce

2 tablespoons butter or
  margarine
2 tablespoons all-purpose flour
1 cup dairy sour cream
2 teaspoons lemon juice
¼ teaspoon salt

1. Melt butter in a 1-quart glass measuring pitcher in microwave oven (**about 30 seconds at High**). Add flour and blend to a smooth paste. Add sour cream gradually, stirring constantly.

2. Cook uncovered in microwave oven **4 minutes at High**, or until thickened; stir vigorously after 2 minutes, then every 30 seconds. Stir in lemon juice and salt.

About 1 cup

Olive Sauce

2 tablespoons butter or
  margarine
2 tablespoons all-purpose flour
1 cup milk
¼ teaspoon salt
¼ cup sliced pimiento-stuffed
  green olives

1. Melt butter in a 1-quart glass measuring pitcher in microwave oven (**about 30 seconds at High**). Add flour and blend to a smooth paste. Add milk gradually, stirring constantly.

2. Cook uncovered in microwave oven **4 minutes at High**, or until thickened; stir vigorously after 2 minutes, then stir every 30 seconds. Stir in salt and olives.

About 1 cup

Cheese Sauce

2 tablespoons butter or
  margarine
2 tablespoons all-purpose flour
1 cup milk
¼ teaspoon salt
¼ teaspoon dry mustard
½ cup (2 ounces) shredded
  sharp Cheddar cheese

1. Melt butter in a 1-quart glass measuring pitcher in microwave oven (**about 30 seconds at High**). Add flour and blend to a smooth paste. Add milk gradually, stirring constantly.

2. Cook uncovered in microwave oven **4 minutes at High**, or until thickened; stir vigorously after 2 minutes, then every 30 seconds.

3. Add salt, dry mustard and cheese to sauce; stir well. Cook uncovered in microwave oven **1 minute at High**; stir.

About 1 cup

Bacon and Chive White Sauce

2 slices bacon, cooked
  (see page 113) and crumbled
2 tablespoons butter or
  margarine
2 tablespoons all-purpose flour
1 cup milk
1 teaspoon chopped chives
½ teaspoon salt

1. Prepare bacon and set aside.

2. Melt butter in a 1-quart glass measuring pitcher in microwave oven (**about 30 seconds at High**). Add flour; mix until smooth. Add milk gradually, stirring constantly.

3. Cook uncovered in microwave oven **4 minutes at High**, or until thickened; stir after 2 minutes, then every 30 seconds.

4. Add crumbled bacon, chives and salt; stir. Serve over fresh vegetables.

About 1 cup

Italian Meat Sauce

1 cup chopped onion
1 clove garlic, minced
1½ tablespoons olive oil
1 pound ground beef
1 can (28 ounces) Italian-style tomatoes, drained and cut in pieces
2 cans (6 ounces each) tomato paste
1 cup water
1½ teaspoons salt
½ teaspoon pepper
1 teaspoon oregano leaves

1. Combine onion, garlic and oil in a 2-quart glass measuring pitcher. Cook uncovered in microwave oven **3 to 5 minutes at High**, or until onion is soft; stir once.

2. Add meat and mix well. Cover with waxed paper. Cook in microwave oven **4 to 5 minutes at High**, or until meat is no longer pink; stir once. Remove excess fat.

3. Stir remaining ingredients into meat mixture. Cook covered in microwave oven **5 to 8 minutes at High**, or until bubbly; stir once.

1½ quarts

Italian Tomato Sauce

¼ cup olive oil
2 medium cloves garlic, halved
1 can (28 ounces) tomatoes, sieved
1 tablespoon snipped parsley
½ teaspoon salt
½ teaspoon oregano leaves, crushed
⅛ teaspoon pepper

1. Heat olive oil and garlic in a 2-quart glass measuring pitcher in microwave oven **3 minutes at High**, or until garlic is lightly browned.

2. Add sieved tomatoes, parsley and dry seasonings to garlic and oil; stir. Cook uncovered in microwave oven **30 minutes at High**; stir twice. Remove garlic.

About 1¾ cups

Mushroom Sauce

8 ounces fresh mushrooms,
  cleaned and sliced
  lengthwise
2 tablespoons butter or
  margarine
¼ cup all-purpose flour
1 cup chicken or beef broth
  (homemade, canned or from
  bouillon cube)
1 cup half-and-half
1 tablespoon snipped parsley
¼ teaspoon salt

1. Put mushrooms and butter into a 2-quart glass measuring pitcher. Cover with plastic wrap. Cook in microwave oven **2 to 3 minutes at High**, or until mushrooms are tender; stir once.

2. Remove from oven. Blend flour into butter and cooked mushrooms. Add broth gradually, stirring constantly. Cook uncovered in microwave oven **6 minutes at High**; stir every minute.

3. Add half-and-half gradually to mushroom mixture, stirring constantly. Heat uncovered in microwave oven to serving temperature (**about 2 minutes at High**); stir once.

4. Remove from oven; stir in parsley and salt.

About 2¾ cups

Béchamel Sauce

2 tablespoons butter or
  margarine
1 teaspoon grated onion
1 tablespoon all-purpose flour
½ cup chicken broth
½ cup half-and-half
¼ teaspoon salt
⅛ teaspoon white pepper
  Dash ground thyme

1. Melt butter in a 1-quart glass measuring pitcher in microwave oven (**about 30 seconds at High**). Add onion and flour; mix well. Add broth and half-and-half gradually, stirring constantly. Cook uncovered **5 minutes at High**, or until thickened; stir after 2 minutes, then every 30 seconds.

2. Remove from oven; stir in seasonings.

About 1 cup

Mock Hollandaise Sauce

1 cup Medium White Sauce
  (see page 188)
2 egg yolks, beaten
2 tablespoons butter or
  margarine
1 tablespoon lemon juice

1. Prepare white sauce. Stir ¼ cup of hot white sauce into egg yolks, then blend into remaining sauce in measuring pitcher. Add butter and lemon juice; mix well.

2. Cook uncovered in microwave oven **1 minute at High**, or until hot and butter is melted; stir once.

About 1¼ cups

Hollandaise Sauce

¼ cup (½ stick) butter or margarine
¼ cup half-and-half
2 egg yolks, beaten
1 tablespoon lemon juice or vinegar
¼ teaspoon salt
   Dash ground red pepper

1. Melt butter in a 1-quart glass measuring pitcher in microwave oven (**about 1 minute at High**). Add half-and-half, egg yolks, lemon juice, salt and red pepper; mix thoroughly. Cook uncovered **2½ minutes at Medium**, or until sauce is thickened; stir.

2. Remove from oven and beat until light.

¾ cup

Barbecue Sauce

1 cup ketchup
¼ cup packed brown sugar
¼ cup white vinegar
¼ cup water
1½ teaspoons celery seed
¼ teaspoon salt
   Dash garlic powder
   Dash pepper
1½ teaspoons Worcestershire sauce
1½ teaspoons prepared horseradish
1 medium onion, chopped

1. Combine all ingredients in a 2-quart glass casserole. Cover with waxed paper.

2. Cook in microwave oven **3 minutes at High**, or until hot; stir once.

About 1½ cups

Orange Barbecue Sauce

¼ cup packed brown sugar
½ teaspoon dry mustard
⅛ teaspoon ground cloves
½ teaspoon Worcestershire sauce
⅓ cup chopped onion
1½ teaspoons grated orange peel
⅓ cup orange juice
¾ cup ketchup

1. Mix all ingredients in a 1-quart glass measuring cup.

2. Cook in microwave oven **4 minutes at High**; stir twice.

About 1½ cups

Chili Sauce

2½ pounds ripe tomatoes, peeled (about 7 medium)
2 medium green peppers, cored
2 medium onions, peeled
1 stalk celery
⅔ cup cider vinegar
⅔ cup sugar
1½ teaspoons salt
¼ teaspoon pepper
¼ teaspoon ground cloves
⅛ teaspoon ground cinnamon

1. Finely chop vegetables. Put into a 4-quart microwave-oven-safe casserole. Add vinegar and a mixture of remaining ingredients.

2. Cook uncovered in microwave oven **40 minutes at High**, or until thick; stir every 10 minutes.

3. Pour sauce into hot sterilized jars; cover. Cool, then store in refrigerator.

About 5 cups

Basic Gravy

2 tablespoons all-purpose flour
¼ cup water
1 teaspoon instant beef or chicken bouillon granules
¾ cup hot water or ¾ cup meat or poultry drippings plus hot water
Salt to taste

1. Combine flour and water in a 2-cup glass measuring cup to make a smooth mixture.

2. Dissolve beef granules in hot water. Add gradually to flour-water mixture, stirring until smooth. Cook uncovered in microwave oven **2½ minutes at High**, or until thickened; stir every 30 seconds for the first minute.

3. Remove from oven; stir in salt.

About 1 cup

Easy Sweet and Sour Sauce

1 cup apricot or peach preserves
2 tablespoons cider vinegar
2 tablespoons ketchup
¼ teaspoon dry mustard

1. Combine all ingredients in a 1-quart glass measuring pitcher.

2. Cook uncovered in microwave oven **2½ to 3 minutes at High**; stir once.

About 1¼ cups

Creamy Apricot Salad Dressing

2 eggs
1 cup apricot nectar
1½ tablespoons lemon juice
⅓ cup sugar
1 teaspoon all-purpose flour
⅛ teaspoon salt
1 tablespoon butter or margarine
⅓ cup chilled whipping cream

1. Beat eggs slightly in a 1-quart glass measuring pitcher. Add apricot nectar and lemon juice; mix.

2. Combine sugar, flour and salt; gradually add to egg mixture, stirring constantly. Cook uncovered in microwave oven **7 minutes at High**, or until thickened; stir every 2 minutes.

3. Add butter to dressing; stir until blended. Cool, stirring occasionally; chill thoroughly.

4. Just before serving, beat cream to soft peaks and fold into chilled apricot mixture. Serve on fruit salad.

About 1⅔ cups

Whole Cranberry Sauce

1½ cups raw cranberries
¼ cup water
½ cup granulated sugar or packed brown sugar

1. Put cranberries, water and sugar into a 1-quart glass measuring pitcher. Cover loosely with plastic wrap. Cook in microwave oven **4 to 5 minutes at High**, or until cranberries have popped; stir once.

2. Remove from oven; let stand several minutes. Stir well and pour into a serving dish.

About 1 cup

Raisin-Pecan Sauce

2 tablespoons butter or margarine
⅓ cup all-purpose flour
2 cups chicken broth (homemade, canned or from bouillon cubes)
½ cup golden raisins
⅓ cup chopped pecans
⅛ teaspoon salt
Dash white pepper

1. Melt butter in a 2-quart glass measuring pitcher in microwave oven (**about 30 seconds at High**). Blend flour into butter. Add chicken broth gradually, stirring constantly. Cook uncovered **4 to 5 minutes at High**; stir vigorously after 2 minutes, then every 30 seconds until sauce comes to boiling and is thickened.

2. Remove from oven. Add raisins, pecans, salt and pepper to sauce; stir. Serve with poultry.

2½ cups

Rosy Applesauce

2 pounds (6 to 8) red-skinned cooking apples (such as McIntosh)
½ cup water
½ to 1 cup sugar (depending on type of apple and sweetness desired)

1. Wash, quarter and core apples. Put apples and water into a 3-quart glass casserole. Cover with an all-glass lid or plastic wrap. Cook in microwave oven **10 minutes at High**; stir once.

2. Force apple mixture through a sieve or food mill. Add sugar and stir until sugar dissolves. Serve warm or chill before serving.

About 1 quart

Lemon Sauce

1 tablespoon cornstarch
¾ cup sugar
¾ cup hot water
2 egg yolks
1 tablespoon butter or margarine
3 tablespoons lemon juice
⅛ teaspoon salt

1. Combine cornstarch and sugar in a 1-quart glass measuring pitcher; add water and mix well. Cook uncovered in microwave oven **2 minutes at High**; stir frequently.

2. Beat egg yolks and add a small amount of hot mixture to egg yolks, then blend into mixture in measuring pitcher. Cook uncovered in microwave oven **1 minute at High**, or until thickened.

3. Remove from oven. Add butter, lemon juice and salt to sauce; beat until blended.

About 1½ cups

Pineapple Sauce

1 can (8 ounces) unsweetened crushed pineapple, drained; reserve 1 tablespoon juice
2 tablespoons light brown sugar
⅛ teaspoon ground cloves

1. Combine pineapple, reserved juice, brown sugar and cloves in a 1-quart glass measuring pitcher. Cook uncovered in microwave oven **2 minutes at High**.

2. Remove from oven. Stir sauce and serve on ham or chicken.

¾ cup

Cherry Sauce

1 can (16 ounces) water-pack pitted red cherries
½ cup sugar
2 tablespoons cornstarch
⅛ teaspoon ground allspice

1. Drain cherries; pour liquid into a 1-cup measuring cup. Add water to make ¾ cup liquid. Reserve cherries.

2. Mix sugar, cornstarch and allspice in a 1-quart glass measuring pitcher. Add liquid gradually, stirring until smooth. Cook uncovered in microwave oven **3 minutes at High**, or until sauce comes to boiling and is thickened.

3. Stir cherries into sauce. Heat uncovered in microwave oven to serving temperature (**about 1 minute at High**). Serve with chicken, duckling or turkey.

About 2 cups

Melba Sauce

1 package (10 ounces) frozen red raspberries
¼ cup sugar
2 teaspoons cornstarch
½ cup currant jelly

1. Put frozen raspberries into a 1-quart glass measuring pitcher. Heat uncovered in microwave oven **1 minute at High**. Stir to break berries apart. Cook uncovered **30 seconds at High**, or until berries are defrosted.

2. Stir a mixture of sugar and cornstarch into raspberries, then stir in currant jelly. Cook uncovered in microwave oven **6 minutes at High**, or until sauce thickens and clears; stir twice.

3. Sieve sauce to remove seeds. Cool before serving.

About 1¼ cups

Chocolate Fudge Sauce

3 ounces (3 squares) unsweetened chocolate
¼ cup (½ stick) butter or margarine
⅔ cup sugar
⅛ teaspoon salt
⅔ cup (1 small can) undiluted evaporated milk
1 teaspoon vanilla extract
Few drops almond extract

1. Melt chocolate and butter in a 2-quart glass measuring pitcher in microwave oven (**about 2 minutes at High**); stir twice.

2. Add sugar, salt and evaporated milk to melted mixture; stir. Cook uncovered in microwave oven **3 minutes at High**, or until mixture comes to boiling; stir every minute.

3. Remove from oven; stir extracts into sauce.

About 1½ cups

Chocolate Peppermint Sauce

3 ounces (3 squares) unsweetened chocolate
¼ cup water
1 cup sugar
½ cup corn syrup
⅛ teaspoon salt
⅔ cup half-and-half
⅛ teaspoon peppermint extract

1. Put chocolate and water into a 2-quart glass measuring pitcher. Cook uncovered in microwave oven **2½ minutes at High**, or until chocolate melts; stir to blend.

2. Add sugar, corn syrup and salt to chocolate mixture; stir well. Cook uncovered in microwave oven **4 minutes at High**; stir every minute.

3. Remove from oven; gradually add half-and-half and peppermint extract, stirring until blended.

About 2 cups

Butterscotch Sauce

1 cup packed light brown sugar
⅓ cup butter or margarine
⅓ cup half-and-half
Dash salt

1. Put brown sugar, butter, half-and-half and salt into a 1-quart glass measuring pitcher. Cook uncovered in microwave oven **2 minutes at High**, or until sugar dissolves and butter melts. Stir until blended. Cook uncovered **45 seconds at High**, or until sauce comes to boiling.

2. Serve warm over cake or ice cream.

About 1¼ cups

Melba Sauce

Chocolate Fudge Sauce

Butterscotch Sauce

Strawberry
Preserves

Peach Preserves

Bread and Butter
Pickles

Grape Jelly

Cranapple Relish

Preserving

Making preserves may not have been on your mind when you bought your microwave oven, but it's nice to know it's possible.

Except for canning, which requires special range-top equipment, several ways of preserving are among your options. You can cook jellies, jams and butters; make pickles; and preserve herbs by drying in the microwave oven. And you can blanch vegetables for freezing, using the chart on page 198.

Jellies and Jams
Small batches of jellies and jams work best in the microwave oven. But for small families and anyone with limited storage space, small recipes work best, anyway. Jellies and jams cooked in the microwave oven won't heat up the kitchen. This is a real plus in the hot months when jellies using fresh fruits are most often made.

It isn't always necessary to postpone jelly-making until harvest time, however. The recipes that follow include some using convenience foods, such as Strawberry Preserves (page 201) made from frozen strawberries, and Grape Jelly (page 200) calling for bottled grape juice. The cooking time is so short that juices won't evaporate, so these recipes include commercial fruit pectin for thickening.

Use a cooking bowl of ample size as sugar mixtures tend to bubble and boil over. Before mixing the jelly ingredients line up all of the equipment and follow manufacturer's directions for sterilizing the jars and lids. Keep the jars filled with hot water until the jelly is ready to pour. (Don't attempt jar sterilization in the microwave oven.) If you want to store at room temperature and use lids, be sure to process following manufacturer's directions. This canning process can not be done in the microwave oven.

After jelly is poured into the jars and paraffin applied, store at room temperature. If paraffin is to be used as a seal, melt it in a double boiler. Paraffin is another "don't" in the microwave oven.

Or, simpler yet, just add lids to the jelly jars and store in the refrigerator; no paraffin or processing needed. The Apricot-Apple Butter on page 201 should be kept in the refrigerator because its low sugar content won't prevent it from spoiling at room temperature.

Pickles
The pickle recipes in this chapter are small batches too. The Freezer Dill Pickles (page 203) should be stored in the freezer and defrosted shortly before serving. All of the other pickles should be ladled into sterilized jars after microwave cooking. Store them covered in the refrigerator.

Blanching Vegetables
Gardeners, and others who like to freeze summer's produce, know that vegetables need to be blanched before freezing to retain bright color and natural texture. Done on top of the stove, this is a steamy job for a summer day. Done in the microwave, only a small amount of water heats the vegetables; the air, oven and equipment don't heat up. After blanching, plunge the vegetables into cold water for the same length of time as they cooked, to stop further cooking. When cool, package for freezing.

Drying Herbs
Herbs are growing in favor with the home gardener. Preserve your harvest for those wintery days by drying herbs in the microwave oven. Make sure the leaves are dried after thoroughly washing; then follow directions on page 199. If our list doesn't include a variety you wish to dry, use the same technique, but experiment with the timing. Start with a short period and add more time, if needed. Remember that your microwave oven is not a dehydrator. Special equipment is needed for proper air circulation and drying of fruits and vegetables.

Friends will love the home-preserved goodies you can make in your microwave oven. Make several batches and share the fruits of your labors with them.

How to Blanch Vegetables

1. Wash and cut vegetables as indicated. Put into a 1½- or 2-quart glass casserole. Add water; do not add salt. Cover with an all-glass lid or plastic wrap.

2. Cook in microwave oven; stir halfway through blanching time and at end of blanching. Plunge into cold water to stop cooking. Allow to cool, then package for freezing.

Type of Vegetable	Amount	Water Amount	Cook at High
Asparagus spears	1 pound	¼ cup	3 minutes
Beans, green (whole or cut)	1 pound	½ cup	3½ minutes
Broccoli (cut in spears)	1 bunch (about 1¼ pounds)	½ cup	3 minutes
Carrots (pared and sliced)	1 pound	¼ cup	3½ minutes
Cauliflower (cut in flowerets)	1 pound	½ cup	3 minutes
Corn (cut from cobs)	cut from 4 ears	¼ cup	4 minutes
Spinach (leaves with stems removed)	1 pound	none	2 minutes
Squash, yellow summer (sliced)	1 pound	¼ cup	3 minutes

Blanching Hints

1. Wash and cut vegetables as indicated. Put into a 1½- or 2-quart glass casserole. Add water; do not add salt.

2. Cover with an all-glass lid or plastic wrap. Cook in microwave oven at High; stir halfway through blanching time and at end of blanching time.

3. Plunge into cold water to stop cooking. Let cool and package for freezing.

How to Dry Herbs

1. Wash herb leaves and pat dry. Spread leaves evenly on paper-towel-lined microwave oven tray. Cover with paper towels.

2. Cook as directed below until almost dry and easy to crumble; rearrange as necessary for even drying. Let stand uncovered to complete drying. Store in covered container away from light.

Type of Herb	Herb Amount	Cook at High
Basil	1 cup leaves	2 to 2½ minutes
Mint	1 cup leaves	1½ to 2 minutes
Parsley (stems removed)	1 cup leaves	2 to 2½ minutes
Celery leaves	1 cup leaves	2½ to 3 minutes

Drying Hints

1. Wash herb leaves and pat dry. Spread evenly on paper-towel-lined microwave oven tray.

2. Cover with paper towel. Cook at High as directed above until almost dry and easy to crumble. Rearrange as necessary for even drying.

3. Let stand uncovered to complete drying. Store in covered container away from light.

Apple-Mint Jelly

2 cups apple juice
3 cups sugar
2 tablespoons dried mint leaves, crushed
1 package (3 ounces) liquid fruit pectin
3 drops green food coloring

1. Combine apple juice, sugar and mint in a 2-quart glass measuring pitcher. Cook uncovered in microwave oven **8 to 9 minutes at High**, or until boiling; stir once.

2. Add liquid pectin and food coloring; stir well. Strain through a fine sieve into hot sterilized jars.

2 half-pints

Grape Jelly

2 cups grape juice
1 cup water
1 package (1¾ ounces) powdered fruit pectin
3½ cups sugar

1. Pour grape juice and water into a 2-quart glass measuring pitcher. Add powdered pectin; stir. Cover with plastic wrap. Cook in microwave oven **8 to 10 minutes at High**, or until bubbles appear at edges of bowl; stir well after 3 minutes.

2. Add sugar gradually to grape mixture, mixing well. Cook covered in microwave oven **6 to 7 minutes at High**, or until mixture has boiled at least 1 minute.

3. Stir well and, if necessary, skim off foam with a metal spoon. Pour jelly into hot sterilized glasses or jars; cover. Cool. Store in refrigerator.

4. If desired, seal jelly with paraffin. Melt paraffin over hot water in a double boiler set over low heat. *Never* melt paraffin over direct heat or in microwave oven. Pour enough melted paraffin on top of jelly to make a layer about ⅛ inch thick. Tilt to seal to edge of glass. Cool, then cover. Store at room temperature, if desired.

4 half-pints

Citrus Marmalade

1 large grapefruit
1 medium orange
1 medium lemon
1 medium lime
1½ cups water
⅛ teaspoon baking soda
5 cups sugar
1 package (3 ounces) liquid fruit pectin

1. Wash fruit. Peel each one, trim off white membrane from peel and cut peel into slivers. Section fruit; discard seeds and dice fruit. Set aside. Combine peel, water and baking soda in a 2-quart glass measuring pitcher. Cover with plastic wrap.

2. Cook in microwave oven **10 to 12 minutes at High**, or until peel is tender.

3. Add sugar and reserved fruit. Cook uncovered in microwave oven **13 minutes at High**, or until sugar is dissolved and fruit is soft; stir 3 times. (Syrup should boil at least 1 minute.)

4. Add liquid pectin and stir well. Let stand uncovered 5 minutes; stir occasionally. Skim off foam with a metal spoon, if necessary.

5. Pour marmalade into hot sterilized glasses or jars; cover. Cool. Store in refrigerator.

6. If desired, seal marmalade with paraffin. Melt paraffin over hot water in a double boiler set over low heat. *Never* melt paraffin over direct heat or in microwave oven. Pour enough melted paraffin on top of marmalade to make a layer about ⅛ inch thick. Tilt to seal to edge of glass. Cool, then cover. Store at room temperature, if desired.

6 half-pints

Strawberry Preserves

1 quart hot water
2 packages (16 ounces each)
  frozen whole strawberries or
  2 quarts fresh strawberries,
  rinsed and hulled
6 cups sugar
1 package (3 ounces) liquid
  fruit pectin

1. Put hot water into a 2-quart glass measuring pitcher. Heat in microwave oven to boiling (**8 to 9 minutes at High**).

2. Spread berries in a single layer in a 15½x10½x1-inch jelly-roll pan. Pour boiling water over strawberries. Let stand in boiling water 2 minutes. Drain berries. Put drained berries into a 4-quart glass bowl. Add 4 cups sugar; combine well.

3. Cook uncovered in microwave oven **20 to 22 minutes at High**, or until mixture bubbles all over; stir 3 times.

4. Stir in remaining sugar. Cook uncovered in microwave oven **5 to 6½ minutes at High**, or until mixture bubbles all over. Let mixture boil **2½ minutes at High**.

5. Remove from oven. Stir in pectin. Pour preserves into a 13x9x2-inch pan. Skim off foam with a metal spoon. Let stand uncovered overnight.

6. Spoon preserves into hot sterilized jars; cover. Store in refrigerator.

7 half-pints

Peach Preserves

4 medium peaches, peeled and
  cut in pieces (about 4 cups)
6 cups sugar
¼ cup lemon juice
1 package (3 ounces) liquid
  fruit pectin

1. Mix peaches, sugar and lemon juice in a 3-quart glass casserole. Cover with an all-glass lid or plastic wrap. Cook in microwave oven **14 minutes at High**, or until peaches are soft and sugar is dissolved; stir every 3 minutes. (Mixture should boil at least 1 minute.)

2. Remove from oven and stir in liquid pectin. Let stand uncovered 10 minutes. Stir to distribute fruit. Pour preserves into hot sterilized jars; cover. Cool. Store in refrigerator.

6 half-pints

Apricot-Apple Butter

2 packages (6 ounces each)
  dried apricots
2 cups apple juice
10 cooking apples (about 2½
  pounds), pared, cored and cut
  in eighths
4 teaspoons lemon juice
½ teaspoon ground cinnamon
  Dash ground cloves

1. Combine ingredients in a 4-quart glass bowl. Cook uncovered in microwave oven **15 to 18 minutes at High**, or until apples are soft; stir every 5 minutes.

2. Purée fruit mixture in blender or food processor. Return to glass bowl. Cook uncovered in microwave oven **15 minutes at High**, or until thick; stir 4 times. Put fruit butter into hot sterilized jars; cover. Cool. Store in refrigerator.

5 cups

Cranapple Relish

2 cups fresh cranberries
1 cup chopped pared apple
1 cup sugar
2 teaspoons grated lemon peel
4 teaspoons lemon juice
½ teaspoon butter or margarine

1. Wash cranberries. Combine all ingredients in a 2-quart glass casserole. Cook uncovered in microwave oven **8 to 10 minutes at High**, or until berries have popped and relish is slightly thickened.

2. Spoon relish immediately into hot sterilized jars; cover. Cool. Store in refrigerator.

3. Serve relish warm or cool.

2 half-pints

Corn Relish

1 can (17 ounces) whole kernel golden corn, drained; reserve ¼ cup liquid
¼ cup white vinegar
1 cup sweet pickle relish
¼ cup minced onion
1 tablespoon diced pimiento
¼ cup sugar
2 teaspoons celery seed
½ teaspoon salt

1. Combine all ingredients in a 2-quart glass casserole. Cover with waxed paper. Cook in microwave oven **10 minutes at High**; stir after 5 minutes.

2. Let stand covered 5 minutes before serving.

3 cups

Watermelon Rind Pickles

½ cup pickling salt
2 quarts water
10 to 12 cups pared watermelon rind cubes (1 inch)*
2 cups white vinegar
6 cups sugar
1 tablespoon whole cloves
2 or 3 sticks cinnamon

1. Mix salt and water in a 3-quart glass casserole; add watermelon rind. Cover and let soak 2 hours. Drain; rinse with cold water. Return rind to casserole.

2. Cover rind with fresh water. Cook uncovered in microwave oven **30 minutes at High**, or until tender; stir twice. Drain; return rind to casserole and set aside.

3. Combine vinegar and sugar in a 2-quart glass measuring pitcher. Tie spices in a cheesecloth bag. Add to vinegar and sugar. Cook uncovered in microwave oven **13 to 15 minutes at High**, or until sugar is dissolved and mixture is boiling; stir 3 times. Remove spice bag.

4. Pour syrup over rind. Cook uncovered in microwave oven **3 minutes at High**.

5. Pack pickles into hot sterilized jars; cover. Cool. Store in refrigerator.

5 pints

*Leave a thin line of pink with the watermelon rind.

Bread and Butter Pickles

2 quarts ¼-inch cucumber
  slices (about 16 cucumbers,
  4 to 5 inches each)
½ cup pickling salt
1 quart boiling water
2 cups chopped onion
2 cups chopped green pepper
¾ cup chopped red pepper
2 cups cider vinegar
2 cups sugar
1 teaspoon celery seed
1 teaspoon mustard seed
½ teaspoon ground turmeric

1. Combine cucumber slices, salt and boiling water in a 4-quart microwave-oven-safe casserole. Cover and let stand at room temperature overnight.

2. The next day, drain the cucumbers and return to the casserole; add chopped vegetables. Set aside.

3. Combine remaining ingredients in a 2-quart glass measuring pitcher. Cook uncovered in microwave oven **8 to 9 minutes at High**, or until sugar is dissolved; stir twice.

4. Pour syrup over cucumber mixture; stir. Cook uncovered in microwave oven **6 minutes at High**; stir once.

5. Pack pickles into hot sterilized jars; cover. Cool. Store in refrigerator.

3 quarts

Freezer Dill Pickles

1 quart ¼-inch cucumber slices
  (about 8 cucumbers,
  4 to 5 inches long)
2 cups sliced onion
4 teaspoons pickling salt
2 tablespoons water
¾ cup sugar
½ cup cider vinegar
1 teaspoon dill weed

1. Mix cucumber, onion, salt and water in a 2-quart glass casserole. Let stand 2 hours.

2. Combine sugar, vinegar and dill weed in a 2-cup glass measuring cup. Cook uncovered in microwave oven **4 minutes at High**, or until sugar dissolves completely. Set aside to cool.

3. Drain cucumber-onion mixture; do not rinse. Return to casserole. Add cooled liquid; mix.

4. Pack mixture into freezer containers; cover. Freeze.

2 pints

Sliced Beet Relish

⅓ cup chopped onion
2 tablespoons water
1 can (16 ounces) sliced beets,
  drained
¾ cup white vinegar
1 cup sugar
½ teaspoon ground allspice

1. Put onion and water into a 1-quart glass casserole. Cover with an all-glass lid or plastic wrap. Cook in microwave oven **2 minutes at High**.

2. Add remaining ingredients to casserole. Cook covered in microwave oven **6 to 7 minutes at High**; stir after 4 minutes and after mixture boils. Cook covered for **2 minutes at Medium-High**, or until sugar is dissolved. Pour into a jar; cover. Refrigerate.

2½ cups

Cherry Pie

Ratatouille

Baked Potatoes

Beef Roast

Complete Meals

Complete meals can be cooked at one time in your new microwave/convection oven. Now you can provide the hot dishes of your breakfast, lunch or dinner at one time without reheating or keeping some foods warm while you prepare others. The complete meal section of this book will start you on your way to using this special feature. The menus included here were tested as given to provide you with the best method of cooking several foods at the same time. It is important to follow directions carefully for best results. Follow the diagrams with each menu for placement of food on racks and ceramic tray.

The utensils mentioned in each menu are the correct size to fit together on the tray or rack and still allow the foods to cook evenly.

Recipes for the foods listed are given with each menu. The directions given for recipe preparation alert you to the advance steps that are needed before the complete meal begins cooking.

The meal completion time given in the directions is only the time needed for the prepared foods to cook simultaneously. In most cases, the foods will be placed in the microwave/convection oven to begin cooking at the same time and will finish at the same time. In some menus for complete meal cooking, you will find that the foods are added to the microwave/convection oven at different times. Occasionally it is necessary to continue cooking one item while another is removed from the microwave oven for its standing time.

When a range of cooking time is given, cook to the minimum time, and check for doneness. It is important to allow for standing time. As in all cooking, there may be slight differences in the time needed, depending on the starting temperatures of the food and your own personal preferences. If a particular food is not finished to your liking, simply return it to the microwave/convection oven for a minute or two while the other foods stand covered.

Microwave Meals
The ceramic tray remains in position in the bottom of the microwave oven during complete meal cooking as well as while cooking single foods. The metal rack can be pulled out to easily add foods, rearrange, or stir foods.

Place the foods on both the ceramic tray and the metal rack to allow microwave energy to reach each food. Placing the food off center allows for better flow of microwave energy. If you wish the foods on the bottom to cook fairly fast, place them where they are not shielded or covered by foods on the rack above. On the other hand, for slow heating of a food on the tray, place it directly under another food. When heating or cooking individual foods (potatoes) or foods in individual dishes (baked apples), arrange them with at least 1-inch space around each for even cooking. For even cooking, all foods should be rearranged, stirred, or the dish rotated at least once during the cooking time. Most foods are cooked covered for uniform cooking.

Convection/Combination Meals
Both metal racks are used when cooking meals in either convection or combination settings. To allow for adequate heat circulation, do not place foods directly on ceramic tray. When using combination cooking, be certain that utensils are suitable for microwave penetration as well as convection heat. In most cases, preheating is not necessary for combination meal cooking.

Creating Your Own Meals
To create your own menus, the following information should be helpful. Place the food requiring the most cooking time on the top metal rack. The food requiring the shortest cooking time should be placed on the bottom (on the ceramic tray for microwave cooking; on the metal rack for convection or combination cooking). Select one of our menus that is similar to your menu, and consult it for the recommended cooking method. In addition, consider these guidelines:
- Select foods of similar serving sizes.
- Select utensils that will fit together (try them empty for fit).
- Select the desired cooking method and determine if utensils are suitable.
- Place foods in the microwave/convection oven where they will cook most efficiently.
- Add food requiring a short heating time near the end of the cooking cycle.

Early Bird Breakfast

Scrambled Eggs
Bacon
Sour Cream Coffee Cake
4 servings

Recipe Preparation

Scrambled Eggs

8 eggs
½ cup milk or cream
2 tablespoons butter or
   margarine

1. Beat eggs; mix in milk. Set aside.
2. Put butter into a 1-quart glass casserole. Set aside.

Bacon

8   slices bacon

1. Arrange bacon, overlapping slightly, on a microwave-oven-safe roast rack set in a 2-quart glass baking dish.
2. Cover with a paper towel. Set aside.

Sour Cream Coffee Cake

1 cup all-purpose flour
1 teaspoon baking powder
½ teaspoon baking soda
¼ teaspoon salt
¼ cup (½ stick) butter or
   margarine
1 teaspoon vanilla extract
½ cup sugar
1 egg
½ cup dairy sour cream
½ cup finely chopped walnuts
1½ teaspoons sugar
1 teaspoon ground cinnamon

1. Combine flour, baking powder, baking soda and salt.

2. Cream butter, vanilla extract and ½ cup sugar thoroughly in a bowl. Add egg and beat well. Add dry ingredients and sour cream alternately to creamed mixture, beating until blended after each addition.

3. Spoon half of batter into a greased 8-inch round glass cake dish.

4. Mix walnuts, 1½ teaspoons sugar and cinnamon. Spoon half of nut mixture over batter in dish. Spoon remaining batter into dish and top evenly with remaining nut mixture. Set aside.

Meal Completion

(Microwave Oven Cooking Time: 16 minutes)

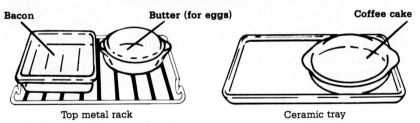

Bacon   Butter (for eggs)   Coffee cake

Top metal rack   Ceramic tray

1. Place coffee cake, bacon and butter for eggs as shown in diagram.

2. Cook in microwave oven **4 minutes at High**.

3. Rotate coffee cake one-quarter turn. Add egg mixture to melted butter and cover with plastic wrap.

4. Cook in microwave oven **4 minutes at High**.

5. Rotate bacon dish one-half turn. Stir eggs. Rotate coffee cake one-quarter turn.

6. Cook in microwave oven **3 minutes at High**.

7. Rearrange bacon in dish. Stir eggs. Rotate coffee cake one-quarter turn.

8. Cook in microwave oven **3 minutes at High,** or until coffee cake is set (a few moist spots will remain).

9. Remove coffee cake. Cover coffee cake with plastic wrap and let stand 10 minutes in dish. Remove eggs and stir (eggs will be soft). Cover with plastic wrap and set aside.

10. Cook bacon in microwave oven **2 minutes at High**. Pat bacon with paper towels.

11. Season eggs to taste; stir.

Fresh-Start Breakfast

Baked Grapefruit
Poached Eggs
Hot Chocolate
4 servings

Baked Grapefruit

2 grapefruit
4 teaspoons brown sugar
2 teaspoons butter or
   margarine

1. Wash grapefruit and cut in half. Remove core and seeds.

2. Set grapefruit halves cut-side-up on a paper towel or in a glass baking dish. Sprinkle each fruit half with 1 teaspoon brown sugar; put ½ teaspoon butter in center. Set aside.

Hot Chocolate

2 ounces (2 squares)
   unsweetened chocolate
1 cup water
3 to 4 tablespoons sugar
   Dash salt
3 cups milk
   Marshmallows

1. Put chocolate and water into a 2-quart glass casserole. Heat uncovered in microwave oven until chocolate melts (**4 to 5 minutes at High**); stir once.

2. Stir chocolate mixture; add sugar and salt. Stir in milk gradually. Set aside uncovered.

3. Reserve marshmallows in serving mugs.

Poached Eggs

2 cups hot water (or enough
   to cover eggs)
4 eggs

1. Put water into a deep 1½-quart glass casserole. Cover with an all-glass lid or plastic wrap.

2. Heat in microwave oven to boiling (**4 to 5 minutes at High**).

(Microwave Oven Cooking Time: 10 minutes)

Hot chocolate   Poached eggs   Grapefruit

Top metal rack   Ceramic tray

1. Place grapefruit, hot chocolate and water for poached eggs as shown in diagram.

2. Cook in microwave oven **5 minutes at High.**

3. Break eggs, one at a time, into a saucer or small dish. Slip each egg carefully into hot water. Cover with an all-glass lid or plastic wrap. Rotate grapefruit one-half turn; stir hot chocolate.

4. Cook in microwave oven **2 minutes at High.**

5. Remove eggs and set aside covered.

6. Cook in microwave oven **3 minutes at High.**

7. Remove hot chocolate from microwave oven and beat with rotary beater. Ladle over marshmallows in mugs.

Hint: If you prefer firmer yolks, continue cooking eggs 1 to 2 minutes.

Quick and Easy Lunch

Easy Vegetable Soup
Hot Dogs
Pineapple Upside-Down Cake
4 servings

Easy Vegetable Soup

1 package (10 ounces) frozen chopped broccoli
1 can (8½ ounces) cut green beans (undrained)
2 cups thinly sliced cabbage
1 cup chopped celery
1 tablespoon instant minced onion
2 cups beef broth (homemade, canned or from bouillon cubes)
1 cup tomato juice

1. Put frozen broccoli into a 3-quart glass casserole. Heat uncovered in microwave oven just until defrosted (**3 to 4 minutes at High**); stir once to separate.

2. Add green beans with liquid, cabbage, celery, onion and broth. Cover with an all-glass lid or plastic wrap. Cook in microwave oven **16 to 18 minutes at High**, or until vegetables are tender.

3. Stir in tomato juice. Set aside.

Pineapple Upside-Down Cake

2 tablespoons butter or margarine
½ cup packed brown sugar
6 slices pineapple
6 maraschino cherries
1 package (18½ ounces) yellow cake mix
⅓ cup unsweetened pineapple juice
   Water

1. Melt butter in an 8-inch round glass cake dish in microwave oven (**about 30 seconds at High**). Mix brown sugar into melted butter. Cook uncovered until brown sugar melts (**about 2 minutes at High**).

2. Arrange pineapple slices and maraschino cherries in dish.

3. Prepare cake batter following directions on package; use pineapple juice and water instead of water called for on package.

4. Fill cake dish half full with batter. (Use remaining batter for cupcakes.) Set aside.

Hot Dogs

4 hot dogs
4 hot dog buns
   Prepared mustard, ketchup or chili sauce

1. Place each hot dog in a bun, spread as desired and wrap in a paper towel.

2. Set aside.

Complete Meals

Meal Completion

(Microwave Oven Cooking Time: 11 minutes)

Cake — Top metal rack

Soup / **Hot dogs** — Ceramic tray

1. Place covered soup, hot dogs and cake as shown in diagram.
2. Cook in microwave oven **3 minutes at Medium-High**.
3. Rotate cake one-half turn.
4. Cook in microwave oven **3 minutes at Medium-High**.
5. Rotate cake one-half turn; stir soup. Rearrange hot dogs.
6. Cook in microwave oven **5 minutes at High**, or until cake is done.
7. Immediately invert cake onto serving plate.
8. Ladle hot soup into bowls.

Fireside Lunch

French Onion Soup
Beef and Cheddar Sandwiches
Lemon Meltaway Cookies
4 servings

French Onion Soup

2 tablespoons butter or
  margarine
3 medium onions, peeled and
  sliced (about 1 quart)
⅓ cup sliced celery
4 cups beef broth (homemade,
  canned or from bouillon
  cubes)
½ teaspoon Worcestershire
  sauce
½ cup (2 ounces) shredded
  mozzarella cheese
4 slices dry French bread

1. Put butter, onion and celery into a 2-quart glass casserole. Cover with an all-glass lid. Cook in microwave oven **6 to 7 minutes at High**, or until vegetables are tender; stir once.

2. Add broth and Worcestershire sauce; stir. Cover with all-glass lid. Set aside.

3. Reserve cheese and bread.

Beef and Cheddar Sandwiches

¾ pound ground beef
¼ cup chopped onion
1 cup (4 ounces) shredded
  Cheddar cheese
3 tablespoons barbecue sauce
1 tablespoon sweet pickle
  relish
  Salt and pepper to taste
4 hamburger buns

1. Combine ground beef and onion in a 2-quart glass bowl. Cook uncovered in microwave oven **5 minutes at High**; stir once. Drain.

2. Add cheese, barbecue sauce, pickle relish, salt and pepper; mix well.

3. Fill hamburger buns with beef mixture. Wrap individually in aluminum foil. Set aside.

Lemon Meltaway Cookies

¼ cup (½ stick) butter or
  margarine, softened
¼ cup confectioners' sugar
1 teaspoon grated lemon peel
1 teaspoon lemon juice
¼ teaspoon vanilla extract
2 teaspoons water
½ cup all-purpose flour
2 tablespoons cornstarch
⅛ teaspoon salt
12 pecan halves

1. Combine butter, confectioners' sugar, lemon peel, lemon juice and vanilla extract in a small mixer bowl. Beat until fluffy. Beat in water. Combine flour, cornstarch and salt; add flour mixture gradually, beating until well mixed.

2. Drop mixture in 12 mounds on a round metal tray. Press pecan half on each cookie. Set aside.

Complete Meals

Meal Completion

(Convection Oven Cooking Time: 19 minutes)

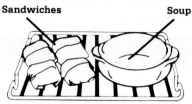
Sandwiches   Soup

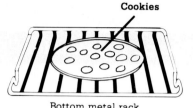
Cookies

Top metal rack   Bottom metal rack

1. Preheat convection oven to 375°F.

2. Place covered onion soup, sandwiches and cookies as shown in diagram.

3. Cook in convection oven **17 minutes at 375°F**.

4. Divide mozzarella cheese evenly on French bread slices. Remove cover from soup; put cheese and bread on soup.

5. Cook in convection oven **2 to 3 minutes at 375°F**, or until cheese is melted.

Hearty Dinner

Baked Chicken 'n' Sausage Dressing
Seasoned Potato Cubes
Creamed Spinach
Chocolate-Nut Brownies
4 servings

Recipe Preparation

Seasoned Potato Cubes

¼ cup fine saltine cracker
  crumbs
1 teaspoon paprika
1 teaspoon garlic salt
1 teaspoon celery salt
  Dash pepper
1 pound potatoes, pared and
  cut in cubes

1. Combine cracker crumbs, paprika, garlic salt, celery salt and pepper in a plastic bag. Add potato cubes and shake to coat well.

2. Put potatoes into a 1½-quart glass loaf dish. Set aside.

Chocolate-Nut Brownies

2 ounces (2 squares)
  unsweetened chocolate
½ cup (1 stick) butter or
  margarine
2 eggs
1 cup packed dark brown sugar
1 teaspoon vanilla extract
¾ cup all-purpose flour
1 cup chopped walnuts, divided

1. Melt chocolate and butter in a 1-quart glass measuring pitcher in microwave oven (**2 to 2½ minutes at High**).

2. Beat eggs until light in a mixer bowl. Add brown sugar and vanilla extract; beat until well mixed. Beat in chocolate mixture. Stir in flour and half of walnuts.

3. Spread batter in a greased 1½-quart glass baking dish. Sprinkle remaining walnuts on top. Set aside.

Baked Chicken 'n' Sausage Dressing

1 tablespoon butter or
  margarine
7 sausage links (about
  ½ pound), cut in chunks
½ cup chopped celery
¼ cup chopped onion
1 teaspoon salt
1 teaspoon poultry seasoning
6 cups bread cubes
¾ cup chicken broth
1 split broiler-fryer chicken
  (2½ to 3 pounds)
2 tablespoons butter or
  margarine

1. Combine 1 tablespoon butter, sausage, celery and onion in a 2-quart glass baking dish. Cover with plastic wrap. Cook in microwave oven **5 minutes at High**; stir after 3 minutes. Drain excess sausage drippings.

2. Sprinkle salt and poultry seasoning over sausage mixture. Stir in bread cubes and broth; spread evenly.

3. Cut each section of fryer in half (to make four pieces). Place on bread cube mixture with meaty portions to outside of dish.

4. Melt 2 tablespoons butter in a 1-cup glass measuring cup in microwave oven (**about 30 seconds at High**). Brush chicken with melted butter. Set aside.

Creamed Spinach

1 package (10 ounces) frozen
  creamed spinach

1. Place pouch of frozen spinach in an 8-inch round glass cake dish. Pierce pouch with fork.

2. Set aside.

Meal Completion

(Microwave/Convection Oven Cooking Time: 62 minutes)

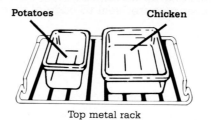

Top metal rack

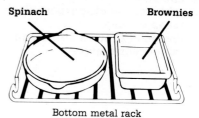

Bottom metal rack

1. Place potatoes, chicken, brownies and spinach as shown in diagram.

2. Cook in microwave/convection oven **30 minutes at Combination II**.

3. Stir potatoes; rotate chicken and brownies one-half turn.

4. Cook in microwave/convection oven **25 minutes at Combination II**.

5. Set brownies on rack to cool. Stir potatoes.

6. Cook in microwave/convection oven **7 to 12 minutes at Combination II**, or until potatoes and chicken are done.

Homestyle Dinner

Paprika Baked Chicken
Scalloped Corn Bake
Pear Meringue Dessert
4 servings

Paprika Baked Chicken

3 tablespoons butter or
   margarine
2 tablespoons all-purpose flour
1 teaspoon paprika
1 teaspoon salt
¼ teaspoon pepper
1 broiler-fryer chicken (about
   2½ pounds), cut in serving
   pieces

1. Melt butter in a 2-quart glass baking dish in microwave oven (**about 1 minute at High**).

2. Combine flour, paprika, salt and pepper in a plastic bag. Add chicken pieces and shake to coat chicken. Arrange chicken with meaty portions to outside in baking dish, turning once to coat with melted butter. Set aside.

Scalloped Corn Bake

2 tablespoons butter or
   margarine
1 package (10 ounces) frozen
   cut corn
2 eggs, beaten
⅔ cup milk
½ teaspoon salt
   Dash pepper
¼ cup dry bread crumbs

1. Melt butter in a 1½-quart glass loaf dish in microwave oven (**about 30 seconds at High**). Set aside.

2. Pierce package of corn with a fork. Place on a paper towel. Cook in microwave oven **4 minutes at High**.

3. Add corn to melted butter. Combine eggs, milk, salt and pepper. Stir into corn mixture. Sprinkle with bread crumbs. Set aside.

Pear Meringue Dessert

2 cans (16 ounces each)
   pear halves, drained and
   quartered
2 eggs, separated
⅔ cup dairy sour cream
½ cup sugar
3 tablespoons all-purpose flour
½ teaspoon salt
½ teaspoon ground cinnamon
2 tablespoons sugar

1. Arrange pears evenly in an 8-inch round glass cake dish.

2. Combine egg yolks and sour cream in a bowl. Stir in ½ cup sugar, flour, salt and cinnamon. Spread over pears.

3. Beat egg whites until foamy. Add 2 tablespoons sugar gradually beating until stiff, not dry, peaks form. Carefully spread meringue over pear mixture; seal to edge of dish on all sides. Set aside.

Meal Completion

(Microwave/Convection Oven Cooking Time: 45 minutes)

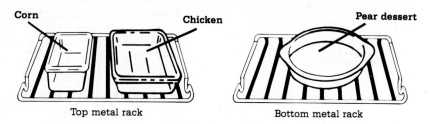

Corn   Chicken   Pear dessert

Top metal rack   Bottom metal rack

1. Place corn, chicken and pear dessert as shown in diagram.

2. Cook in microwave/convection oven **45 minutes at Combination II**, or until chicken is thoroughly cooked and meringue is lightly browned.

Special Dinner

Stuffed Turkey Breast
Acorn Squash
Cherry-Pineapple Cobbler

6 servings

Acorn Squash

3 acorn squash (1¼ to
  1½ pounds each)
2 tablespoons butter or
  margarine

1. Pierce squash and set aside.
2. Reserve butter.

Stuffed Turkey Breast

1 medium apple
2 cups cooked long-grain and
  wild rice
1 frozen turkey breast (about
  3 pounds), defrosted

1. Core and chop apple. Combine apple and rice.

2. Rinse turkey breast and pat dry. Stuff rice mixture under neck skin and in cavity between ribs. Place stuffed breast on its side in a 2-quart glass baking dish. Set aside.

Cherry-Pineapple Cobbler

1 can (30 ounces) cherry pie
  filling
1 can (20 ounces) crushed
  pineapple, drained
1 cup all-purpose biscuit mix
1 tablespoon sugar
¼ teaspoon ground cinnamon
⅓ cup milk

1. Combine cherry pie filling and pineapple in a 1½-quart glass baking dish.

2. Combine biscuit mix, sugar and cinnamon in a bowl. Stir in milk just until moistened. Drop from tablespoon onto top of cherry mixture in 6 biscuits. Set aside.

(Microwave/Convection Oven Cooking Time: about 60 minutes)

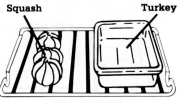

Squash   Turkey

Top metal rack

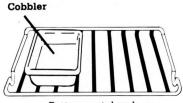

Cobbler

Bottom metal rack

1. Place turkey, squash and cobbler as shown in diagram.

2. Cook in microwave/convection oven **30 minutes at Combination I**.

3. Turn turkey over and insert Temperature Probe in thickest portion of turkey breast without touching the bone.

4. Cook in microwave/convection oven set at **170°F (Temperature Probe) and at Combination I (about 30 minutes)**, or until turkey, biscuits and squash are done.

5. Remove turkey from oven. Cover with foil and let stand 10 minutes for heat to equalize.

6. Let squash stand 5 minutes. Cut each squash in half. Scoop out seedy centers. Put 1 teaspoon butter into each cavity.

Family Dinner

Meatloaf
Baked Potatoes
Green Peas
4 servings

Meatloaf

1½ **pounds ground beef**
 ½ **cup fine dry bread crumbs**
 1 **egg, beaten**
 ¾ **cup milk**
 ¼ **cup finely chopped onion**
1½ **teaspoons salt**
 ¼ **teaspoon pepper**
 ½ **cup ketchup**

1. Mix ground beef lightly with bread crumbs, egg, milk, onion, salt and pepper in a bowl. Pack and mound mixture lightly into a 1½-quart glass loaf dish. Cover with waxed paper. Set aside.
2. Reserve ketchup.

Baked Potatoes

4 **medium baking potatoes (about 1½ pounds)**

1. Scrub and pierce potatoes.
2. Set aside.

Green Peas

1 **package (10 ounces) frozen green peas**

1. Put frozen peas into a 1-quart glass casserole.
2. Cover with an all-glass lid or plastic wrap. Set aside.

(Microwave Oven Cooking Time: about 34 minutes)

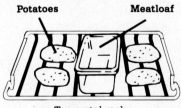

Potatoes   Meatloaf

Top metal rack

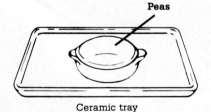

Peas

Ceramic tray

1. Place peas, meatloaf and potatoes as shown in diagram.
2. Cook in microwave oven **7 minutes at High**.
3. Spread ketchup on meatloaf and rotate one-half turn.
4. Cook in microwave oven **7 minutes at High**.
5. Rotate meatloaf one-half turn. Turn potatoes over. Stir peas.
6. Cook in microwave oven **7 minutes at High**.
7. Rotate meatloaf one-half turn. Rearrange potatoes. Stir peas.
8. Insert Temperature Probe in meatloaf.
9. Cook in microwave oven set at **160°F (Temperature Probe) and at High (approximately 13 minutes)**.
10. Remove meatloaf, cover with aluminum foil and let stand 5 minutes.

Hint: Larger potatoes require more cooking; if necessary, add 3 to 4 minutes to cooking time.

Oriental Style Dinner

Beef Kabobs
Quick-Cooking Rice
Vegetable Stir-Fry
4 servings

Recipe Preparation

Beef Kabobs

¾ cup soy sauce
¼ cup honey
1 pound beef sirloin, cut in
   1-inch pieces
24 pineapple chunks, fresh or
   canned
1 green pepper, cored and cut
   in squares
8 cherry tomatoes

1. Combine soy sauce and honey in a bowl. Add meat; stir to coat. Marinate 1 hour.

2. Remove meat and reserve marinade.

3. Alternate beef, pineapple and green pepper on 8 skewers. Arrange kabobs in a 2-quart glass baking dish and brush with marinade. Cover with waxed paper. Set aside.

4. Reserve cherry tomatoes.

Vegetable Stir-Fry

1 tablespoon vegetable oil
1 slice fresh ginger (⅛ inch),
   peeled
1 small clove garlic, peeled and
   crushed
¼ cup sliced onion
½ cup fresh broccoli flowerets
½ cup cauliflower slices
½ cup red or green pepper
   strips
½ cup sliced fresh mushrooms
1 package (6 ounces) frozen
   pea pods
¼ teaspoon salt

1. Put oil, ginger and garlic into a 1½-quart glass casserole. Cook uncovered in microwave oven **1 minute at High**.

2. Add onion, broccoli, cauliflower, pepper, mushrooms, pea pods and salt to casserole; stir. Cover with an all-glass lid or plastic wrap. Cook in microwave oven **4 to 5 minutes at High**, or until vegetables are crisp. Set aside.

Quick-Cooking Rice

1½ cups hot water
1 teaspoon salt
1 teaspoon butter or margarine
1½ cups packaged precooked rice

1. Combine water, salt and butter in a 1½-quart glass loaf dish. Cover with plastic wrap.

2. Heat in microwave oven to boiling (**about 4 minutes at High**).

3. Set aside covered.

Meal Completion

(Microwave Oven Cooking Time: 7 minutes)

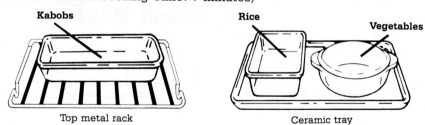

Kabobs

Top metal rack

Rice   **Vegetables**

Ceramic tray

1. Place covered boiling water for rice, covered vegetables and covered kabobs as shown in diagram.

2. Cook in microwave oven **3 minutes at High.**

3. Rotate kabobs. Stir rice into water. Cover with plastic wrap; stir vegetables.

4. Cook in microwave oven **4 minutes at High**.

5. Place a cherry tomato at the end of each skewer for garnish.

Hint: The time on Beef Kabobs is for medium meat; continue cooking 2 to 3 minutes for well-done meat.

Sunday Dinner

Roast Beef
Baked Potatoes
Ratatouille
Cherry Pie
4 servings

Recipe Preparation

Cherry Pie

Pastry for 2-crust pie
2 cans (16 ounces each) red tart pitted cherries packed in water
¾ cup sugar
¼ cup cornstarch
   Dash salt

1. Prepare pastry for one crust; fit into a 9-inch glass pie plate.

2. Drain cherries; reserve ¾ cup liquid.

3. Combine sugar, cornstarch and salt in a 1-quart glass measuring pitcher. Add liquid gradually, stirring constantly. Cook in microwave oven **3 minutes at High**, or until thickened; stir once. Mix in cherries.

4. Fill pastry-lined pie plate with cherry mixture; spread evenly. Prepare pastry for second crust. Cut into lattice strips and arrange in crisscross woven fashion on top of pie. Trim and seal edges. Set aside.

Ratatouille

2 tablespoons butter or margarine
1 medium onion, peeled and sliced
1 medium zucchini, sliced
1 small green pepper, sliced
1 small eggplant, pared and cut in cubes
1 large tomato, cut in chunks
½ teaspoon salt
½ teaspoon marjoram leaves
¼ teaspoon oregano leaves
¼ teaspoon garlic salt
⅛ teaspoon pepper

1. Put butter and onion into a 1½-quart glass loaf dish. Cook in microwave oven **3 minutes at High**, or until onion is tender; stir after 1 minute.

2. Combine zucchini, green pepper, eggplant, tomato, salt, marjoram, oregano, garlic salt and pepper in a large bowl. Add onion and butter; mix well. Turn mixture into loaf dish. Set aside.

Roast Beef

1 teaspoon onion salt
½ teaspoon dry mustard
   Dash pepper
1 beef sirloin tip roast (3 to 4 pounds)

1. Combine onion salt, dry mustard and pepper. Rub mixture on all sides of beef roast.

2. Place beef roast on a roast rack suitable for microwave and convection heat; set in a 2-quart glass baking dish. Set aside.

Baked Potatoes

4 baking potatoes (about 1½ pounds)

1. Pierce potatoes with a fork.

2. Set aside.

Complete Meals

(Microwave/Convection Oven Cooking Time: about 75 minutes)

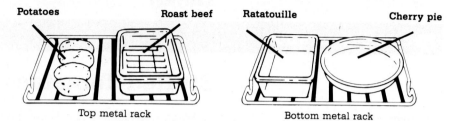

Potatoes   Roast beef   Ratatouille   Cherry pie

Top metal rack   Bottom metal rack

1. Preheat convection oven to 400°F. Place pie on bottom metal rack. Cook in convection oven **15 minutes at 400°F**. Reduce temperature to 325°F.

2. Place pie, ratatouille, roast beef and potatoes as shown in diagram.

3. Insert Temperature Probe in center of meat.

4. Cook in microwave/convection oven set at **130°F (Temperature Probe) and at Combination I (about 60 minutes)**. Stir ratatouille after 40 minutes.

Champion Dinner

Sirloin Steak 'n' Blue Ribbon Sauce
Buttered Noodles
Stuffed Tomatoes
6 servings

Recipe Preparation

Stuffed Tomatoes

6 firm ripe tomatoes
3 tablespoons butter or
   margarine
⅓ cup finely chopped green
   onion
2¾ cups soft bread crumbs
¼ teaspoon poultry seasoning
   or dash sage
1 teaspoon sugar
¾ teaspoon salt
   Dash pepper
   Paprika

1. Wash tomatoes, cut a ¼-inch slice off top of each and cut out stems. Scoop out and reserve ¾ cup of pulp; chop any large pieces.

2. Put butter and onion into a 1-quart glass casserole. Cook uncovered in microwave oven **3 to 4 minutes at High**, or until tender; stir after 1 minute.

3. Add bread crumbs, poultry seasoning, sugar, salt, pepper and reserved tomato pulp to cooked onion; toss lightly. Fill tomatoes with stuffing and put into a 1½-quart glass baking dish. Sprinkle with paprika. Cover with waxed paper. Set aside.

Buttered Noodles

1 quart hot water
1 teaspoon salt
8 ounces uncooked wide
   noodles
2 tablespoons butter or
   margarine

1. Combine water and salt in a 1½-quart glass loaf dish. Cover with plastic wrap. Heat in microwave oven to boiling (**8 to 9 minutes at High**).

2. Add noodles and stir through water. Cover with plastic wrap. Set aside.

3. Reserve butter.

Sirloin Steak 'n' Blue Ribbon Sauce

1 beef sirloin steak (2 pounds),
   cut about 1 inch thick
1 cup thinly sliced onion
1 medium lemon, thinly sliced
¼ cup (½ stick) butter or
   margarine
2 tablespoons prepared
   mustard
1 cup chili sauce
1 tablespoon Worcestershire
   sauce
1 teaspoon chili powder
1 can (6 ounces) cocktail
   vegetable juice

1. Trim fat from steak. Cut steak into serving pieces and put into an 8-inch square glass baking dish. Arrange onion and lemon slices over meat.

2. Melt butter in a 1-quart glass measuring pitcher in microwave oven (**about 30 seconds at High**). Blend in mustard, chili sauce, Worcestershire sauce, chili powder and vegetable juice. Pour mixture over onion and lemon. Cover with plastic wrap. Set aside.

Meal Completion

(Microwave Oven Cooking Time: 26 minutes)

Noodles   Steak   Stuffed tomatoes

Top metal rack   Ceramic tray

1. Place covered tomatoes, covered noodles and covered steak as shown in diagram.

2. Cook in microwave oven **7 minutes at High**.

3. Rotate steak, noodles and tomatoes one-half turn.

4. Cook in microwave oven **7 minutes at High**.

5. Rearrange steak; rotate noodles and tomatoes one-half turn.

6. Cook in microwave oven **5 minutes at High**.

7. Rotate steak, noodles and tomatoes one-half turn.

8. Cook in microwave oven **5 minutes at High**.

9. Remove steak and let stand covered 5 minutes before serving. Remove noodles, drain and rinse with warm water. Toss noodles with butter. Remove metal microwave oven rack.

10. Cook tomatoes in microwave oven **2 minutes at High**.

11. Remove tomatoes, discard waxed paper and cover with plastic wrap. Set aside.

Hint: The time on Sirloin Steak 'n' Blue Ribbon Sauce is for medium-rare steak; if a more well-done steak is desired, increase the cooking time.

Holiday Dinner

Baked Ham
Sweet Potatoes
Mixed Vegetables
4 servings

Baked Ham

1½-pound fully cooked ham

1. Place ham in a 1½-quart glass baking dish.
2. Cover with waxed paper. Set aside.

Sweet Potatoes

4 medium sweet potatoes (about 1¾ pounds)

1. Scrub potatoes and pierce.
2. Set aside.

Mixed Vegetables

1 package (10 ounces) frozen mixed vegetables

1. Put frozen vegetables into a 1-quart glass casserole.
2. Cover with an all-glass lid or plastic wrap. Set aside.

(Microwave Oven Cooking Time: 17 minutes)

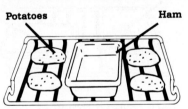

Top metal rack

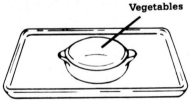

Ceramic tray

1. Place covered ham, covered vegetables and potatoes as shown in diagram.

2. Cook in microwave oven **6 minutes at High**.

3. Rotate ham one-half turn, rearrange potatoes and stir vegetables.

4. Insert Temperature Probe in thickest section of ham.

5. Cook in microwave oven set at **115°F (Temperature Probe) and at High (about 6 minutes)**.

6. Remove ham, cover with aluminum foil and let stand 10 minutes.

7. Cook potatoes and vegetables in microwave oven **5 to 6 minutes at High**, or until potatoes are done.

8. Let potatoes and vegetables stand 5 minutes.

Company Dinner

Pineapple-Stuffed Pork Chops
Broccoli-Cheese Casserole
Orange-Glazed Apples
Chewy Granola Bars
4 servings

Broccoli-Cheese Casserole

1 pound fresh broccoli, cut in
  bite-size pieces
2 tablespoons water
1 can (11 ounces) condensed
  Cheddar cheese soup
¼ cup mayonnaise
¼ cup milk
¼ teaspoon salt
4 slices bacon, cooked and
  crumbled, divided
¼ cup fine saltine cracker
  crumbs

1. Put broccoli and water into a 1½-quart glass casserole. Cover with an all-glass lid or plastic wrap. Cook in microwave oven **6 minutes at High**. Drain and set aside.

2. Combine Cheddar cheese soup, mayonnaise, milk, salt and half of bacon. Stir into broccoli.

3. Combine cracker crumbs and remaining bacon. Sprinkle on top of broccoli mixture. Set aside.

Pineapple-Stuffed Pork Chops

2 tablespoons chopped celery
1 tablespoon chopped onion
1 tablespoon butter or
  margarine
1 cup dry bread cubes
1 can (8¼ ounces) crushed
  pineapple, drained
¼ cup chopped walnuts
¼ teaspoon salt
¼ teaspoon poultry seasoning
4 pork loin chops, 1¼ to 1½
  inches thick (cut for stuffing)
2 tablespoons soy sauce

1. Combine celery, onion and butter in a 1-quart glass measuring pitcher. Cook uncovered in microwave oven **1½ minutes at High**. Stir in bread cubes, crushed pineapple, walnuts, salt and poultry seasoning.

2. Stuff chops with mixture. Arrange chops with meaty portions to outside in a 2-quart glass baking dish.

3. Brush with soy sauce. Set aside.

Orange-Glazed Apples

8 medium apples, pared, cored
  and cut in chunks
½ cup orange marmalade
2 tablespoons honey

1. Combine apples, orange marmalade and honey in a bowl.

2. Turn into a 1½-quart glass loaf dish. Set aside.

Chewy Granola Bars

1 cup packed light brown sugar
6 tablespoons vegetable oil
½ teaspoon vanilla extract
2 eggs
1 cup granola-type cereal
¾ cup all-purpose flour
1 teaspoon baking powder
½ teaspoon salt
½ cup golden raisins

1. Combine brown sugar, oil and vanilla extract in a mixer bowl; beat until blended. Mix in eggs. Stir in cereal.

2. Combine flour, baking powder, salt and raisins; stir into cereal mixture. Turn mixture into a 1½-quart glass baking dish; spread evenly. Set aside.

Complete Meals

Meal Completion

(Microwave/Convection Oven Cooking Time: 55 minutes)

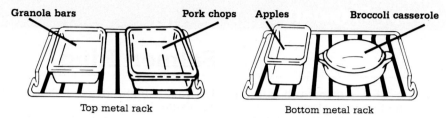

Granola bars   Pork chops   Apples   Broccoli casserole

Top metal rack   Bottom metal rack

1. Arrange granola bars, pork chops, apples and broccoli casserole as shown in diagram.

2. Cook in microwave/convection oven **55 minutes at Combination I;** stir apples after 30 minutes and rotate granola bars.

3. Stir apples before serving. Cool granola bars before cutting.

Convenience Dinner

Salmon Ring
Creamed Peas
4 servings

Salmon Ring

1 can (15½ ounces) red salmon
½ cup chopped celery
½ cup chopped green pepper
2 tablespoons minced onion
1 cup fine dry bread crumbs
1 tablespoon lemon juice
1 cup undiluted evaporated milk
1 egg, beaten

1. Drain salmon; discard skin and bones, if desired. Flake salmon and set aside.

2. Combine celery, green pepper and onion in a 2-quart glass casserole. Cook uncovered in microwave oven **2 minutes at High**, or until tender.

3. Add flaked salmon, bread crumbs, lemon juice and a mixture of evaporated milk and egg to cooked vegetables; mix well.

4. Carefully spoon salmon mixture into a 5½- to 6-cup microwave-oven-safe ring mold. Cover with waxed paper. Set aside.

Medium White Sauce

2 tablespoons butter or margarine
2 tablespoons all-purpose flour
1 cup milk
¼ teaspoon salt

1. Put butter into a 1-quart glass casserole. Set aside.

2. Reserve remaining ingredients.

Green Peas

1 package (10 ounces) frozen green peas

1. Put frozen peas into a 1-quart glass casserole.

2. Cover with an all-glass lid or plastic wrap. Set aside.

(Microwave Oven Cooking Time: 18 minutes)

Sauce   Salmon ring   Peas

Top metal rack   Ceramic tray

1. Place covered peas, butter for sauce and covered salmon ring as shown in diagram.

2. Cook in microwave oven **6 minutes at High**.

3. Rotate salmon ring one-half turn; add flour to melted butter and blend to a smooth paste. Add milk gradually, stirring constantly. Stir peas.

4. Cook in microwave oven **6 minutes at High**.

5. Rotate salmon ring one-half turn; stir salt into white sauce and stir peas.

6. Cook in microwave oven **6 minutes at High**; stir white sauce after 3 minutes.

7. Unmold salmon ring on a platter. Mix peas with white sauce; let stand 1 minute and spoon into center of ring.

Seafood Dinner

Fillet of Sole Amandine
Dilly Squash
Fudge-Frosted Cake
4 servings

Fillet of Sole Amandine

1 package (16 ounces) frozen fillet of sole
1 tablespoon butter or margarine
¼ cup slivered almonds
¼ cup (½ stick) butter or margarine
¼ teaspoon salt
2 teaspoons lemon juice

1. Heat package of fish in microwave oven **4 minutes at Medium-Low**; turn package over after 2 minutes. Let stand 5 minutes.

2. Put 1 tablespoon butter and almonds into a 9-inch glass pie plate. Cook uncovered in microwave oven **5 to 6 minutes at High**; stir every minute just until almonds are lightly toasted. Set aside.

3. Melt ¼ cup butter in a 2-cup glass measuring cup in microwave oven (**about 1 minute at High**).

4. Place fillets in a 2-quart glass baking dish and lightly brush with melted butter. Cover with waxed paper. Set aside.

5. Add almonds, salt and lemon juice to remaining melted butter; stir and reserve.

Dilly Squash

2 tablespoons butter or margarine
1 pound yellow summer squash, sliced
1 tablespoon dried parsley flakes
¼ teaspoon dried dill weed
¼ teaspoon salt
Dash onion powder

1. Melt butter in a 1½-quart glass loaf dish in microwave oven (**about 30 seconds at High**). Add remaining ingredients; stir well.

2. Cover with plastic wrap. Set aside.

Fudge-Frosted Cake

1 package (6 ounces) semisweet chocolate pieces
2 tablespoons water
⅔ cup sweetened condensed milk
1 teaspoon vanilla extract
1 cup all-purpose biscuit mix
½ cup sugar
2 tablespoons vegetable shortening
1 egg
½ cup milk
1 teaspoon vanilla extract
½ cup chopped walnuts

1. Line an 8-inch round glass cake dish with waxed paper cut to fit. Set aside.

2. Melt semisweet chocolate in a 1-quart glass measuring pitcher in microwave oven (**about 2½ minutes at High**); stir once. Add water, sweetened condensed milk and 1 teaspoon vanilla extract; stir with a spoon until smooth. Pour into lined dish.

3. Combine biscuit mix, sugar, shortening, egg and ¼ cup milk in a small bowl; beat 1 minute. Add remaining ¼ cup milk and vanilla extract; beat 1 minute. Pour batter over chocolate mixture. Cover with waxed paper. Set aside.

4. Reserve walnuts.

Meal Completion

(Microwave Oven Cooking Time: 13 minutes)

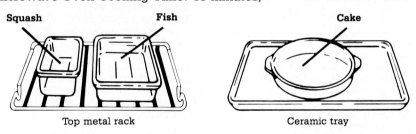

Squash   Fish   Cake

Top metal rack   Ceramic tray

1. Place covered cake, covered squash and covered fish as shown in diagram.

2. Cook in microwave oven **5 minutes at High**.

3. Reverse positions of cake and fish and rotate each dish one-half turn.

4. Cook in microwave oven **5 minutes at High**.

5. Rotate cake and fish one-half turn and stir squash.

6. Cook in microwave oven **3 minutes at High**, or until cake tests done with a wooden pick.

7. Immediately invert cake onto a serving plate. Remove waxed paper and sprinkle with reserved chopped walnuts.

8. Remove squash from oven and stir. Remove fish from oven and pour almond sauce over fish.

Index

Index

Index

Index

Index

Complete Meals